PayPal For Dummies®

Cheat Sheet

Fee Schedule

Activity	Personal Account	
Opening a PayPal account	Free	
Sending money	Free	
Withdrawing funds from your account	Withdrawing to a US bank is free; the fee for withdrawing to an international bank account varies by country.	by country.
Adding funds to your account	Free	Free
Receiving funds	Free	$0.01 to $2999.99: 2.9% plus $0.30 per transaction
		Merchant Discounts:
		$3000.01 to $10,000.00: 2.5% plus $0.30 per transaction
		$10,000.01 to $100,000.00: 2.2% plus $0.30 per transaction
		Over $100,000: 1.9% plus $0.30 per transaction
Converting from one currency to another	2.5% fee	2.5% fee

D0573475

Your PayPal E-mail Might Be a Fraud If. . .

You get an e-mail sent to "Dear PayPal Member" instead of addressing you by name.

The e-mail contains an attachment.

You're asked for your username, password, or other personal information.

The e-mail contains a link that does not take you to https://www.paypal.com.

The subject of the e-mail is "PayPal Random Account Verification," or something similar.

The e-mail has not been sent to the e-mail account you use as your PayPal account.

"PayPal" is offering to deposit funds into your account.

The PayPal logo image looks fuzzy, pixelated, or slightly different from the logo on the PayPal website.

The body of the e-mail has odd-looking formatting like everything centered, multiple fonts used throughout, and strange paragraph spacing.

For Dummies: Bestselling Book Series for Beginners

PayPal For Dummies®

API Error Codes

Error String or Number	Description
10001	Unexpected error.
10002	Authentication error.
10003	Missing Required Arguments.
10004	Invalid Argument.
10005	Unsupported feature.
10006	Unsupported version.
10007	Permission Denied.
10009	Server refused request.
11001	Invalid argument warning.
11002	FYI warning.
PA_Long_Error_ACH_Not_Verified	Your ACH is not verified.
PA_Long_Error_Authentication	Your username or password is incorrect.
PA_Long_Error_Authentication_Not_Authorized	You don't have the correct permission to call the API.
PA_Long_Error_Authentication_Invalid_Token	Your token is invalid.
PA_Long_Error_Counterparty_Locked_Or_Inactive	The account of the other person in the transaction is either locked or inactive.
PA_Long_Error_Currency_Invalid	The payment currency is invalid.
PA_Long_Error_Currency_Not_Supported	The currency of the payment is not supported.
PA_Long_Error_Memo_Invalid	Invalid characters have been entered into the memo field.
PA_Long_Error_Soap_Header_Null	Your SOAP header is null.
PA_Long_Error_Transaction_Could_Not_Load	The transaction could not be loaded.
PA_Long_Error_Transaction_Id_Invalid	The ID of the transaction is invalid.
PA_Long_Error_User_Locked_Or_Inactive	Your account is either locked or inactive.
PA_Long_Error_User_Restricted	Your account is restricted.
PA_Long_Error_Version_Not_Supported	You are trying to make a call to an unsupported version.
PA_Long_Error_Version_Not_Valid	The version is invalid.
PA_Long_Warning_Encryption_Failed	A warning message letting you know the transaction ID may be incorrect.
PA_Long_Warning_Memo_Truncated	The content of the memo was too long and had to be truncated.
PA_Long_Error_WS_Security	The necessary WS security elements were not found.
PA_Long_Error_Security	The security header is invalid.
PA_Long_Error_Invalid_Account_Number	The account number is not valid.

For Dummies: Bestselling Book Series for Beginners

PayPal®
FOR
DUMMIES®

PayPal® FOR DUMMIES®

by Victoria Rosenborg

Foreword by Marsha Collier
Author of *Starting an eBay® Business For Dummies®*

WILEY

Wiley Publishing, Inc.

PayPal® For Dummies®

Published by
Wiley Publishing, Inc.
111 River Street
Hoboken, NJ 07030-5774

Copyright © 2005 by Wiley Publishing, Inc., Indianapolis, Indiana

Published by Wiley Publishing, Inc., Indianapolis, Indiana

Published simultaneously in Canada

For general information on our other products and services, please contact our Customer Care Department within the U.S. at 800-762-2974, outside the U.S. at 317-572-3993, or fax 317-572-4002.

For technical support, please visit www.wiley.com/techsupport.

Wiley also publishes its books in a variety of electronic formats. Some content that appears in print may not be available in electronic books.

Library of Congress Control Number: 2005921023

ISBN: 0-7645-8392-1

Manufactured in the United States of America

10 9 8 7 6 5 4 3 2 1

1O/RR/QT/QV/IN

WILEY

About the Author

Victoria Rosenborg is the author of *ePublishing For Dummies* and co-owner of SmallBusinessOnline.net (`www.smallbusinessonline.net`), a business that develops e-commerce and marketing Web sites for small businesses. She is experienced in using PayPal both as a merchant and in conjunction with other shopping cart software. Victoria worked for six years at Microsoft as a technical evangelist and program manager. Part of the launch team for MSNBC, Victoria managed the MSNBC.com Web development teams for *Dateline*, *Nightly News with Tom Brokaw*, *The Today Show*, and *Meet the Press*. She was also the Director of Technology for iPublish, the Time Warner Book Group's division responsible for publishing eBooks.

Victoria is married, has two children, and lives in Connecticut.

Dedication

This book is dedicated to my husband, Neil, who took on everything house-related (cooking, washing, driving the children to after-school activities, and just about everything else you can think of) so I could have the time I needed to finish this book. He is a wonderful man and my best friend and I'm very lucky to have him!

This book is also dedicated to my children, Jessica and William, who tried hard to understand when Mommy couldn't play with them, read to them, help them with the homework (and all the other things I couldn't do during the three months I was writing.) I'm so lucky to have such great kids!

Author's Acknowledgments

Even though the author's name goes on the front cover, it takes a lot of effort on the part of many people to actually get a book out of the author's mind and into the books stores. I'm lucky to have had a group of great people behind me who made this book a reality.

First, I would like to thank my agent, Carole McClendon, from Waterside Productions. Not only did she help me with great suggestions for improving the book in the proposal stage, she gave me support and encouragement whenever I needed it; I couldn't have completed this book without her. I would also like to thank Tom Heine, the Acquisitions Editor for this book. Tom understood the target audience I wanted to reach and because of his support, I was able to write the book I wanted to write. Tim Borek, the Project Editor for this book, also deserves credit; Tim worked hard to ensure the content of the book was both accurate and up-to-date. I would also like to thank Consulting Editor Marsha Collier and Technical Editor Kerwin McKenzie; I feel very fortunate to have had these two checking up on me to ensure I didn't embarrass myself!

Publisher's Acknowledgments

We're proud of this book; please send us your comments through our online registration form located at www.dummies.com/register/.

Some of the people who helped bring this book to market include the following:

Acquisitions, Editorial, and Media Development

Project Editor: Tim Borek

Acquisitions Editor: Tom Heine

Copy Editor: Jerelind Charles

Technical Editor: Kerwin McKenzie

Editorial Manager: Robyn Siesky

Media Development Supervisor: Richard Graves

Editorial Assistant: Adrienne Porter

Cartoons: Rich Tennant, (www.the5thwave.com)

Composition Services

Project Coordinator: Maridee Ennis

Layout and Graphics: Andrea Dahl, Lauren Goddard, Stephanie D. Jumper, Lynsey Osborn, Heather Ryan, Ron Terry, Julie Trippetti, Erin Zeltner

Proofreaders: Leeann Harney, Jessica Kramer, Joe Niesen, Brian H. Walls, TECHBOOKS Production Services

Indexer: TECHBOOKS Production Services

Special Help

Marsha Collier, Steven Hayes

Publishing and Editorial for Technology Publishing

    Richard Swadley, Vice President and Executive Group Publisher

    Barry Pruett, Vice President and Publisher, Visual/Web Graphics

    Andy Cummings, Vice President and Publisher, Technology Dummies

    Mary Bednarek, Executive Acquisitions Director, Technology Dummies

    Mary C. Corder, Editorial Director, Technology Dummies

Publishing for Consumer Dummies

    Diane Graves Steele, Vice President and Publisher

    Joyce Pepple, Acquisitions Director

Composition Services

    Gerry Fahey, Vice President of Production Services

    Debbie Stailey, Director of Composition Services

Contents at a Glance

Table of Contents

Foreword

*T*oday, when an eBay buyer clicks the PayPal logo to pay for their purchase with PayPal, they don't think twice. PayPal is so deeply ensconced in the day-to-day transactions on eBay that it has become second nature. Perhaps this is because they are now owned by eBay, or perhaps it's because PayPal was the first and the best in envisioning an online payment service.

When Pierre Omidyar formed eBay, it was based on the fact that there would be a level playing field for all: that the big guys would have no advantage over the little guy. But the "big" guys had a big advantage the little guy couldn't counter; they could accept credit cards from their customers. The little guy (most likely a home-based or part-time seller) didn't have the gross sales to qualify for a business merchant account to accept credit cards in payment for their goods, and most likely didn't have a profit margin large enough to allow for the percentage that would be charged.

The founders of PayPal were planning on "beaming money to the world" through the use of Palm Pilots (and all future PDAs). Their first transaction was a highly touted media event when $3 million seed money (from the venture investors at Nokia) was beamed to the Palm Pilot of PayPal founder Peter Thiel in 1999. Here was born the nugget of the idea that electronic commerce would take over the world.

It was only accidentally that PayPal discovered online auctions — eBay to be exact — and to solicit new customers using a very lucrative referral program. PayPal gave each user a $10 credit for every customer that signed up as a member. This $10-per-person cash payment was enough to launch one of the most successful viral marketing campaigns in history. It made PayPal a major player in a very short span of time.

Although my PayPal account says I've been a member since February 2, 2000, I feel like I've been a PayPal devotee since its inception. I remember when the site bore the title of x.com and it seemed much more of a casual operation. At least it *appeared* as such, it was always a forward-thinking organization that knew someday they would be the premier money mover on the Internet. They were very on target — at the right time.

PayPal has become *de rigueur* as a payment system on eBay, but not enough of the budding online entrepreneurs know that PayPal can enable their Web-based businesses to accept credit cards at a comparatively low cost point.

The fact that PayPal offers a wealth of tools that are easily accessible by any Web site owner is a well-kept secret. With a little knowledge of HTML, any Web site owner can install automatic buttons for subscriptions, donations, shopping carts, and payments (the elements for which Web hosting companies can charge big bucks).

The best part is that these tools are free. The downside is you have to learn how to use them, and in our instant gratification society, very few people care to take the time to learn the tools they need to improve their lot in life. This book demystifies the "missing" PayPal tools.

Victoria Rosenborg has done a heck of job in this book translating PayPal-geek into everyday, easy-to-understand language. Okay, so maybe all that HTML coding is still there, but this book breaks it down into its simplest form. If you want to take advantage of the tools, one of the simplest ways to get there is by reading and studying this book.

Bookmark it. Write in it. Bounce from one chapter to the next. But most importantly, keep it next to you when you build your Web site. It'll save you well over the price you pay in solid information on using the magic PayPal tools.

Marsha Collier
Author *eBay For Dummies*, *Starting an eBay Business For Dummies*, and *eBay Timesaving Techniques For Dummies*

Introduction

• •

*L*ike many people, I was introduced to PayPal, one of the Web's most valuable resources, by purchasing items through eBay auctions. After winning an auction, I was able to send payment with just a few taps of the keyboard and a couple of clicks with the mouse. PayPal made everything so easy!

As time went on, I started to sell items through eBay and discovered the value that PayPal offers to merchants. If you already have a PayPal account, this book shows how to get the most out of using PayPal. If you don't have a PayPal account, I hope this book encourages you to open one and get started!

About This Book

Whether you want to use PayPal to purchase goods and services, offer PayPal as a payment option when selling on eBay, add PayPal buttons to an existing Web site, or create custom PayPal applications, this book is designed to help you. It's divided into sections, which demonstrate how to sign up for, buy with, and sell from using your PayPal account. In these pages, I show you how to

- Choose which PayPal account is right for your needs and open the account.
- Protect your money and your privacy from people who are seeking to steal your identity or rip you off.
- Use PayPal as you would a bank account (whether you want to deposit money, spend money, or purchase on credit).
- Set up your PayPal account to sell goods and services on eBay, through a PayPal shop, or from your Web site.
- Send an invoice, request money, and use PayPal to simplify your shipping.
- Take advantage of PayPal's ability to send and receive funds in different currencies.
- Create and customize PayPal buttons to use with your eBay auctions.
- Integrate the PayPal Shopping Cart and transactions into your existing Web site.
- Develop online applications, using PayPal Web Services.

Foolish Assumptions

This book may have caught your eye because you want to use PayPal but worry whether your money will be safe. Or you sell on eBay and want to make your auctions more successful by taking advantage of PayPal's advanced features. Perhaps you're a webmaster who wants to turn a marketing Web site into an e-commerce Web site. Or you're a developer who wants to know more about PayPal's new Web Services, a set of application programming interfaces (APIs) that let you create applications with integrated PayPal technology. If any of these assumptions describe you, then there's something in this book to help you.

I'm going to make some other assumptions about you:

- ✔ You have access to a computer. (You may be able to determine from this book's illustrations that I use Windows XP, but if your computer runs Mac or Linux, you can still follow the instructions in this book.)

- ✔ You know how to use a Web browser and can access the Internet.

- ✔ You have an e-mail account.

- ✔ You're over age 18. (PayPal won't let a minor open a PayPal account.)

- ✔ You want to use PayPal services for buying or selling items, or you want to incorporate PayPal technology into Web sites or software you develop.

- ✔ You want tips and strategies for using PayPal effectively to manage your money and earn interest on your money.

- ✔ You are concerned with the security of your PayPal account and maintaining your privacy.

How This Book Is Organized

This book has seven parts, each of which was designed to stand alone. This means you can jump ahead and read Chapter 5 without first having to read Chapter 3.

You can read every chapter, in no particular order, or read just those chapters with information you want and ignore the rest. If you're new to PayPal and haven't yet opened an account, I strongly suggest that you read the first four chapters to get a sense of how PayPal works and how to set up an account.

If you've been using your PayPal account for awhile and you're ready to "kick it up a notch," you can jump around to your heart's content. Take what you like and leave the rest!

Part 1: Powerful, Practical PayPal

In this part, I give you an overview about what PayPal is, and more importantly, all the things you can do with your PayPal account. I help you decide which type of PayPal account is right for you and take you through the process of opening your account. I give you an overview of the PayPal User Agreement (just in case you haven't actually read it) and warn you about fees PayPal may charge you. Perhaps most importantly, I show you how to be safe and smart when using your PayPal account, so you don't get your identity stolen by unscrupulous buyers or sellers.

Part 11: Purchasing with PayPal

In this section of the book, I show you how to use your PayPal account to purchase goods and services and how to send money via e-mail. I give you an overview about how to pay for items you purchase through eBay and how to use mass payments to pay many vendors with a single PayPal transaction. I show you how to get a PayPal debit card, so you can withdraw your money from ATMs; how to write eChecks; and how to add funds to your account. Finally, I show you how to apply for, and use, PayPal Buyer Credit (just in case your funds can't cover all the purchases you want to make!).

Part 111: Selling with PayPal

Here I show you how to make money by selling goods and services. I also show you how to set up your preferences as a seller, including payment preferences (so you don't get paid in Euros, when you want payment in U.S. dollars). I show you how to list an item on eBay and customize the PayPal logo associated with your auction. You learn how to organize your auctions through the PayPal Selling Manager and even how to earn 1.5 percent cash back when making purchases yourself! I explain how to send an invoice through e-mail, and create an invoice template to speed up your billing process. You can even use PayPal to organize your shipping . . . you can select a shipper and print a shipping label without ever leaving the PayPal Web site. Finally, I show you how to download information about your transactions, review your sales, and analyze your transaction data.

Part IV: Getting Money in the (e)Mail

It's not enough to know how to sell products and invoice buyers using PayPal, you also need to know the different ways you can receive money through PayPal. In Part IV, I explain the difference between requesting money and sending an invoice. I introduce you to eChecks and show you the difference between eChecks and instant transfers. I show you how to accept payment in the form of eChecks and how to block eChecks, when necessary. I also show you how to work with different currencies, if you plan on selling to buyers outside of the United States. Finally, I help you understand the currency conversion process, to help you avoid unnecessary conversion fees.

Part V: Integrating PayPal into Web Sites and Applications

Are you ready to get more sophisticated about using PayPal? I show you how to create and customize PayPal buttons and integrate PayPal into an existing Web site. I show you how to add the PayPal Shopping Cart to your Web site so users can purchase multiple items before beginning the checkout process. You learn about PayPal wizards, which work with many of the applications you may currently use (including Outlook). If you design Web sites with Adobe GoLive, Microsoft FrontPage, Macromedia Dreamweaver or Flash, there's a PayPal wizard designed to save you many hours of hand-coding. In this book, I show you how to get the most out of these tools.

Part VI: PayPal Web Services

For developers, this section contains information about PayPal's newly published Web Services. I show you how to get an account on the PayPal Developer Central Web site, and how to set up your testing environment. I also talk you through some sample code and give you an overview of the APIs you'll be working with.

Part VII: The Part of Tens

It wouldn't be a *For Dummies* book without the Part of Tens, and this book is no exception. In this section, I give you ten reasons to add PayPal to an existing Web site and provide ten helpful PayPal resources for you to check out when you want more information.

Icons Used in This Book

This book utilizes three core icons:

The Remember icon highlights information you'll want to keep in mind as you read the book.

When I offer some good-to-know information, I flag it with a Tip icon.

Look out for the Warning icon, because it can help save you from a problem, or keep you from wasting time.

Where to Go from Here

Now that you know what you'll find in each section of the book, take a few moments to glance through the Table of Contents. Jump to any chapter that interests you and start reading. You'll be on your way to using PayPal more effectively to send, manage, and make money!

Keep in mind as you read that PayPal is constantly changing its Web site — improving the interface and offering new services. If a screen I describe looks somewhat different than the screen you see on your computer, don't let it throw you. The link you need will be somewhere on the new screen; just look around and you should be able to find it!

I Want to Hear from You!

If you learn about a new PayPal service or a trick I haven't mentioned in this book, please let me know! I would love to get feedback from you and I always like learning new details about PayPal. If you would like to get a monthly newsletter, filled with PayPal tips and tricks, you can sign up at my Web site, www.PayPalBook.com.

I also want to hear about any topics you want to get more information about. Contact me at vr@PayPalBook.com.

Part I
Powerful, Practical PayPal

The 5th Wave — By Rich Tennant

"Hmm, I'm sure SOMEONE will give you a few bucks for them."

In this part . . .

1 give you an overview about what PayPal is, and more importantly, all the things you can do with your PayPal account. I help you decide which type of PayPal account is right for you, and take you through the process of opening your account. I give you an overview of the PayPal User Agreement (just in case you haven't actually read it) and warn you about fees PayPal may charge you. Perhaps most importantly, I show you how to be safe and smart when using your PayPal account, so you don't get your identity stolen by unscrupulous buyers or sellers.

Chapter 1

Getting to Know PayPal

. . . .

In This Chapter

▶ Sending and receiving money via e-mail with PayPal

▶ Discovering benefits of PayPal

▶ Managing your money (and making money in the process) with PayPal

▶ Protecting yourself when buying or selling with PayPal

▶ Utilizing PayPal as a buyer or seller

▶ Customizing PayPal for your Web site or application

. . . .

*W*ith over 50 million members, you probably already know what PayPal is, or have heard something about it, even if you're not using the service yet. But if you're one of those people who are a little fuzzy on what PayPal actually does, or can do for you, keep reading. You won't be a PayPal expert at the end of this chapter, but I hope you are intrigued enough to want to know more.

You know that great feeling you get when you go to the mailbox and discover an envelope with a check in it? PayPal can give you that same thrill when you discover somebody's sent you money via e-mail. At its most basic level, that's what PayPal is — a way to transfer money over the Internet without the hassle of going to a bank to wire money to somebody else's bank account.

In this chapter, I tell you what PayPal is, a little bit about how the service works, and how you can best use the service to send and receive money. To be able to access PayPal, you need a computer with an Internet connection, you need to be at least 18 years old, and you need an e-mail account that you can use with the service. That's it!

Discovering PayPal

PayPal is an online payment service (which functions somewhat like an online bank) that lets people send and receive payments via their e-mail accounts. More than 50 million people currently use the service, and PayPal adds approximately 28,000 new user accounts each day. Over 42,000 Web sites now accept PayPal.

PayPal is a global service and is available in over 45 countries. PayPal supports sending and receiving payments in U.S. dollars, Canadian dollars, euros, pounds sterling, and yen, and lets you convert money from one currency to another.

Signing up for a free personal PayPal account is as simple as going to `www.paypal.com` and clicking the Sign Up link. Figure 1-1 shows the Sign Up link in the upper-right corner of the screen, and in the center of the page.

After signing up for an account, you can send and receive payments, send online invoices, accept credit card payments for goods and services (even if you don't have a merchant account with a bank), and use PayPal in conjunction with auctions.

Figure 1-1:
You can sign up for a PayPal account, right from the PayPal home page.

In the beginning was the Palm Pilot

PayPal was cofounded by Peter Thiel and Max Levchin in December 1998. Originally called Confinity (a blend of the words Confidence and Infinity), PayPal started with the idea of creating a secure microwallet system. Microwallets could be used to store credit card information on Palm Pilots, allowing Palm Pilot users to securely beam money to one another.

From Palm Pilots, the idea evolved into an online payment system to let users send money via e-mail. Max Levchin wrote up a business plan and the rest, as they say, is dot-com history. PayPal had its Initial Public Offering (IPO) in February 2002.

eBay acquired PayPal in October 2002, making millionaires of Peter and Max. PayPal is now the world leader in secure online payment solutions.

Most people access PayPal from a standard desktop or laptop computer, but PayPal can also be viewed with a WebTV browser and Web-enabled portable devices such as cellphones. The future plans of PayPal include availability on Web-enabled pagers and handheld devices, such as Palm Pilots.

The most important factor in PayPal's success is that it enables you to make payments securely. All payment information is encrypted when users send and receive payments, and PayPal offers protection services for both buyers and sellers. Additionally, PayPal takes an active role in preventing fraud. For in-depth information on how to protect yourself when using PayPal's services, see Chapter 3.

Determining What PayPal Can Do for You

If you're slightly cynical and have a "Show me the money" attitude, let me jump right into the benefits that PayPal offers, when compared to a traditional bank or money market account:

- ✔ Opening a PayPal account is fast and easy.
- ✔ You can conduct transactions (that is, send or receive money) with anyone who has an e-mail account.
- ✔ Sending or receiving cash in different currencies is easy (compared to converting currency at a traditional bank).

✔ Money in your PayPal account can be invested in a money market fund, which offers competitive returns compared to the interest rates of many banks.

✔ You can use PayPal for business transactions without needing to qualify for a business checking account. (If you've ever opened one of these, you know how much documentation you have to provide and how many forms you need to fill out!)

✔ Sending an invoice is as simple as filling out an online form — no stamps needed!

✔ With instant payments, you can send and receive money in real time. There's no more waiting a couple of days for the check to clear.

✔ Setting up a Web page to accept donations for a charity is easy.

✔ Accepting payments for an online auction is easy and you get paid immediately, instead of waiting days to get a check in the mail.

✔ PayPal has a variety of tools to let you manage your eBay auctions more efficiently; it even offers online tools to help with tracking and shipping!

✔ PayPal buttons and shopping carts can be integrated into existing Web sites so you can accept payments online.

✔ If you're a developer, you can write applications using PayPal's newly published APIs (application programming interfaces).

You can find out about all of these conveniences later in the book. Just keep reading to find out more.

PayPal versus paying online with a credit card

A credit card can also be used for online payments, but PayPal offers you several advantages:

✔ When you pay with your PayPal account, you don't wrack up expensive interest charges.

In fact, if you invest in a PayPal Money Market account, you can earn interest on your money, right up until the time it is deducted from your account.

✔ When you want to purchase items through eBay, most sellers accept PayPal even when they don't accept credit cards.

✔ You can send payments via e-mail, something not supported by most credit card companies.

✔ You can use PayPal to send someone a gift certificate (perfect if you're one of those people who wait until the very last minute)!

> ✔ No fees are associated with sending or receiving money through a Personal PayPal account. However, there are fees for receiving money when you have a Premier or Business PayPal account.
>
> ✔ You can see a list of transactions in your PayPal account as soon as they have gone through, making it easier to track your cash flow.

In fact, PayPal makes it so easy to spend your money, you may find yourself trying to take advantage of its ease a little too often!

PayPal problems

As great as PayPal is, nothing in life is without problems and that includes PayPal. Some problems that plagued PayPal in its infancy have been ironed out, but there are still a few of which you should be aware. Keep reading to make sure you don't get stung unexpectedly, because you didn't know how the PayPal systems works.

When you have a dispute with a merchant about an item you paid for with a credit card, or when someone has used your credit card without your authorization, you can request your credit card company to do a *chargeback*. A chargeback means your credit card company will not hold you accountable for the payment until after the dispute has been resolved. PayPal does not let you chargeback, although they do have a Buyer Protection program. Unfortunately, the Buyer Protection program covers only $1,000. For expensive purchases above $1,000, you may want to use a credit card instead of your PayPal account.

Freezing funds in your account

If PayPal puts a limit on your account for some reason, it may be 180 days before PayPal gives you access to the money in your account. Prior to June 2003, you had to request the return of the funds, but now PayPal returns these funds automatically.

The best way to avoid having a limit put on your account is to read your PayPal User Agreement carefully to make sure you understand all of its terms. But you do that with all legal documents — right?

Some users have complained that it can be difficult to find the PayPal phone number for customer support. But it is possible! For support, you can call 402-935-2050 during the hours shown in Table 1-1.

Table 1-1	PayPal Customer Service	402-935-2050
Day	**Opens**	**Closes**
Monday–Friday	4:00 AM PDT	10:00 PM PDT
Saturday	6:00 AM PDT	8:00 PM PDT
Sunday	8:00 AM PDT	6:00 PM PDT

Please note that PayPal Customer Service only discusses issues with the account holder, so be prepared to provide verification in the form of your telephone number, your e-mail address, or the last four digits of the credit card or bank account you registered with PayPal.

Finding Out How PayPal Works

Like many great ideas, the fundamentals of PayPal are pretty easy to grasp. Your PayPal account is much like any savings or checking account, except PayPal was designed specifically for online transactions. Before you can start using PayPal, the first thing you need to do is open a PayPal account. I recommend you start with a Personal account, because you have no fees associated with sending or receiving money. After you get your feet wet, you can always upgrade to a Premier or Business account.

You are required to upgrade from a Personal account to a Premier or Business account if you send payments totaling $2,000 or more. This limit may vary, depending upon whether you have a U.S. or International account. There may also be limits on how much money you can transfer from your PayPal account to your bank account. To see what limits apply to your account, click the View Limits link, located to the right of your account balance box, on your Account Overview page. Chapter 2 provides information about which type of account is right for you.

Money makes the (PayPal) world go 'round

Okay, you're convinced and you opened a Personal account. Now what? An account without funds is like a cone without ice cream — what's the point? You need to get money into your PayPal account before you can start doing anything.

You add funds to your PayPal account in one of three ways:

✔ By receiving payments from other PayPal members

✔ By linking a savings or checking account to your PayPal account and using Electronic Funds Transfer (EFT)to transfer money

✔ By getting interest payments on the funds that are in your PayPal account

When you make a payment with PayPal, you have several funding sources from which to choose to finance the transaction. These sources include the following:

✔ If you have enough funds in your PayPal account to cover the payment you want to make, the funds are deducted directly from your PayPal account.

✔ If you have linked a checking or savings account to your PayPal account, the funds can be deducted directly from your bank account in the form of an eCheck.

✔ If you link a credit card to your PayPal account, the payment amount can be deducted from your credit card after you've depleted the funds in your PayPal account balance. The payment shows up on your monthly credit card bill.

The process for buying a good or service using PayPal is very straightforward:

1. **After winning an auction or purchasing an item, if you opt to use PayPal for payment, PayPal deducts the amount of your purchase from funds in your PayPal account or authorizes payment from the credit card you have linked to your PayPal account.**

2. **PayPal credits the seller's account with the funds deducted from your account (less any applicable transaction fees).** Fees only apply to sellers with Premier and Business accounts. See Chapter 2 to read about Premier and Business accounts.

3. **PayPal generates e-mails to you (the buyer) and the seller to confirm the transaction and the transfer of funds.**

Chapter 4 describes the payment process in greater detail, if you want to know the exact steps involved, but the actual transfer of funds is no more complicated than if you were to pay for an item with a check from your checking account.

How PayPal makes money

Just like a bank, PayPal makes money off the "float" of the funds they manage. In other words, PayPal is earning interest against the money that you (and millions of others) have placed into their accounts, but not spent yet.

Think of it this way: PayPal has roughly 50 million members. If each member left $10 in their account for a year, the accrued interest would total around $500 million dollars. Even at an interest rate as low as 1.75 percent, PayPal would be earning $8,750,000 every year, just for letting the money sit there!

Additionally, PayPal makes money by charging transaction fees for Premier and Business accounts: There's no charge to send money, but when you receive money, PayPal takes a percentage of the amount (between 1.9 percent and 2.9 percent) plus a 30-cent USD transaction fee. For more detailed information about the PayPal fee structure, see Chapter 2.

Knowing How PayPal Protects Buyers and Sellers

PayPal makes member security one of its top priorities; an entire section of the PayPal Web site is dedicated to security issues (see Figure 1-2). The Security Center gives valuable information about how PayPal safeguards your money and protects your privacy, and describes steps you can take to protect yourself from fraud.

PayPal maintains special programs designed to protect sellers and buyers. For sellers, PayPal offers annual fraud protection coverage, up to $5,000. There are a number of criteria a seller must meet to ensure coverage. The PayPal Web site list these requirements and you can find them in Chapter 3.

PayPal also offers a PayPal Buyer Protection plan, which provides $500 of coverage for qualified purchases. When there is a problem, PayPal first works with both the buyer and seller to solve a dispute. If that doesn't work, the buyer can file a claim to recover the payment. For more information on how the PayPal Buyer Protection program works, see Chapter 3.

Most disputes are a matter of miscommunication and can be resolved without anyone needing to file a claim. Unfortunately, scam artists are out there who are trying to steal your money.

PayPal has an extensive list of security tips. These tips cover a great deal of information, including

- Recognizing e-mail that claims to be from PayPal (but isn't)
- Keeping your password safe
- Using your account wisely
- Determining whether you're actually on the PayPal site, or on a fraudulent site

Figure 1-2:
PayPal's
Security
Center
provides
you with
important
safety
information,
whether
you're a
buyer or a
seller.

I generally receive a fake "PayPal e-mail" every nine months or so. An example of a fake e-mail is shown in Chapter 3, along with an explanation of how I knew it was a fake (and how you can spot a fake, too!).

Discovering the Scope of PayPal's Tools and Services

When I told a friend that I was writing *PayPal For Dummies,* she offered her congratulations and then paused for a second.

"That's great," she asked, "but is there really enough about PayPal to fill a whole book?"

Yes! And that's what I hope you realize, as you scan the rest of these pages. PayPal is much more than a simple service that lets you send money via e-mail. There's so much you can do to get the most out of PayPal and really make it work for you. As a buyer, PayPal lets you

✔ Create a Personal account for free.

✔ Manage your money as effectively as you can with regular banking accounts.

✔ Obtain PayPal credit, using your line of credit and calculating your monthly payments.

✔ Get interest on the money that's in your account.

For sellers, PayPal offers an even greater range of services. You can

✔ Upgrade to a Premier account when you want to accept credit card payments from buyers.

✔ Set your account up with specific selling preferences and select how you prefer to receive payments.

✔ Obtain a Business PayPal account, with multiple users and different levels of access for your employees.

✔ Add PayPal logos to your eBay auctions and sell your items in PayPal shops.

✔ Invoice users, ship with PayPal, and track non-PayPal payments through PayPal's online tools.

Discovering more about PayPal's rich set of features and tools is worth the time because they can save you time, save you money, and help you make money. And who doesn't want to do that?

Making PayPal Work for You

Some of PayPal's real power lies in the ability to customize the way it works and integrate PayPal features into a Web site. You need to know HTML and be comfortable working with scripting languages (such as ASP or PHP) to take advantage of these features. If you are a Webmaster or developer, PayPal lets you

✔ Integrate PayPal buttons and shopping carts into an existing Web site and turn it into an e-commerce Web site.

✔ Work with different types of buttons (including Donations buttons) and create customized buttons with the Button Factory.

✔ Use PayPal wizards that are available for other software applications. Wizards are available for Adobe GoLive, Microsoft Outlook, Microsoft FrontPage, Macromedia DreamWeaver, and Macromedia Flash.

✔ Work with the newly published PayPal APIs (Application Programming Interfaces). The chapters that address the APIs are written for software developers.

Chapter 2

Sign Me Up!

*I*f you haven't opened a PayPal account before, it may be easiest to start with a Personal account, just to get a sense of how PayPal works and what you can do with it. Later, when you're ready, you can always upgrade to a Premier or Business account.

On the other hand, if you're the type of person who likes to jump right in, you may want to pass "Go" and go straight to Premier (or Business, for that matter). All three types of accounts are quick and easy to open and your choice depends upon the type of flexibility you need when conducting financial transactions.

Types of PayPal Accounts

No matter which type of account you open — Personal, Premier, or Business — they all give you a basic set of functionality. Each of the accounts lets you do the following things:

✔ Send and receive payments via e-mail.

✔ Incorporate PayPal buttons into online auctions. The buttons let you accept PayPal payments, automatically invoice the winner of your auctions, and send e-mail payment reminders.

✔ Pay with PayPal for goods and services you purchase online.

✔ Add PayPal buttons to items you sell through your own Web site.

✔ Earn interest on the funds in your account, through the PayPal Money Market Fund.

✔ Use a virtual debit card. You can pay merchants who don't accept PayPal with a "virtual" debit card number and the funds are taken from your account as if you were using a debit card from a traditional bank.

✔ Insure your account. PayPal deposits the funds in your PayPal account into an FDIC-insured bank. Your funds are protected up to a total amount of $100,000, in the event that the bank fails. Unfortunately, this insurance is not passed on to your PayPal account. If PayPal were to close, your funds are not insured.

✔ Download a log, containing information about your PayPal transactions.

✔ Use e-mail–based customer service.

In addition to these core features, you get added benefits from having a Premier or Business account. Table 2-1 shows the features available with each type of account.

Table 2-1	PayPal Account Features		
Feature	*Personal Account*	*Premier Account*	*Business Account*
Core features (see the list of core features in the preceding paragraphs)	X	X	X
Accept credit card payments from people who aren't using a PayPal account		X	X
Flexibility in how you choose to receive payments		X	X
Ability to set up subscriptions/recurring payments		X	X
Ability to add a PayPal Shopping Cart to your Web site(s)		X	X
Ability to apply for an ATM/Debit Card, which lets you pay for goods and services offline and get money from ATMs		X	X
Ability to make mass payments (pay up to 10,000 people at once)		X	X

Feature	Personal Account	Premier Account	Business Account
Download logs with your PayPal account information (with advanced options for the type of data to be downloaded)		X	X
Ability to open a PayPal Shop		X	X
Toll-free customer service seven days a week		X	X
Do business under your business, corporation, or group name			X
Have multiple users access your account			X
Set different permission levels for the users of your account			X

The account benefits described previously are available for people who have opened U.S. PayPal accounts. There are restrictions on accounts opened in other countries. To see if there are any account restrictions for your country, or to see whether PayPal is available in your country, review the Non-U.S. Account Information available on the PayPal Web site. Here's how:

1. **From the PayPal home page, click the <u>Help</u> link located at the upper-right corner of the page.**

   The PayPal Help Center screen displays a list of categories, located on the left side of the screen.

2. **Click the <u>Non-U.S. Accounts Category</u> link.**

   The Non-U.S. Accounts Help section has a series of questions and answers that give you more information about International accounts.

3. **Click one of the questions to see the corresponding answer.**

For more information about opening an account from outside the United States, see the section "Accounts Outside of the United States," later in this chapter.

Before choosing your account type, you need to be aware that there are some fees associated with Premier and Business accounts, as well as non-U.S. accounts. Make sure you read the "PayPal Fees" section of this chapter before making your decision.

After you decide which type of account is right for you, you're ready to open your account!

Setting Up Your Profile

You start setting up your PayPal profile during the process of registering for a PayPal account. Open up your browser and type **www.paypal.com** into the Address Bar. The PayPal home page has multiple links that let you sign up for your free account. You can find one <u>Sign Up</u> link in the upper-right corner of the screen, and the other can be found in the middle of the screen.

Opening a Personal account

You can open a Personal account in just a few steps; the entire process doesn't usually take more than five minutes. Here's how:

1. **At the PayPal Account Sign Up page, make sure the Personal Account option is selected.**

   If you're wondering what happened to the Premier account, just hang on. You have the option of upgrading a Personal account to a Premier account later on. Figure 2-1 shows the PayPal Account Sign Up page.

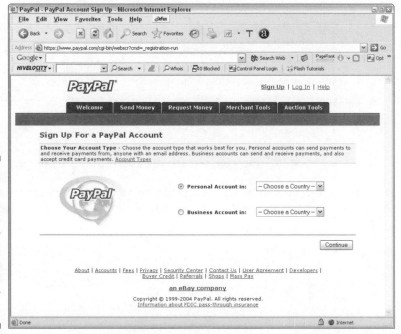

Figure 2-1:
From the Sign Up page, you select either a Personal or Business account and choose your country.

2. Select your country from the list and click the Continue button.

You're ready to start giving PayPal your personal information. Figure 2-2 shows the Account Sign Up page.

3. Start building a PayPal profile by filling in the fields shown on the Account Sign Up page.

The information you need to give PayPal includes

- Your first name, last name, and full address, including city, state, zip code, and country. PayPal requires a zip code for U.S. accounts, but may not require one if you create an International PayPal account.

- Your home telephone number for verification purposes; you have the option of entering a work number.

- Your e-mail address. You need to enter this twice so PayPal can ensure you didn't mistype it the first time.

- A password to use with your PayPal account.

  This password must be at least eight characters long and is case-sensitive. (This means you need to pay attention to whether you use uppercase and/or lowercase characters when you create your password. PayPal won't accept *PASSWORD123* as a valid password if you typed *password123* as your password when you created your account.) Just as you did when you entered your e-mail address, you need to type your password a second time. Picking a password that you don't use with other accounts you may have is also important. If you pick your e-mail password to use as your PayPal password and your e-mail password is compromised, you may find someone making unauthorized use of your funds! It's better to be safe and think up a unique password.

- You are asked to pick two questions from a list of four security questions. The answers you give to these questions are used to verify your identity if you lose or forget your password. You get to choose from the following questions: your mother's maiden name, the last four digits of your driver's license number, the last four digits of your Social Security number, and the city of your birth.

- Deciding whether you want to open a Personal or Premier account. The big advantage of having a Premier account is that you can accept credit card payments from people who don't have or use a PayPal account. Be sure to review the "PayPal Fees" section of this chapter before making your decision.

- You need to read and accept the PayPal User Agreement and Privacy Policy, or you won't be able to open your account. More information is given later in this chapter, but it's *vital* that you read both documents before checking the Yes option, indicating that you agree to the terms. Knowing what can or may happen to your account is important before transferring your money into the account.

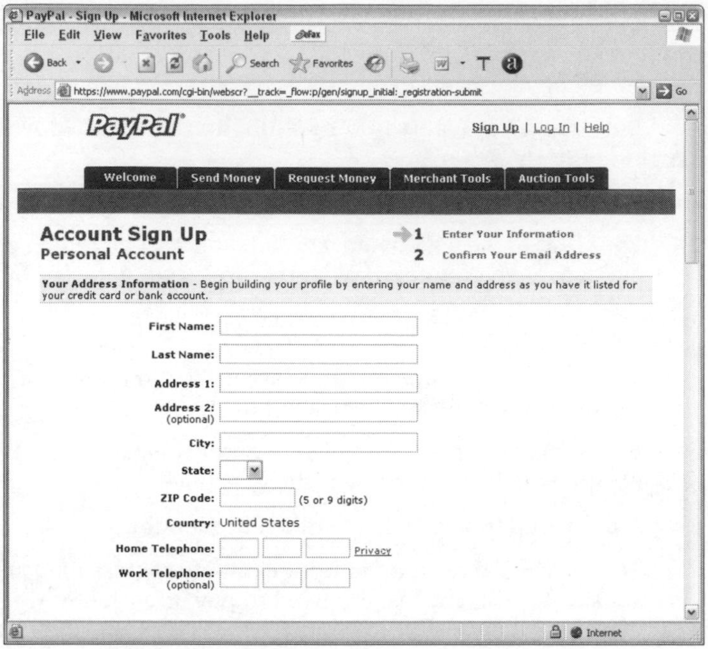

Figure 2-2:
At the
Personal
Account
Sign Up
page, you
enter
personal
information
in the form,
and then
confirm your
e-mail
address.

- PayPal also asks you to indicate that you understand your rights with regard to the arbitration of claims as outlined in the Legal Disputes section of the User Agreement. A link is provided to the document, which describes how legal disputes should be handled in the event that there are problems between you and PayPal. As with any legal document, it's important that you read it before signing and contact a lawyer if you're unsure as to what the document means.

- You have one final security step to go through before the account opens. PayPal displays a sequence of characters in a box with a boxed background. You must type in the characters, exactly as shown, in a text box to the right of the sequence. See Figure 2-3 for an example of what the box looks like. This step is to prevent automated programs from trying to sign up for PayPal accounts. Although a program can fill out the fields on the Account Sign Up page, it can't read the sequence and type it into the box.

- If you are visually impaired, you can still type the correct character sequence into the box, even if you can't read the characters as shown against the background. Click the Help link displayed at the end of the "Security Measure" paragraph to open the PayPal Registration Security Help page. At the end of the page is a listen to the security characters link. Click the link to hear an audio clip that says the characters aloud. You can then type the characters into the box correctly to finish the registration process. In the case of these security characters, it doesn't matter whether you type in the letters as uppercase or lowercase, as long as you get the letters and numbers in the correct sequence.

4. **Click the Sign Up link at the bottom of the page to submit your regis-tration information.**

   After filling out the registration form, you're taken to a page that tells you the process is almost complete except for the confirmation of your e-mail address. After you click the Sign Up link from the previous screen, PayPal sends you an e-mail.

5. **Open your e-mail program and look for an e-mail from PayPal.**

   If your e-mail inbox is anything like mine, you have to search hard to find the PayPal e-mail amidst all the spam. Look for an e-mail from service@ paypal.com with a subject heading of "Activate Your PayPal Account!"

6. **Click the Click here to activate your account link, which can be found in the body of the e-mail.** (Alternatively, you can copy the link and paste it into the address bar of your browser.)

   Clicking the link takes you to a page where you are prompted to enter the password you designated when you registered for the account.

7. **Type your password and click the Confirm button.**

   Congratulations! You just opened your PayPal account.

PayPal gives you the option of linking a checking or savings account to your PayPal account, but wait to do this until you have a chance to review the information in Chapter 5.

Upgrading to a Premier account

Assuming you didn't opt for a Premier account when you signed up for a PayPal account, you can always upgrade at any time. After logging on to your PayPal account, follow these steps:

1. **Click the** Upgrade Account **link, which you find on the left side of the page.**

   The Upgrade Your Account page gives you information about what a Premier account can offer and has a link to a page detailing the fees associated with having a Premier account.

2. **After reviewing the information, click the Upgrade Now button.**

   The Choose a Name to Do Business As page gives you the option of upgrading to a Premier or Business account.

3. **Select one of the options and click the Continue button.**

   That's it! You've successfully upgraded to a Premier account!

Opening a Business account

The process of opening a PayPal Business account is very similar to opening a Personal or Premier account, except for the following:

- ✔ **You need to provide the name of your business and indicate the type of business you have.** You pick the type from a list of business categories. You also need to provide your business address.

- ✔ **You need to give customer service contact information (e-mail, phone number, and your Web site address, if your company has a Web site).**

- ✔ **You need to give contact information for the business owner (name, work telephone number, home telephone number, and address).**

Updating your profile

After you open a PayPal account, keeping your user profile up-to-date is very important. To update your profile, log on to your account and click the Profile link under the My Account tab. You have the option of updating any of the following:

- **Account Information:** You can update your basic contact information (e-mail, address, password, time zone, and so on).

- **Financial Information:** You can change the credit cards or bank accounts associated with your PayPal account, set up online bill paying, see your account balances, redeem gift certificates, and more. The options that are available are dependent upon the type of account that you have.

- **Selling Preferences:** Here you can set up preferences for setting up auctions, registering your Web site as a PayPal shop, setting shipping preferences, setting up invoice templates, and so on. The options available depend upon the type of PayPal account you have.

Accounts Outside of the United States

PayPal will let you open an account in 45 countries and sends or receives payments in U.S. dollars, Canadian dollars, euros, pounds sterling, and yen.

You should be aware that certain countries have restrictions on what you can do with your PayPal account. Additionally, there may be added fees for transactions that are free to U.S. PayPal accounts. Table 2-2 shows countries where PayPal is accepted and whether any restrictions apply. Although not listed in the table, you can open an account in Anguilla and send, but not receive, payments. To find out more about specialized fees that apply to non-U.S. accounts, see the information on fees, later in this chapter.

Table 2-2	Countries Where PayPal Is Accepted
Countries That Do Not Support Withdrawals from Local Bank Accounts	*Countries That Permit Withdrawals from Local Bank Accounts*
Argentina	Australia
Brazil	Austria
Chile	Belgium
China	Canada
Costa Rica	Denmark
Dominican Republic	Finland
Ecuador	France
Greece	Germany
Iceland	Hong Kong

(continued)

Table 2-2 (continued)

Countries That Do Not Support Withdrawals from Local Bank Accounts	Countries That Permit Withdrawals from Local Bank Accounts
India	Ireland
Israel	Italy
Jamaica	Japan
Luxembourg	Mexico
Malaysia	Netherlands
Monaco	New Zealand
Portugal	Norway
Thailand	Singapore
Turkey	South Korea
Uruguay	Spain
Venezuela	Sweden
Switzerland	
Taiwan	
United Kingdom	

PayPal and Privacy

PayPal takes your privacy so seriously that there's a link to their Privacy policy at the bottom of every page on the site; and you have to agree to the Privacy Policy before you are able to sign up for your PayPal account.

The privacy policy lists the circumstances under which PayPal will share your private information. You can learn more by reading the policy. PayPal also shares your information with marketing partners.

Before you jump up and down and yell, "I knew it!" you should know that you can be taken off the list of people who get marketing pitches. Here's how:

1. **Click the Profile link under the My Account section of the home page.**

2. **Click the Notifications link, located under the Account Information column.**

3. **On the Notifications page, you can select who you want to let contact you.**

   If you don't want to hear from third-party marketing organizations, you can take yourself off their lists!

PayPal wants to make sure that you're comfortable with their privacy policy. If you have any questions, they encourage you to contact them by filling out an online form, available at `www.paypal.com/ewf/f=ci_prv`. (You can find this link at the end of their privacy policy.) PayPal also encourages you to call them at 402-935-7733, or write to them at PayPal, P.O. Box 7022, Mountain View, CA 94039.

The PayPal User Agreement

As with the Privacy Policy, you can find a link for the PayPal User Agreement at the bottom of every page of the Web site. Unlike the Privacy Policy, the User Agreement covers so much ground and gets updated so often, that trying to summarize it in a book is a little ludicrous. Figure 2-4 shows the first page of the PayPal User Agreement.

Figure 2-4:
The PayPal User Agreement is so comprehensive that the first page contains a series of links to pages that give detailed information about the subpolicies that are a part of the larger User Agreement.

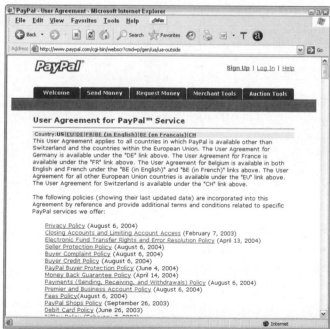

The PayPal user agreement covers the following topics:

- Who is eligible for a PayPal account
- The legal relationship between you and PayPal
- The fees you are required to pay PayPal for use of their services
- Residency in one of the countries where PayPal accounts are available
- How payments are sent and received
- The information you must provide to PayPal
- Restrictions that PayPal can place on your account and activities
- Access to, and use of, the service in ways other than how PayPal intended it to be used
- Your privacy and security
- Termination and closing of your account
- Remedies (in the case of wrongdoing) and the right of PayPal to collect from you
- Assignability, legal compliance, and notices
- How legal disputes are handled, general policies, and disclosures

Covering as much ground as the User Agreement covers (I'm talking ground cover roughly the size of Alaska), the following PayPal policies are included as a part of the larger User Agreement:

- Privacy Policy
- Closing Accounts and Limiting Account Access Policy
- Electronic Fund Transfer Rights and Error Resolution Policy
- Seller Protection Policy
- Buyer Complaint Policy
- Buyer Credit Policy
- PayPal Buyer Protection Policy
- Money Back Guarantee Policy
- Payments (Sending, Receiving, and Withdrawals) Policy
- Premier and Business Account Policy
- Fees Policy
- PayPal Shops Policy
- Debit Card Policy
- BillPay Policy

- ✔ Acceptable Use Policy
- ✔ Bonus Policy
- ✔ Merchant-Initiated Payments Policy

As with the Privacy Policy, you should review the User Agreement before you sign it and check with a lawyer if you have questions about anything.

If you happen to be one of the 50 percent of users who click Yes to accept User Agreements without actually reading what you're signing, here are a couple of tips to keep in mind.

PayPal allows you to have one Personal account and one Premier or Business account. You are allowed to add additional e-mail addresses, bank accounts, and credit or debit cards to your existing accounts.

If there is a dispute involving your account, PayPal will notify you by e-mail and freeze the funds in your account that are related to the dispute. PayPal then investigates the dispute. If they find the dispute in your favor, access to the limited funds is restored to you. If they find against you, they can do any of the following:

- ✔ Return the funds to the sender (and restore the rest of your account).
- ✔ Freeze all the funds in your account for 180 days.
- ✔ Close your account and send you a check for the money in your account (minus the disputed amount).

If you discover someone has gained access to your account and/or password, and you notify PayPal within two business days, you won't lose more than $50 if unauthorized funds are taken from your account. (If you wait longer than two days, you can be liable for up to $500!) If you wait more than 60 days, you give up the ability to recover any money that was taken from your account.

If there's a problem with your account, resulting from a PayPal error, PayPal will make things right, except under the following conditions: if you didn't have enough funds in your account to fulfill the transaction in the first place, if you used an ATM or system that you knew had problems before starting to use it, or if circumstances beyond PayPal's control (they give floods and fires as examples) prevent PayPal from making a transaction.

PayPal used to allow online gambling, but changed their policy after they were acquired by eBay. If you use PayPal's services for gambling, adult content, or buying/selling prescription drugs from noncertified sellers, you're in violation of PayPal's User Agreement. In September 2004, PayPal announced that it would start fining users up to $500 for violation of the Agreement. Not only that, PayPal may take legal action in addition to levying the fines. If you engage in any of these activities, stop using PayPal unless you want to start paying hefty fines.

PayPal Fees

For U.S. PayPal accounts, whether you have a Personal, Premier, or Business account, you can do the following for free:

- ✔ Open a second PayPal account
- ✔ Send money
- ✔ Withdraw funds from your account
- ✔ Add funds to your account

For Personal accounts, receiving payments from other PayPal members is free, but you can't accept credit card payments. Premier and Business accounts can accept credit card payments, but fees are charged, depending on the volume of transactions you receive each month.

- ✔ The standard rate, if you receive less than $3,000 U.S. dollars per month, is 2.9 percent of the transaction, plus 30-cent per transaction fee. It works like this . . . if you sell two items in a month, each worth $50, you will pay $3.50 in fees:

```
$50 x 2 items = $100
$100 x 2.9% = $2.90
2 items x $0.30 transaction fee = $0.60
$2.90 + $0.60 = $3.50
```

- ✔ After you receive more than $3,000 a month, you qualify for a Merchant rate, which means you get a discount on the variable rate fee. You still have to pay $0.30 per transaction, but the 2.9 percent gets discounted according to the schedule shown in Table 2-3.

Table 2-3	Merchant Rate Fees (USD)
Monthly Volume	*Fee Amount*
$3,000.01 to $10,000.00	2.5% plus $0.30 per transaction
$10,000.01 to $100,000.00	2.2% plus $0.30 per transaction
Over $100,000	1.9% plus $0.30 per transaction

If you make an eCheck payment, there's a fee of $5.00 USD. You can find more information about eChecks in Chapter 12.

For U.S. PayPal accounts, receiving payments in currencies other than U.S. dollars, the percentages stay the same, but the $0.30 per transaction fee varies according to currency:

- ✔ $0.55 CAD for Canadian dollar payments
- ✔ €0.35 EUR for euro payments
- ✔ $0.20 GBP for pound sterling payments
- ✔ ¥40 JPY for yen payments

Fees for currency conversions are the retail foreign exchange rate, as determined by PayPal, plus 2.5 percent of the amount exchanged. As with any currency exchange rate, the amount varies according to market conditions.

For non-U.S. accounts, depending upon the country, there may be fees for activities, such as withdrawals, returns, receiving funds through Personal accounts, and so on. To see the fee structure for your country, click the <u>Fees</u> link shown at the bottom of every PayPal page. Click the <u>Fees for Other Banks</u> link, shown in the center of the page.

PayPal as Your Money Market Manager

After you log on to your PayPal account, you see a <u>Money Market</u> link at the bottom of every page. Clicking the link shows you information about investing your money in the PayPal Money Market Fund.

Funds in regular PayPal accounts don't earn any interest, as they would if you had your money in a standard checking or savings account in a bank. If you want any return on your money, you need to invest in the PayPal Money Market Fund, which is run by Barclays Global Fund Advisors.

Barclays takes the combined monies of PayPal users who invest in the fund, and invests in high-quality, short-term securities (such as treasury bills and bank notes) rather than stocks, which have historically been riskier investments. The returns made from the fund are then distributed to PayPal investors.

Although the PayPal Money Market Fund has traditionally yielded more than the interest paid by the average checking account, you have to remember that you are investing your money, and investments always carry some risk. If the fund doesn't do well over a period of time, not only will you not earn money — you could actually lose money. As with any investment, you need to do some research before deciding if the PayPal Money Market Fund is right for you. Click the <u>prospectus</u> link, located on the Money Market page, to read about the fees and expenses associated with the fund, along with information about the fund's goals, how the money is managed, and information about how the fund has performed in the past.

The option to invest in the PayPal Money Market Fund is available only to U.S. accounts. If you decide that the Money Market Fund is right for you, enrolling is very easy.

1. **Log on to your PayPal account and click the <u>Money Market</u> link at the bottom of the page.**

2. **Click the <u>Start Earning a Return Today</u> link.**

3. **Enter your Social Security number and check the "I have read the prospectus" option.**

4. **Finally, click the Submit button.**

   You're enrolled!

It sounds obvious, but I want to remind you of a little fact. Even if you enroll in the PayPal Money Market Fund, you won't earn anything on your account unless you add funds to your PayPal account!

Refer a Friend

Periodically, PayPal offers bonuses to members who get friends or family to sign up for an account. The $5.00 Refer-a-Friend bonus was very popular, but unfortunately this program ended in September 2003. Currently, PayPal offers a bonus when you sign up a new *merchant*. A merchant is defined as someone with a Premier or Business account who sells at least $3,000 of goods or services a month. If you sign up a merchant, you'll earn 0.5 percent of the merchant's revenue for a 12-month period, up to a cap of $1,000 USD.

Because the PayPal Referral Programs come and go, it's worthwhile to review the What's New items on the home page, whenever you log on to your account. You may discover a program that can help bring you some money!

Closing Your PayPal Account

I hope that once you try PayPal, you'll want to keep using it. But if PayPal isn't right for you, or if you find you opened too many PayPal accounts (which happened to me in the course of writing this book), it helps to know how to close an account when you need to. Here's how:

1. **Log on to your PayPal account.**

   Locate the My Account section.

2. **Click the <u>Profile</u> link.**

3. **Click the <u>Close Account</u> link.**

PayPal displays a page that tells you what to expect when you close your account.

- Any unclaimed payments or pending money requests associated with your account are automatically cancelled.

- If you have a balance in an eBay Anything Points account, or if you have Gift Certificate points in your account, these are forfeited.

- PayPal sends you a check for the funds that are in your account, minus any fees that you still owe. The check is mailed to your street address.

- The check that PayPal mails you has a $1.50 processing fee. If there is less than $1.50 in the balance of your account, you will not receive a check.

4. **If you still want to close your account, click the Continue button.**

   If you want to share information with PayPal about why you're closing your account, select the reason(s) from the list PayPal displays.

5. **After you select your reason(s), click the Continue button.**

   You go to a page with the PayPal customer service number, in case there are any account concerns that you want to discuss with them.

6. **If you're still committed to closing the account, click the Continue button.**

7. **At the final Close Account page, click the Close Account button.**

   You have successfully closed your account.

In a few days, PayPal sends you an e-mail, letting you know that they're sorry to lose you as a customer. The e-mail message contains a link to let you sign up again if you ever have a change of heart.

Chapter 3

Protecting Yourself

*I*magine the following scenario. You're walking along a crowded city street, and you notice a man selling watches that are displayed on a folding table. On closer inspection, one of the watches appears to be a Rolex! Savvy bargain hunter that you are, you ask how much the watch costs and are very excited to learn you can get a "genuine Rolex" for just $100! Opening your wallet, you hand the man five twenties and walk off the proud owner of . . . well . . . total junk.

After you get over your anger and disappointment, what's your next move? Do you go to your bank and demand reimbursement for the $100 you lost because you bought a fake from a disreputable vendor? I don't think so! But many people would expect PayPal to provide reimbursement if they bought the fake Rolex from an online auction.

In fact, PayPal does offer you a certain amount of protection from disreputable sellers, but you need to use common sense when purchasing online. Not to be a cynic, but if it looks too good to be true, it probably *is* too good to be true.

Protecting Yourself As a Buyer

Protecting yourself as a buyer starts with using the same common sense you use to protect your identity and credit cards in the physical world, and then applying a few additional strategies to protect yourself when purchasing online.

Problems, which can, and unfortunately do, occur when buying online, include these:

- ✔ Not receiving items that you purchased.

- ✔ Receiving items that are not what you expected, based on the description you read before making the purchase.

- ✔ Having your e-mail address sold to third parties, causing hundreds of spams to show up each time you open your mail program.

- ✔ *Phishing* and *spoofing,* where you receive an e-mail that seems to come from a trusted source (such as PayPal), instructing you to click a link. The link takes you to a Web site that seems to be valid, but isn't really PayPal.com, or eBay.com, or another vendor you trust. Unfortunately, these e-mails and sites seem so real that you may enter personal information without realizing you've helped a scam artist steal your identity.

Receiving shoddy goods (or not receiving any goods)

PayPal has multiple programs in place to protect you against sellers who don't deliver the goods, or deliver goods that were clearly misrepresented. The section of this chapter describes the PayPal Buyer Protection program and gives information about what to do if you feel you've been taken advantage of.

Selling your e-mail to third parties

Even trustworthy merchants may sell your e-mail address to third parties, as a way of making money. But a smart merchant doesn't want to offend you, or risk driving your business away in the future. Take a long, careful look at the fields shown on a purchase form when you're ordering an item.

Many times you see check boxes, which give the seller permission to share your information with "trusted marketing partners" or let you choose to "be informed about other exciting offers." Usually, these check boxes are already checked.

"Trusted marketing partners" and "exciting offers" are marketing double-speak for "we're planning on selling your e-mail address to the highest bidder." Make sure to uncheck these boxes before clicking any Submit or Purchase Now buttons. Unless you're one of those people who feels really popular when you see hundreds of e-mails in your inbox . . . these e-mails will come from your new buddies who want to help you make money, introduce you to new friends, help you purchase medication, and want to show you lots of pictures. I'm sure you get where I'm going with this joke, so in the interest of good taste, I'm going to stop now.

Phishing and spoofing

Identity theft, which is when someone steals your personal or financial information, isn't limited to online situations, but the Internet can make it much easier for a criminal to steal from you. Phishing and spoofing are two methodologies used by criminals to persuade you to give them personal information.

Phishing is when you get an e-mail that seems to come from a trusted source and directs you to a Web site that asks for personal information. The Web site is a fake, but is designed to look like the real thing and includes fake versions of company logos, and links to the real company Web site.

Spoofing is the process of faking an e-mail header (that is, who the e-mail is from) so it looks like an e-mail from a valid company representative. Spoofing works because you're much more likely to be fooled by an e-mail that appears to come from `validation@paypal.com` instead of `bob@hackersrule.com`. If you trust the source, you may be fooled into clicking a link that takes you to the phony Web site.

Beware of fake PayPal e-mail

Scam artists send out many fake PayPal e-mails, so being wary is important. I usually receive a couple every year. Some of them are pretty clever, but there are a few ways you can tell whether you received a valid PayPal e-mail or someone is trying to scam you:

- ✓ **A real e-mail from PayPal greets you with your first and last name, or the name of your business (if you have a business account).** If you get an e-mail with the greeting "Dear PayPal Member," you know it's a fake.

- ✓ **PayPal e-mails do not contain attachments.** If an e-mail instructs you to download something, or open an attachment, the e-mail isn't really from PayPal.

- ✓ **PayPal e-mails do not ask you to respond to the e-mail with personal information.** If you get an e-mail asking for your PayPal password, Social Security number, checking account information, and so on, you know the e-mail is a fake and it should be reported to PayPal. You can find more information on reporting problems later in this chapter.

- ✓ Valid PayPal e-mails instruct you to open a new browser window and type **https://www.paypal.com** before logging on. This ensures that you're entering your username and password into the real PayPal Web site instead of a spoof Web site.

A "genuine" fake PayPal e-mail

Figure 3-1 shows a spoofed PayPal e-mail that I received last year.

Figure 3-1:
This e-mail contains several clues that tell you it came from a scam artist instead of PayPal.

Here are the clues I noticed, which alerted me that the e-mail was fake:

- **The subject of the e-mail is "PayPal Random Account Verification."** PayPal doesn't do random account verification.

- **The e-mail has been addressed to Vrosenborg.** Valid e-mails from PayPal are sent to the e-mail account associated with the PayPal account.

- **The PayPal logo image in the upper-left corner of the e-mail looks a little fuzzy.** I'm sure PayPal would use a better version of their logo image, if they were really sending me this e-mail.

- **The text in the e-mail's main paragraph is centered, which looks a little odd.** Real PayPal e-mails are designed by professionals and the layout of the e-mail would look better than this! PayPal also sends e-mails that are formatted as plain text. If you get a plain text e-mail, it may actually be from PayPal — keep looking for other clues to make the determination.

- **The e-mail contains a bunch of typos.**

- **The e-mail asks me to click a link instead of instructing me to open a new browser window and log on to my PayPal account.** Now for the big giveaway. . . .

> ✔ **The link in the e-mail starts with** `http://www.paypal.com`, **instead of** `https://www.paypal.com`. The `s` after `http` in an e-mail address means the site uses Secure Sockets Layer (SSL) technology to encrypt your data and keep it safe. If the e-mail address doesn't start with `https`, it can't be from PayPal.

As soon as I received this e-mail, I alerted PayPal so they could start researching the fake e-mail. Later in this chapter, I show you how to report fake e-mails. Although reporting fake e-mails is a little more work than just hitting the delete key, letting PayPal know when you get one of these is important to help them ensure the perpetrator is caught and prosecuted.

The PayPal Security Center

PayPal has a Security Center section of their Web site that is accessible from every page by clicking the <u>Security Center</u> link. The Security Center contains links to many resources to help you stay safe when using your PayPal account. Some of the helpful information includes these topics:

> ✔ General safety tips and whitepapers you can download to learn more about conducting safe online transactions

> ✔ How PayPal encrypts your data to keep it secure

> ✔ The PayPal buyer and seller protection programs

> ✔ Obtaining account insurance

> ✔ Verifying your account (see Chapter 5)

> ✔ Links to pages where you can report buyer and seller problems

PayPal Buyer Protection

Caveat Emptor — the only Latin I know . . . meaning "let the buyer beware" — should be the guiding principle when purchasing an item online. Sometimes, however, you can experience problems, no matter how careful you've been about the purchase. The PayPal Buyer Protection program offers some measure of defense against sellers who are out to swindle you. Qualified items are insured up to $1,000 coverage at no added cost to you. (The qualifications are pretty stringent, so review the list shown in the next section to see whether your purchase is covered.)

General Security Tips

You don't want to get taken advantage of, so keep these tips in mind when you buy an item online or when you get an e-mail requesting you to give personal information:

Look before you buy. The more you know about a vendor, the more confidence you have when making a purchase. To learn about a vendor, you should:

> **Make sure the vendor's address and phone number are displayed on their Web site.** The Web site should also have the name of a real person you can contact in the event of a problem.
>
> **Google the vendor.** Type the name of the business into google.com (or yahoo.com or your search engine of choice) and see if anything comes up. If the search engine can't find any references, you should be cautious before buying something. (As a rule, you want to do business with a company that's been in business more than five minutes!)
>
> **Compare the vendor's prices to prices given by other sellers.** You don't want to pay twice as much as you have to in order to purchase an item. (You should also be wary of the "bargain of the century." Established vendors have prices that are close to those of their competition.)
>
> **The vendor's return policies should be clearly stated on the Web site.** If you can't return an item (particularly a defective item), you should probably look elsewhere to make your purchase.

If you're buying from an auction, instead of an online store, take the time to review information about the seller and determine whether he or she seems trustworthy. On eBay.com, you can get information about the seller:

> **Seller information is located in a blue box on the right side of the screen.** It shows the seller's feedback number (the number of times users have left feedback after conducting business with this seller). Under the seller's name is a feedback percentage. This percentage shows how often the seller has gotten positive feedback. (Generally, I don't deal with sellers who have a feedback lower than 98 percent.)
>
> **You can also click the Read Feedback Comments link.** On this page you can read the detailed comments left by other users, in reverse chronological order.

Use a secure password for all online transactions. Having a unique password for your PayPal account is a good idea. (Your PayPal password should be different from your e-mail password, or the one you use to log on to your company's network.) Some passwords are more secure than others. Never use your name (or the names of your spouse, significant other, or children) when creating a password. Create a password that has a combination of numbers, uppercase letters, and lowercase letters.

Don't share your password with anyone (not even your best friend)!

Change your password on a regular basis (but write the new password down somewhere safe — just in case you forget it!).

Only make purchases from Web sites that use SSL. SSL stands for Secure Sockets Layer, a technology that encrypts your credit card and other information before transmitting it. (Unencrypted information is too easy for a hacker to steal.) To tell whether a Web site is secure, look at the Web site address. Secure Web sites start with `https://` instead of the usual `http://`. See the examples shown below:

```
https://www.paypal.com (Secure)
http://www.nonsecurewebsite.com
          (Not Secure)
```

Whenever you go to the PayPal Web site, start by opening a new browser window and typing `https://www.paypal.com` **into the address bar.** This ensures you don't get to the "spoofed" version of the PayPal Web site.

Do not give your PayPal username and password to anyone. Even if the person asking claims to be a PayPal representative, don't share your information with them. If PayPal has to contact you for any reason, they will not ask for your password.

To qualify for Buyer Protection, an item must meet all of the following criteria:

- The item needs to be listed on eBay. Purchases made through other Web retail outlets do not qualify.

- The PayPal Buyer Protection logo needs to be displayed under the seller's information on the right side of the screen with the item's description.

- PayPal must be used to purchase the item after you win the auction, and the payment needs to go to the e-mail address associated with the auction listing.

- If your item never arrives, and it meets the other criteria, it will be covered by Buyer Protection. Alternatively, it may also be covered if what you receive is significantly different from what was described in the auction listing. "Significantly" is the important word in the previous sentence; you're not protected just because you don't like an item or it's a little more beat up than you expected.

- The item has to actually be a tangible good (in other words, something you can touch). Services and intangible goods are not covered under the policy.

Not only must the item meet the Buyer Protection criteria, you have limitations on how you file a claim. The Buyer Protection Rules require the following conditions:

- **Only one claim can be filed per PayPal payment.**

- **A claim must be filed within 30 days of making the payment.** If you've been waiting three weeks for your eBay item to arrive, you should get your claim in right away, or you could miss the window of opportunity.

- **You only get three Buyer Protection refunds a year.** After that, PayPal makes no guarantees that you'll be refunded a third time.

- **You have to provide PayPal with all the information they require while they investigate the claim.**

The process for getting a refund under the Buyer Protection program is the same as filing for a claim that is not covered. See the section of this chapter called "How to complain or report a problem" for information on how to file a claim.

If you applied for PayPal's Buyer Credit and purchased an item using your credit line, you may be covered for the full value of the item and not just up to $1,000. See the terms of your PayPal Credit Agreement for more information about this coverage. See Chapter 6 for more information about PayPal credit.

Eligibility for Buyer Protection

If you're a seller who wants to qualify for the Buyer Protection logo, you need to meet the following criteria:

- You need at least 50 feedback comments from users you bought from or sold to on eBay.
- At least 98 percent of your feedback needs to be positive.
- You must be a verified member of PayPal. See Chapter 5 for more information about getting verified.
- You need a Premier or Business PayPal account, which you use when accepting payments for items you sold on eBay.
- You need to have a U.S., U.K., German, or Canadian PayPal account, and the account must be in good standing.

The item you're selling must meet some criteria as well:

- You must accept PayPal as one of the payment options when listing the item on eBay.
- The item must be listed on the U.S., U.K., Canadian, or German versions of the eBay Web site.
- The item must be a physical good, not a service or intangible item (like a psychic reading!).
- Payment for the item must come to the PayPal account associated with the eBay listing.

In addition to the PayPal Buyer Protection program, your purchase may be covered by the eBay Buyer Protection program, up to $250. You can read more about this program by going to www.ebay.com and clicking the Services link in the eBay navigation bar. On the left side of the page under Bidding and Buying Services, click the Buyer Protection link.

The Money Back Guarantee

If the PayPal Buyer Protection policy isn't enough for your peace of mind, PayPal will let you purchase a Money Back Guarantee for selected items. This guarantee is a form of insurance you can purchase while using PayPal to pay for an item.

For goods that qualify for the guarantee, you see a Money Back Guarantee check box on the Confirm Details payment page. The price of the insurance appears next to the check box. If you want to purchase the insurance, just click the box before finishing the payment process.

The Money Back Guarantee covers tangible goods that cost less than $1,000. To take advantage of the guarantee, you need to return the merchandise you purchased, within 30 days of paying for the item, to PayPal (not the seller). PayPal then refunds your money.

The Money Back Guarantee is a good way to ensure you'll be satisfied with the item on which you're bidding. If you're not satisfied and want to file a claim, follow these steps:

1. **Log on to your PayPal account.**
2. **Click the <u>Security Center</u> link.**

   This link appears at the bottom of every page.
3. **On the Security Center page, click the <u>Resolution Center</u> link shown in the For Buyers column.**
4. **Click the <u>File a Claim</u> link, fill out the form, and click the Continue button to file your claim.**

How to complain or report a problem

You may have several reasons to contact PayPal about a problem: you received a spoofed e-mail, someone hasn't mailed the item you paid for, and so on. This section of the chapter walks you through the process of filing a complaint or reporting a problem.

Filing a Buyer Complaint

If the item you purchased doesn't meet all the criteria for the PayPal Buyer Protection, you can still file a Buyer Complaint. PayPal investigates your complaint and works to settle your dispute. In general, if they find the seller should give your money back, they'll try to recover the money for you, within 30 days after you file the complaint.

Before filing a complaint, make sure you meet the following criteria:

✔ You used PayPal to purchase the item.

✔ The item is MIA (missing in action). Even if the product differs grossly from its description, PayPal won't investigate a claim unless the item has not been delivered.

✔ You filed a claim within 30 days of paying for the item.

✔ The item is a tangible good (not an intangible item or a service).

Before filing a Buyer Complaint, PayPal encourages you to contact the seller to see if the two of you can work things out. If that doesn't work, follow these steps to file a Buyer Complaint:

1. **Log on to your PayPal account and click the <u>Security Center</u> link, which is shown at the bottom of every page.**

2. **Click the <u>Resolution Center</u> link.**

3. **Click the <u>File a Claim</u> link and then click the Continue button, shown on the next page.**

4. **Review the Filing a Claim requirements listed on the page.**

   Make sure you can provide PayPal with the information they require to investigate the complaint.

5. **Enter your PayPal Transaction ID in the box shown at the bottom of the page.**

6. **If you don't have the Transaction ID, click the Get PayPal Transaction ID button, shown next to the box.**

   Clicking the button brings up your PayPal account history, listing all of your recent transactions. A column showing all the Transaction IDs is shown in the middle of the page. After copying the Transaction ID, close the window to continue filing your claim.

7. **Enter your Transaction ID and click the Continue button.**

   PayPal confirms whether you really want to file a complaint.

8. **Click Continue.**

   At the Merchandise Dispute – Buyer Protection page, PayPal shows the transaction details (the name and e-mail of the buyer, the name and e-mail of the seller, the amount of the transaction, and so on).

9. **You are asked to supply details of the transaction.**

   Try to be as specific as possible.

PayPal tries to resolve all complaints within 30 days. You may be asked for additional information before the claim can be finalized.

Does the process really work or is it a waste of time? I had to file a complaint once, when an eBay item was not delivered. (The item had no reserve and I was the only bidder. My bid was $1.00. I think the seller decided to ignore the entire transaction.) I wasn't concerned about losing a dollar but it irked me that someone wasn't playing by the rules. PayPal was able to get my dollar back, less than a week after I filed the complaint.

Reporting a problem

If you receive a fake PayPal e-mail, or you realize you've been swindled, you should report the incident to PayPal right away. To report a problem, you need to follow these steps:

1. **Click the <u>Security Center</u> link, which is shown at the bottom of every page.**

2. **At the bottom of the For Buyers column, click the <u>Report a Problem</u> link.**

3. **Choose Report Fraud from the first list of topics.**

   Figure 3-2 shows the Ask Your Question page and the list of top-level items from which to choose. The Report Fraud topic is at the end of the list.

4. **Choose a subtopic and then explain why you need to contact PayPal in one sentence.**

   Don't worry; you get a chance to be more verbose on the next screen.

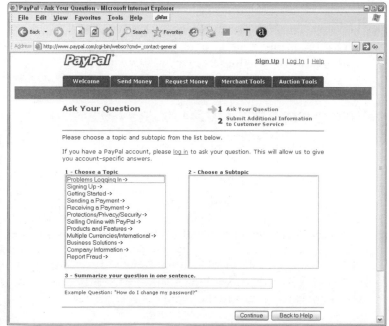

Figure 3-2:
You report a problem to PayPal by picking a topic from the first list and a subtopic from the second list.

5. **At the next screen, give detailed information about the incident you're trying to report and then click the Continue button.**

   PayPal contacts you to let you know they received the message. Sometimes they request additional information (such as asking you to forward a copy of a suspicious e-mail).

When PayPal is the problem

You can use the <u>Report a Problem</u> link if you think PayPal has made an accounting error or has done something unexpected with your account. At the Ask Your Question screen, select the topic that most closely matches your issue and choose a subtopic from the list on the right. If you really need to contact someone right away, you can always call PayPal customer support; the phone number is 402-935-2050.

Protecting Yourself As a Seller

Protecting yourself as a seller can be more difficult than protecting yourself as a buyer. When you're buying, you get to decide whether you want to risk purchasing from a vendor with a low eBay feedback score. You can decide whether you're uncomfortable with the lack of contact information on an e-commerce Web site. But when you're a seller, you have no control over who buys from you.

Luckily, you always have the option not to ship an item until PayPal has transferred funds into your account. But unscrupulous users can claim to have not received goods that you mailed to them.

Selling smart: Tips for sellers

The following tips can help you when you sell online:

✔ **When possible, only ship to confirmed addresses.** A confirmed address means PayPal has checked the address in a user's profile against the billing address used by the member's credit card company. You can check whether the buyer's address has been confirmed: From the Account Overview page, click the transaction details and scroll down to the middle of the page to see the shipping address. If the address is confirmed, you see the word "confirmed" under the address. Unfortunately, only U.S. and Canadian addresses can be confirmed.

✔ **Use a shipping service that lets you track delivery online.** FedEx, UPS, or the U.S. Post Office all offer methods that let you see whether your package has arrived at the correct destination.

✔ **If you sold the item through eBay, check the buyer's reputation on the Feedback Forum.**

   1. **After logging on to eBay, scroll down to the bottom of the page and click the <u>Feedback Forum</u> link.**

   2. **Enter the eBay user ID of the person who won your auction and click the Find Member button.**

      The eBay Member Profile shows you the feedback score and percent of positive feedback. You can also read the feedback comments to see if there are recurring problems with the buyer.

✔ **If someone trying to purchase from you wants to use multiple PayPal accounts to make the payment, don't accept the payment.** You'll be in violation of the PayPal User Agreement and it's more likely that the buyer may be trying to commit a fraud.

✔ **Don't accept credit card payments.** This option can be turned on or off by clicking the <u>Payment Receiving Preferences</u> link found under your Account Profile.

✔ **If the buyer is buying a high-ticket item, do a little extra research about the buyer (especially if the buyer wants the item shipped overnight).** You can look up the buyer on the eBay forum or search with Google for the buyer's name and the purchased item. You may discover your buyer has a history of buying antiques, but not paying for them, or claiming they never arrived.

✔ **Show extra caution when shipping items internationally.** According to PayPal, you run a higher risk of being swindled. In fact, the PayPal User Agreement prohibits you from selling to countries that are not on their approved countries list. To see the list of approved countries, look at Table 2-2 in Chapter 2.

If you have a questionable buyer, request a signed receipt for delivery of the item you ship. This helps protect you if the buyer tries to file a complaint against you.

The PayPal Seller Protection Policy

For eligible transactions, PayPal offers Seller Protection up to $5,000 USD. (The $5,000 is an annual limit, not a limit per transaction.) In order to qualify for Seller Protection, the following criteria must be met:

✔ You need to have a Premier or Business PayPal account.

✔ International criteria:

   • You must be a U.S. or Canadian seller and have sold to someone in the U.S.; or

   • You must be a seller from the U.K. who has sold to someone in the U.K. or U.S.

✔ You need to have shipped the item to the address shown on the transaction details page.

✔ You have to ship the item in a timely manner. (Unfortunately, PayPal doesn't specify what constitutes as "timely.")

✔ You need to have "reasonable proof of postage" and be able to track delivery online. (Translation: Use FedEx, UPS, or USPS and don't throw away those receipts!)

✔ If the item is worth more than $250, you need to request a signature when the shipping service delivers the item to the buyer.

✔ The item must be a tangible good (not an intangible item or service).

✔ The buyer must have paid for the item using a single PayPal account. (But you already knew this was a requirement — right?)

✔ You agree not to surcharge the buyer. According to the PayPal User Agreement, you're not allowed to charge any additional fees beyond the payment for the item.

✔ You provide timely responses to any questions asked by PayPal during the course of the investigation.

Blocking payments

Because the requirements for getting reimbursed through Seller Protection are pretty stringent, you may choose to block payments from international users, or users who do not have a confirmed address. Figure 3-3 shows the Payment Receiving Preferences screen, where you can block certain types of payments.

To set up your Payment Receiving Preferences, go to your account profile and click the Payment Receiving Preferences link (found in the middle of the Selling Preferences column). Please note: You will need to upgrade to a Premier or Business account to see this link.

When you block a payment, you're given the option of not blocking buyers, blocking all buyers who don't meet a specific set of criteria, or getting asked whether you want to block a specific buyer. Blocking options include:

✔ Blocking payments from buyers who do not have a confirmed address.

✔ Blocking payments not made in U.S. dollars (that is, any buyer who wants to purchase your item with yen is blocked from buying).

When blocking buyers based on currency, you have the option of blocking the payments, not blocking the payments, or accepting the payments and having the currency converted to U.S. dollars. (You can find more information about currency conversion in Chapter 4.)

✔ You can block payments from anyone who does not have a U.S. PayPal account. Alternatively, you can choose to require that non-U.S. buyers use the Pay Anyone option when sending money. More information about this option is found in Chapter 7.

✔ You can block payments from sellers who have a bank account linked to their PayPal account but choose to pay with a credit card instead. This helps you avoid selling an item to someone who is trying to pay with a stolen or invalid credit card.

✔ You can prevent someone from sending an eCheck to pay for a purchase.

If you are selling an item at auction, you want to get as large a group of people bidding as possible. When you block certain types of payments or buyers, you're limiting the universe of people who might bid on your item. You need to balance caution with practicality when deciding to block payments.

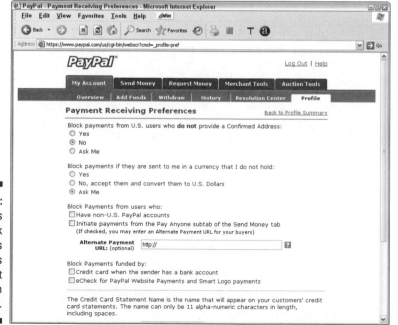

Figure 3-3:
PayPal lets
you block
payments
from buyers
who don't
meet certain
criteria.

Reporting a problem

The process for reporting a problem when you're the seller is identical to the process of reporting a problem as a buyer.

1. **Click the <u>Security Center</u> link, which is shown at the bottom of every PayPal page.**

2. **Click the <u>Report a Problem</u> link found at the bottom of the For Sellers column.**

3. **On the Ask Your Question page, select a topic from the first set of options and then choose a subtopic.**

4. **Summarize your problem in a single sentence.**

5. **Fill out additional information on the next page, which is sent to PayPal customer service.**

PayPal tries to resolve your issue in 30 days. During this time, you may be asked for additional information to help PayPal investigate the complaint.

Part II
Purchasing with PayPal

The 5th Wave   By Rich Tennant

"Guess who found a Kiss merchandise site on the Web while you were gone?"

In this part . . .

Here I show you how to use your PayPal account to purchase goods and services, and how to send money via e-mail. I give you an overview about using PayPal when paying for items you purchase through eBay, and how to use mass payments to pay many vendors with a single PayPal transaction. I show you how to use PayPal as if it were a bank: getting a PayPal Debit card to withdraw money from ATMs; writing eChecks, and adding funds to your account. Finally, I show you how to apply for, and use PayPal Buyer Credit (just in case your funds can't cover all the purchases you need to make).

Chapter 4

Paying with Your PayPal Account

*A*lthough it's nicer to get money than to send it, most people start using their PayPal accounts by making a payment. Maybe you just won an auction on eBay and decided to try PayPal instead of using your credit card. Perhaps you received an online invoice. Whatever the reason or type of payment, it helps to know the ins and outs of paying with PayPal.

Sending Money

I think PayPal is one of those ideas that will continue to evolve in years to come. I envision a world where all bills will be paid online. Instead of paying for small purchases with cash, we'll beam a buyer to a vendor, using our cellphones. (Okay, beam me up Scotty.)

Actually, the future isn't *that* far away — and you can already access your PayPal account with your cellphone, even if you can't pay via cellphone yet! You can use PayPal to pay for a variety of things, but some of the most common uses include

✔ Sending money to other people (much easier than getting a money order and mailing it)

✔ Paying for purchases you buy online

✔ Paying for purchases you buy offline

✔ Paying bills online

Account Optional

With PayPal's Account Optional feature, you can make a purchase even before you open a PayPal account! For Web sites and auction sales that offer this option, you can pay for an item with your credit card.

1. **When you check out after buying an item, you are redirected to the PayPal Web site to complete the transaction.**

2. **At PayPal's Payment Details page, you can log on to your PayPal account to complete the purchase by entering the PayPal username and password and clicking the Continue button.**

3. **If you want to complete the purchase and you don't have a PayPal account, click the Click Here button.**

4. **On the Shipping Information page, you can select a shipping preference and confirm your shipping address.**

5. **Click the Continue Checkout button.**

6. **At the Billing Information page, you're asked to enter your credit card and billing information, along with an e-mail address and phone number.**

7. **You're also asked to type a string of characters, which is displayed in a box over a checked background as an added security measure.**

8. **Click the Continue Checkout button.**

If you try to pay through the Account Optional method, but you already have a PayPal account associated with the e-mail account and/or credit card that has been linked to a PayPal account, PayPal prevents you from completing the transaction.

9. **The Make Your Payment screen shows the confirmation details of the order: the e-mail address of the PayPal seller, the number of items and the amount, your shipping information, and your credit card information. If the details are correct, click the Pay button.**

The You Have Completed Your Transaction page appears. It gives a receipt ID for the transaction. It also gives the e-mail address for the PayPal seller and a contact e-mail.

✔ When the transaction shows on your credit card statement, the seller is listed as "PAYPAL *NAME_OF_PAYPAL_ACCOUNT_HOLDER". If, for example, the seller's PayPal account was sellersname@e-mail.com, the credit card statement lists the transaction as "PAYPAL *SELLERSNAME".

✔ If you want to sign up for a PayPal account, all you have to do is click the Save My Info button and your PayPal account is created using the information you provided during the payment process.

✔ If you don't want to sign up for an account, just click the Return to Merchant link to return to the e-commerce Web site where you started the purchasing process.

You can send (or spend) money in a variety of ways, including e-mailing money, responding to an invoice or request for money, and purchasing items with a PayPal debit card.

Sending money through the mail

Sending someone a payment (if you're not responding to an invoice) is a very quick and easy process.

1. **Log on to your PayPal account and click the Send Money tab.**

2. **At the Send Money page shown in Figure 4-1, enter the e-mail address of the person to whom you want to send money.**

   You can type the e-mail address in the box or select from a list of people to whom you recently sent a payment.

3. **Enter the amount of money you want to send and select a currency.**

   You can pick from U.S. dollars, Canadian dollars, euros, pounds sterling, or yen.

4. **Select the reason you're sending this person money from a list of options including**

   • **You're purchasing an eBay item.**

   • **You're purchasing an item from an auction other than eBay.**

   • **You're buying goods online (but not through an auction).**

   • **You're paying for a service.**

   • **You want to send Quasi-cash.**

      You hear more about Quasi-cash later in the chapter.

5. **You can enter a subject, which becomes the subject header of the e-mail PayPal generates when sending your payment.**

6. **You can also enter a note, which is included in the body text of the e-mail that PayPal generates.**

7. **Click the Continue button.**

8. **On the Check Payment Details page, you have the opportunity to check whether the payment information is correct:**

   • **You can check the basic payment information.** Information includes e-mail address, user status, type of payment, amount of payment, e-mail subject header, and message.

   • **You can see the source of funds that will be used to make the payment.** You can find more information about different types of funding options and how to get funds into your PayPal account in the next chapter.

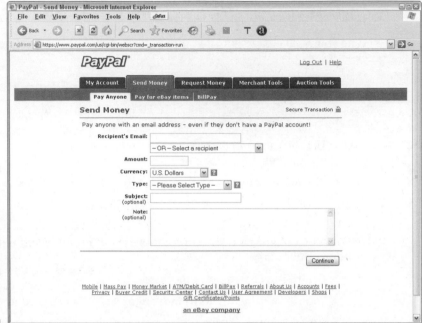

Figure 4-1:
With
PayPal,
sending
money to
anyone with
an e-mail
address is
a snap.

9. **If the recipient is a PayPal member, the shipping address will show under Shipping Information, or you can add a new address if needed.** If you are sending Quasi-cash, or purchasing an intangible item, you should select the "No shipping address required" option.

10. **Click the Send Money button to send your payment.**

I've sent a payment, now what?

After clicking the Send Money button, you see a page that tells you the money has been sent. If you want to see details of the transaction, click the My Account tab in the main navigation bar. This page shows you recent activity in your account.

If you need funds from your bank account or credit card to cover the payment you just sent, you see a Transfer transaction near the top of the transaction list. You should also see a Payment transaction at the top of the list; this shows the payment you just sent. Click the Details link for more information about the payment.

User Status

User Status is a new feature PayPal has added to help protect your security. To see the User Status when sending a payment, click the <u>User Status</u> link (which you find on the Check Payment Details page). A new window opens and displays member information about the person to whom you're sending the payment.

You can see the Seller Reputation, Account Status, Account Type, Account Creation Date, and how long that person has been a PayPal member. (Of course if you're a math whiz, you don't need to see how long the person has been a member, because you've already figured that out, based on the date the account was created.)

Seller Reputation: This shows the number of verified PayPal members who have sent a payment to the person you are paying. Transactions take 30 days before they show up in a member's "reputation" and new accounts may not have a number yet. If someone has a high seller reputation score, the chances are high that your transaction with this person will proceed smoothly.

Account Status: This shows whether the member is verified (has confirmed a bank account which they linked with their PayPal account). Just because a member hasn't been verified, it doesn't mean the person isn't reputable. There are a number of reasons why someone may not be verified: the account is new, they don't use their PayPal account often enough to bother with verification, or they have a non-U.S. account.

Account Type: This shows whether the recipient has a Personal, Premier, or Business account. Although recipients with Personal accounts can receive money, sellers of goods and services should have a Premier or Business account. Premier and Business accounts are required if you want to accept credit card payments.

For How Long the Person Has Been a Member: It makes sense that the longer someone has been a member, the more likely that person is to be reputable (but don't forget that length of membership should not be treated as a guarantee).

How does the recipient get paid?

Next, the recipient gets an e-mail, saying the money has been sent. If you sent money to a PayPal member, the funds will be deposited directly in the recipient's PayPal account. See Figure 4-2 for an example of what the e-mail looks like.

You also get an e-mail (from `service@paypal.com`) letting you know that the money's been sent. You can click a link in the e-mail to see the details of the transaction.

If the person you sent payment to doesn't have a PayPal account, the recipient's e-mail will contain a link with instructions to complete the PayPal easy registration form to claim your money.

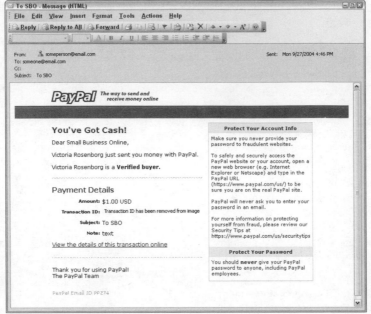

Figure 4-2:
The recip-
ient of your
payment
gets an
e-mail from
PayPal.

This is an example of viral marketing's finest hour . . . of course the person is going to fill out the form to get the cash, and PayPal gets a new member. Viral marketing occurs when users pass along marketing messages during the course of using a product.

PayPal Debit Card

With a PayPal Debit Card, paying for offline purchases is also easy; you can use your card anywhere MasterCard or Visa is accepted; in other words, pretty much everywhere. To apply for a debit card, you need to be a PayPal member for at least 60 days.

1. **Click the ATM/Debit Card link, which you find at the bottom of every page.**

   You can read some introductory material about the card. The terms may change, but right now the card is free.

2. **Click the Continue button to start the application process.**

   You need to be a Premier or Business member to apply. You also need to link a credit card to your PayPal account and confirm a checking account. (You can find more information about becoming verified in the next chapter.) If you haven't met these requirements, PayPal will display a list of the steps you still need to take before applying.

3. **If you meet the requirements, you'll see your name and address, along with a box you need to check to indicate you read and agree to the debit card agreement.**

4. **Click the Submit button and you're done!**

   PayPal lets you know your daily spending and withdrawal limits and will mail you your debit card.

After you receive your debit card, you can use it as you would a bank debit card. When you use the card to pay for an item or to withdraw cash from an ATM, the amount is deducted from your PayPal account. If you try to spend or withdraw more than you have in your PayPal account, the card may be refused for "insufficient funds," so checking your PayPal balance before you start spending is important.

The virtual debit card

Even if you don't have a PayPal debit card, you can still buy goods and services online, even from merchants who don't accept PayPal, as long as they accept MasterCard. The PayPal Debit Bar gives you a "virtual" MasterCard number you can use to make a payment. Like a PayPal debit card, the funds are withdrawn from your PayPal account.

The qualifications for using the Debit Bar are similar to the requirements you must meet for getting a Debit card. You must have a verified U.S. bank account, have linked a credit card to your PayPal account, have money in your PayPal account, and be a PayPal member in good standing.

When you use the Debit Bar, you have a $150 USD limit per day (assuming you have at least $150 in your PayPal account!). It's free to install and use the Debit Bar, and you can use the Debit Bar even if you already have the PayPal Debit Card. (But you don't really need to use the Debit Bar if you already have a Debit Card you can use.) Another benefit of the Debit Bar is its added security; it is a virtual number which you can only use on the Web.

Before you can start using the Debit Bar for purchases, you need to follow these steps:

1. **Click the <u>Shops</u> link, which you can find at the bottom of every PayPal page.**

2. **Click the <u>Shop Anywhere</u> link.**

   At the time this chapter was written, the link can be found in the middle of the right column, but the page layout may be different when you read this. Look carefully around the page and I'm sure you can find the link.

3. **To start using the Debit Bar, enter the Web address of the shop from which you want to purchase.**

   PayPal has a list of shops to choose from, or you can type in the Web address of a different store. (See Figure 4-3, which shows how you can start shopping with the Debit Bar.) In Figure 4-4 example, I type **www. amazon.com** into the text box.

Figure 4-3:
PayPal gives you a list of preferred shops to choose from before you can start using the Debit Bar, or you can enter the Web address of a different online store.

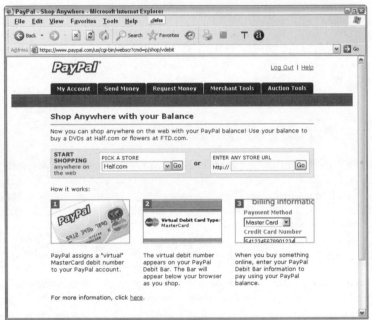

4. **Click the Go button.**

   Two browser windows open. The top (and larger) windows show the Web site you selected during the last step. In this example, the amazon. com store is shown in the top browser window. The Debit Bar shows in the second browser window, at the bottom of the screen. (See Figure 4-4 for an example of what the screen looks like.)

   Even if you go to a different Web site, the Debit Bar continues to show at the bottom of your screen until you close its browser window. Make sure you close this window before leaving your computer to ensure someone else doesn't use the number to purchase items by using the money in your PayPal account.

5. **Shop at the Web site the way you would normally.**

   You won't need to think about the Debit Bar until it's time to pay for the purchases in your shopping cart.

Figure 4-4:
When opened, the PayPal Debit Bar shows at the bottom of your screen. It gives you a virtual debit card number you can use for purchases and shows how much money is left in your PayPal account.

6. **When you're ready to pay, click the Web site's Check Out button or link.**

7. **Select MasterCard from the list of available cards (MasterCard, Visa, Amex, and so on).**

8. **To enter the credit card number, copy and paste the Virtual Debit Card Number shown on the PayPal Debit Bar screen.**

9. **Enter the expiration date shown on the PayPal screen.**

   This date is usually a year from the day the Debit Bar was opened.

10. **Enter the card holder's name, as shown in the Debit Bar.**

11. **After filling in the payment information, submit your order.**

   This process varies, according to the site from which you're purchasing. Please note: The balance in the Debit Bar does *not* change as soon as you submit your order. You need to mentally remember that your balance has been reduced until you see the payment show up on your PayPal transaction list.

Unfortunately, the Debit Bar does not give you the three-digit credit card verification number found on the back of a plastic MasterCard or Visa credit card. For sites that require this number (and many do these days, for security purposes), you need to use a PayPal Debit Card.

Quasi-cash

In PayPal lingo, Quasi-cash is not money you use when paying Monopoly, but is money you send to someone, when you are not paying for a specific good or service.

Quasi-cash is easy to send — after clicking the <u>Send Money</u> link in the PayPal navigation bar, select Quasi-cash from the list of payment types.

Although PayPal never charges you for sending someone Quasi-cash, if the funds are taken from a credit card to make the payment, you may be charged a "cash advance" fee by the bank that issued the credit card. This is similar to the fee you get when you withdraw money from a bank ATM, where you don't have an account.

This fee is taken out of the amount you send the recipient. (If you sent someone $50, for example, they would only receive $48.25, because $1.75 will be used to pay the fee.) If you owe someone money, you need to factor in the fee when deciding how much money to send.

Picking a Currency

PayPal makes it easy for you to send and spend money, and you're not limited just to U.S. dollars when making a payment. Chapter 13 covers how to accept payment in multiple currencies, so if you want to know more about currency conversion, skip ahead to that chapter.

If all you need to know is how to send a payment in a different currency, keep reading.

Sending a payment in pounds sterling or yen starts like any other payment — by clicking the Send Money tab in the PayPal main navigation bar. When you're ready to select a currency, you can pick U.S. dollars, Canadian dollars, Euros, Pounds Sterling, or Yen from the list. Make the other selections that pertain to your payment and click the Continue button.

The recipient of the payment does not need to have that currency in his or her PayPal account in order to accept the payment. (So if I want to pay you in yen, it's no problem, even if you only have U.S. dollars in your PayPal account.)

On the Check Payment Details page, you see the details about the payment you're making, along with information about the currency exchange. Under the Total Amount section of the page, you see the total amount, along with what the equivalent would be in U.S. dollars.

The Source of Funds section of the page shows how much money will be deducted from your account. If you have that particular currency in your account, the money will be deducted from the selected currency first. (If you were sending someone five Canadian dollars, for example, and had $10 Canadian, plus $20 U.S. in your account, the $5 Canadian payment would come out of the $10 Canadian, rather than your funds in U.S. dollars.) If you do not have enough money in the international currency, the funds are taken from your U.S. account and a currency conversion rate is applied before the payment can be made.

The Source of Funds section of the page also shows PayPal's daily currency conversion rate. If you're the one sending the payment, you don't have to pay the currency conversion fee, but the person you're sending the money to will get stuck with the fee. Here's how it works:

1. I decided to send Bob Smith $5.00 Canadian. (I know he's planning a trip to Montreal soon.) Both Bob and I have U.S. PayPal accounts.

2. The PayPal conversion rate, on this day, is one U.S. dollar for every 1.24156 Canadian dollars. (Time to whip out the calculator!) At this conversion rate, PayPal deducts $4.03 U.S. out of my account to cover the cost of sending $5 Canadian to my buddy Bob.

3. Bob receives an e-mail notifying him that I transferred $5 Canadian to his PayPal account. A link is in the e-mail, which shows him the transaction details of the payment.

4. Unless Bob is blocking payments in other currencies, the transaction details give him the choice of:

    • Accepting the payment and converting the Canadian dollars to $3.82 U.S. and transferring the amount into his PayPal account. (You notice that I paid $4.03 for the five Canadian dollars, but Bob only gets $3.82 when he converts the payment back to U.S. dollars because he gets stuck with the $0.21 currency conversion fee.)

    • Bob can also choose to accept the payment in Canadian dollars. In this case, $5.00 Canadian gets deposited into his account (and he saves the $0.21 conversion fee).

    • Bob can choose not to accept the payment and the money returns to my account.

Making Payments

In addition to using PayPal to send money to other people, PayPal can also be used to pay your bills. Try this:

1. **To get started, click the <u>BillPay</u> link shown at the bottom of every PayPal page.**

   You can select the biller to be paid from a list. PayPal has some generic billers, such as Southwestern Bell or Sprint, but these are just to start you off. If you don't have an account with one of the listed companies, or you don't want to use PayPal to pay these companies, just ignore them.

2. **If you want to add a biller to the list of options shown, click the <u>Add New Biller</u> link.**

   This brings you to a page where you can search for the name of your biller. Over a thousand companies can be selected from the list. You browse for the biller's name or search for a specific company.

3. **When you find the name of your biller, click the name.**

   You can enter a nickname for the biller (this is optional), your account number with the biller, and the biller's zip code.

4. **Click the Add Biller button to add the biller to the list.**

   If you're ready to pay right away, you can click the Add & Pay button instead of the Add Biller button.

5. **A <u>Can't find your Biller?</u> link is at the bottom of the page.**

   Clicking this link opens a form you can send to ask your biller to start accepting PayPal. (Gotta love that viral marketing!)

6. **After you select the biller from the list, click the Pay button.**

   The BillPay screen appears.

7. **On the Bill Pay screen, enter the amount you want to pay and click the Continue button.**

   On the Check BillPay Details page, you can see the biller to be paid, the account number (for security's sake, only the last four digits of the number are shown), the source of the funds used to pay the bill, and the amount. This page also shows you when the payment is expected to reach the biller. (It usually takes two to three days, so don't wait until the last minute to pay a bill!)

8. **If you are satisfied with the details, click the Pay Bill button.**

Paying bills through PayPal is great, but it requires you to have an account with the company to be paid. In the case of a credit card company, setting up the payment is easy, but it's not as easy if you're trying to pay a retailer directly.

When you need to, you can edit your biller information (or remove a biller) by clicking the <u>BillPay</u> link at the bottom of the PayPal page and clicking the <u>Edit My Billers</u> link. Click next to the biller's name to either edit the information or remove from the biller list.

Buying from eBay Auctions

Before eBay acquired PayPal, using PayPal to pay for an item on eBay was relatively simple. Because eBay acquired PayPal, paying with your PayPal account has become the easiest way of paying after you win an item.

Describing the whole process of buying and selling items on eBay could fill an entire book. (In fact, it has filled an entire book! I give a quick overview to show you how to pay for eBay items with PayPal. If you want in-depth information on how to acquire or sell items through eBay, I recommend you look at *eBay For Dummies* by Marsha Collier.)

Open your browser and type **eBay.com**. You can search for an item using the search box in the upper-right corner of the page or browse for an item by clicking one of the categories shown on the left side of the page. In the list of available items, click one to see more detailed information and have the opportunity to bid.

On the detailed item description page, you see a link called <u>Shipping, payment details, and return policy</u>. Click this link to see the payment options (assuming you win the bidding!). If the seller accepts PayPal, it is listed as one of the options.

PayPal icons are sprinkled all over eBay, if you know where to look. (See Figure 4-5, which shows the eBay icon help page where you can learn the meaning of the icons used in eBay auctions. To see the page in your browser, go to `http://pages.ebay.com/help/find/icons.html`.)

- ✔ **In the list of available items, some have a double "P" icon next to the item name; this means the user accepts PayPal.** If you see a listing without out the double "P" icon, the user may still accept PayPal but you need to check in the item description to find out.

- ✔ **A double "P" with a shield means the user accepts PayPal and the item listed qualifies for the PayPal Buyer Protection program.** For more information about the PayPal Buyer Protection program, see Chapter 2.

- ✔ **When the seller accepts PayPal for payment, the PayPal logo displays to the left of the credit card icons under the "Payment methods accepted" section of the page.**

- ✔ **You can opt to search only for auction items that accept PayPal.** On the page that shows a list of items, look for the Search Options section in the left column. One of the options lets you search just for items that accept PayPal as a form of payment.

When you win an auction, you receive a congratulatory e-mail from eBay. The e-mail contains payment options, which you access by clicking the Pay Now button. When you click the button, you are asked to log on using your eBay username and password.

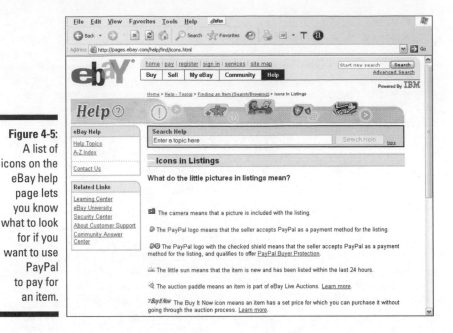

Figure 4-5:
A list of icons on the eBay help page lets you know what to look for if you want to use PayPal to pay for an item.

The eBay Review Your Purchase page shows the address the item is to be shipped to and the price (including shipping and handling). Under the Select a Payment Method section of the page, you can select PayPal from the list of payment options and click the Continue button. You are redirected to a PayPal page, where you can complete the payment process. Follow these steps:

1. **Log on to your PayPal account by entering your username and password.**

2. **Review the payment and shipping details of the transaction.**

3. **Click More Funding Options if you want to change how you will pay for the item.**

   Options include taking the funds from your PayPal balance, paying by eCheck (you can find more information about eChecks in Chapter 12), or using PayPal Buyer Credit. Not all of these options may be available to you, depending on how your PayPal account has been set up and which PayPal options you signed up for.

4. **Click the Pay button to complete the transaction.**

   The Payment Complete page shows that the item has been paid for; you can also see other items available for sale from the same seller.

If you purchased multiple items from a single seller on eBay, you can opt to combine all the purchases into a single invoice and pay with a single PayPal transaction. (The prices must all be in the same currency.)

Tracking Payments

Each time you log on to your PayPal account, you are taken to an Account Overview page, which shows information about your recent account activity. The Account Overview page shows transactions from the last seven days, or the last 15 transactions (whichever number is the lesser). A message at the top of the screen tells you what category of transactions you're looking at. For each transaction, you can see the following information:

- Type of activity, which can include payments, denied payments, transfers, virtual debit card purchases, and so on.
- Whether the payment was "To" you or "From" you. (Myself, I prefer the payments "To" me!)
- The name or e-mail address of the other party involved in the transaction.
- The date of the transaction.
- The status of the transaction. (Completed, denied, pending, unclaimed, and so on.)
- The amount of the transaction.
- Any fees charged by PayPal for completing the transaction.

When viewing the records in the recent activity list, you can check the box to the left of the transaction type and click the File Selected Items button, found at the bottom of the list. The recent activity list is refreshed, but the items you filed are no longer shown.

You can get detailed information about a specific transaction by clicking the Details link shown for every record. Transaction details include

- Contact information about the person with whom you're doing business.
- The date and time of the initial transaction.
- Information in the e-mail sent by PayPal to the other party in the transaction.
- The type of payment.
- The source of funding.
- Any backup funding used if you didn't have enough money in your PayPal account.

If the transaction was payment for an eBay auction item, the item number, title, quantity, and winning bid will also be shown. The shipping and handling charges are shown, along with the total amount paid out of your PayPal account to fund the purchase.

Ancient History

If you want to see account transactions that are older than seven days, click the My Account button and then click the History button. The History page shows all transactions for the last month. Use the search tools to see history before the last month. The search tools give you a number of ways to view your transactions — by payment type, by fee, by currency, and by date.

If you have a Premier or Business account, you can also get monthly account statements by clicking the Monthly Account Statements button. Each statement is ready on the 15th of the month, and you can view and print statements for a three-month period, before the statement gets deleted from the PayPal server.

You can find more information about how to download your account history and review the data in Chapter 11.

Canceling a Payment

Every so often, you may need to cancel a payment. PayPal has stringent requirements you must meet before you can cancel a payment. The payment must be unclaimed (that is, no one has tried to collect the payment yet) and sent to a recipient who does not yet have a PayPal account. If a transaction meets these criteria, you'll see a status of Unclaimed when looking at that record in the Account History.

Any transaction with an Unclaimed status shows a Cancel button in the Action column of the Account Overview or Account History pages. To cancel a payment, just click the Cancel button. You are asked to confirm the cancellation; click the Cancel Payment button and you're done. The status of the transaction becomes Cancelled and the funds return to your account.

If you made a payment that does not have a status of Unclaimed, you cannot automatically request a refund through PayPal. PayPal recommends you contact the recipient of the funds to try to get a refund. If that doesn't work, you may have to file a complaint or go through the PayPal Sellers Protection program.

Pay Many at One Time with Mass Payments

If you have a Premier or Business account, you have the option of making *Mass Payments,* which enable you to pay multiple vendors — up to 10,000 — at a single time. To make a Mass Payment, you start by creating a file containing the payment information, which you upload to PayPal. (Paying this way is much quicker than writing hundreds of checks!)

Although a Mass Payment is free for the recipient, PayPal charges you a fee of 2 percent of the total payment. There's a $1 USD cap, per payment, for each payment made through Mass Payments.

Before making a Mass Payment, you need to make sure you have enough funds in your account to cover all of the payments. (This may sound obvious, but it's something you want to check before you upload the file!) Mass Payments cannot be funded by a credit card you linked to your account; you need to transfer money from your checking account into your PayPal account before beginning the process.

You can make Mass Payments in any currency supported by PayPal, but you can use only one type of currency per file you create. Converting your funds to the currency you'll be using for the Mass Payment before starting the process is a good idea.

Here's the process for making Mass Payments:

1. **Click the <u>Mass Payment</u> link, which you find at the bottom of every PayPal page.**

2. **Create a tab-delimited text file containing information about the people you want to pay.** You can easily create this file with Excel.

   a. **Open Excel.**

   b. **Enter data.** In a new spreadsheet, put the recipient's e-mail address in the first column, the amount to be paid in the second column (the payment number should have two decimal places), and the currency code in the third column. Valid three-digit country codes are USD for U.S. dollars, EUR for euros, GBP for pounds sterling, CAD for Canadian dollars, and JPY for yen.

   c. **Enter optional information.** The fourth and fifth columns are optional: the fourth column can contain a unique identifier (such as your account number to the company you're sending payment). In the fifth column, you can write a short message to the person you're paying.

      d. After filling in the spreadsheet, select Save As from the Excel File menu.

      e. In the Save As window, select the Text (Tab delimited)(*.txt) option from the Save as type list.

      f. Name the file and click the Save button.

3. **On the PayPal Web site, click the <u>Make a Mass Payment</u> link.**

4. **Click the Browse button to locate the text file you saved using Excel.**

5. **Enter an e-mail subject header and message to go with the payments.** The header and message is sent to every recipient on the Mass Payment list.

6. **Click the Continue button.** You see a page that confirms the number of payments to be made, the total amount of the payments to be made, the fees associated with making the mass payment, and a confirmation window, showing the contents of your text file. You also see the e-mail header and message you entered on the previous screen.

7. **If everything is correct, click the Send Money button.**

That's all you need to do. The recipients of the payments receive PayPal notification e-mails and the funds are deposited into their accounts.

Chapter 5

Using PayPal Transactions

*O*n the Web site, PayPal describes itself as the "world's largest online payment service." Although PayPal is not a bank, it allows you to perform many banklike transactions. Still, as you read the remainder of this chapter, it's important to remember that your money is not as safe as when you place it in a standard U.S. bank account. PayPal funds are invested in an FDIC-insured bank, but the funds are only covered if the bank fails — not if PayPal itself fails.

To get access to the full range of PayPal services, you need to upgrade from a Personal account to a Premier or Business account, and you need to get verified. The next section of this chapter tells you what it means to get verified and how you can do it.

Becoming Verified

Being verified by PayPal means you're a U.S. PayPal member who has linked ("added" in PayPal lingo) a savings or checking account to your PayPal account. PayPal then confirms that the bank account is valid. Basically, it's like getting the PayPal "Seal of Approval."

Banks are legally required to screen people who try to open an account. If you have a bank account, PayPal is able to "verify" your identity (they know you really are who you say you are). Verified PayPal members are less likely to be a security risk with which you have to deal.

Just because a PayPal member is verified doesn't mean that dealing with the member is a risk-free proposition. Anyone with a bank account can get verified, so you still have to use common sense when conducting transactions. See Chapter 3 for tips on how to use PayPal safely.

After you're a verified PayPal member, PayPal lifts some of the account restrictions you have when you first signed up:

- As an unverified member, you have a limit of $1,000 USD that you can receive within a month.

- As an unverified member, you can withdraw only $500 per month from your PayPal account.

- Unverified members have a sending limit of $2,000 over the life of their account.

After becoming verified:

- You can send PayPal payments and the funds can be withdrawn directly from your checking or savings account. Monies from your accounts can also be used to pay any PayPal fees you may have incurred.

- You qualify for the Seller Protection Policy on items that meet the Seller Protection criteria. (To read more, see Chapter 3.)

- You can use PayPal's BillPay service to pay your bills online.

- You can qualify for Buyer Protection on items that meet the criteria.

- If you sell items, you can use the PayPal "Verified" seal and logo on your auctions and your Web sites. (This seal increases buyers' comfort levels when they decide to purchase from you.)

- You can qualify for a PayPal debit card, which lets you withdraw funds from an ATM.

Getting verified only takes a few steps, but completing the process can take several days.

1. **From the PayPal home page, click on the Get Verified link.**

2. **Click the Add Bank Account link to continue.**

   The Add U.S. Bank Account page appears. Figure 5-1 shows what the page looks like.

3. **To link your bank information to PayPal, you need the following information:**

   • **The name of your Bank:** The name of your bank must contain only alphanumeric characters (that is, letters or numbers only). If your bank uses any other characters, leave them out of the name.

   • **Whether you have a checking or a savings account.**

- **The Routing Number for your account:** The routing number uniquely identifies your bank. The number is the first nine digits shown at the bottom of your check.

- **The next series of numbers are your check number or your account number:** To determine which it is, look at the upper-right corner of your check. The three- or four-digit number shown there matches the check number shown at the bottom of the check. The other number is your account number.

- **Your checking or savings account number:** This number is usually between 3 and 17 digits.

4. **After entering this information into the form, click the Add Bank Account button to continue.**

   PayPal then shows a page that describes the rest of the process. (They also send you an e-mail with this information.)

5. **PayPal makes two small deposits into the account you just linked.**

   In this case, PayPal is really a pal who pays! (Don't get too excited, the deposits are just a few pennies, each.) It generally takes two to three days before these deposits show up in your account. You can determine when they've been credited to the account by looking at your bank statement, calling your bank, or — if you have online access to your bank account — looking the deposits up online.

6. **After you see the deposits, log on to your PayPal account and click the <u>Confirm Bank Account</u> link.**

7. **Click the Confirm button.**

   PayPal displays a page where you can enter the amount of each deposit made to your bank account.

8. **Click the Submit button and you're verified!**

In rare cases, PayPal lets you become verified without adding a bank account to your PayPal account, but you need to be a publicly-traded corporation or a well-known public entity. (Translation . . . if you're not GE or Tom Brokaw, you might as well go ahead and link your bank account.)

Verification and non-U.S. accounts

If you have a non-U.S. PayPal account, you can still become verified, although the process is a little more time-consuming. You need to confirm your e-mail address, link a credit card to your account, and give PayPal your *expanded use number*.

An expanded use number is a four-digit code that shows up on your credit card statement. When applying for verification, PayPal requires you to pay a $1.95 fee, which is charged to your credit card. When you get your credit card statement, look for the expanded use number next to the $1.95 payment. You are asked to enter this number into a PayPal form, as a way of verifying your identity. (You are refunded the $1.95 fee after you complete the verification process; the money shows up in your account as a bonus.)

Certain countries have more stringent requirements before you can get verified. If you want to find the requirements for a specific country, click PayPal's <u>Help</u> link (found at the top of every page), type **non-U.S. verification** into the search box, and then click the Search button. PayPal displays a list of articles in response to the search. Click the <u>Can non-U.S. members become Verified?</u> link to see the additional requirements.

Linking a credit card to your account

Although it's not, strictly speaking, part of the verification process, you may also want to link a credit card to your PayPal account. Having a credit card added to your PayPal account lets you do a number of nifty functions, such as apply for a PayPal Debit Card or send an Instant Transfer. To link a credit card to your account, just follow these steps:

1. **From PayPal's home page, click the <u>My Account</u> link and then click the <u>Profile</u> link.**

2. **Click the <u>Credit Cards</u> link.**

3. **At the Add Credit Card or Debit Card page, enter your credit card information (as if you were making an online purchase):**

   - First and last name

   - Card type (Visa, MasterCard, Discover, American Express, and eCheck are accepted)

   - Card number and expiration date

   - Your card verification number (the three- or four-digit security code that you find on the back of your credit card)

   - Your billing address. (You can use the address you used when you signed up for PayPal or add a new address, but the address must match the one where you receive your credit card bills.)

4. **Click the Add Card button, and you just linked a credit card to your PayPal account!**

Adding Funds

Before you can do anything with your PayPal account, you need to get money into the account. After you become verified and link a bank account to your PayPal account, transferring funds into your PayPal account is free. The process, which can take between three and four days to complete, is pretty simple. Here's how:

1. **Click the <u>Add Funds</u> link, which you find under the My Account tab.**

   On the Add Funds page, PayPal shows the different options for transferring money. (The number of options you see depends on whether you're verified, if you have a credit card linked to your account, and so forth.)

2. **Click the <u>Transfer Funds</u> link.**

   It can take as long as three or four days to transfer money from a bank account to your PayPal account.

3. **Select which account to transfer funds from (you also have the option of adding a new bank account to the list) and the amount of money to be transferred. (See Figure 5-2.)**

4. **Click the Continue button.**

   PayPal shows you the transaction details.

5. **Click either the Cancel button (if the information is incorrect) or click the Submit Money button to transfer the money.**

Figure 5-2:
If you've
linked a
bank
account to
your PayPal
account,
you can opt
to transfer
funds
between
the two
accounts.
(Just be
aware that
it takes
a few days
for the
transfer
to be
completed.)

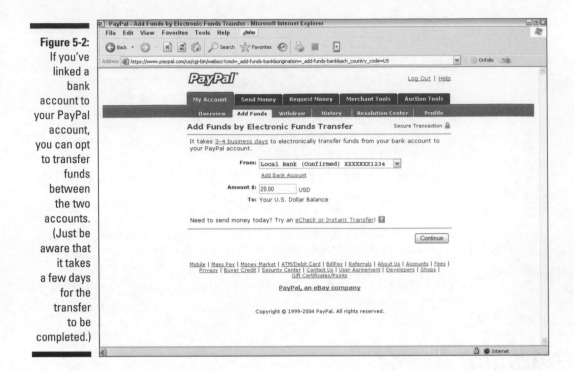

6. **You can view the transaction details of the transfer by clicking the** <u>Go</u> <u>to My Account</u> **link.**

   The transaction has a status of "pending" until the money transfers.

Withdrawing Funds

Funds can be withdrawn from your PayPal account in one of three ways: You can request a check, which is drawn from the funds in your account; you can request an electronic funds transfer to your banking account; or you can use Instant Transfer to send a payment to another PayPal member. These processes don't happen overnight, so if you're going to need the money quickly, don't wait until the last minute.

The check's in the mail

Most of us are used to paper checks, and you may prefer to get a check from PayPal instead of using an electronic funds transfer when you withdraw money from your account. The process is a slow one; according to PayPal, it will be one to two weeks before your check arrives in the mail. If you're in no hurry and prefer a paper check when receiving funds, follow these steps:

1. **Click the <u>My Account</u> link.**

2. **Click the <u>Withdraw</u> link.**

3. **On the Withdraw Funds page, click the <u>Request a check from PayPal</u> link.** (See Figure 5-3.)

   PayPal charges you a $1.50 USD fee each time you request a check. The Withdraw Funds by Check page shows the amount of money in your PayPal account, available for transfer.

4. **Enter the amount to be transferred in the Amount field.**

   Even if you have a credit card and/or bank account linked to your PayPal account, the amount of money you can transfer must be less than the amount of money in your PayPal account. The funds must be mailed to you, not a third party. PayPal shows you a list of *confirmed addresses* to which you can send the check. (A confirmed address, in this case, is one where you get a credit card bill.)

5. **If you want to add an additional address, click the <u>Add an Address</u> link.**

   In addition to adding the address, you need your credit card information so PayPal can check the address against the address on file with your credit card company.

Figure 5-3:
You can transfer funds from your PayPal account by requesting a check to be sent to you. This process can take up to two weeks and you are charged a $1.50 fee per check.

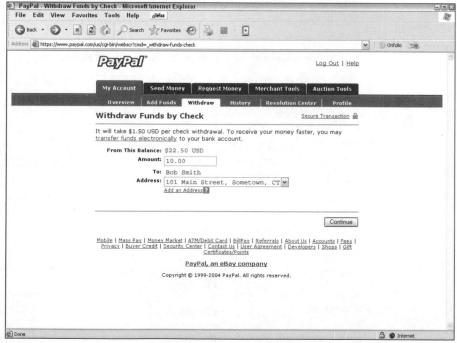

6. **After picking the address, click the Continue button.**

   PayPal shows you a confirmation page. Please note that the $1.50 processing fee is taken out of the check amount. This means if you entered $25.00 as the amount of the check, the actual check you receive will only be for $23.50.

7. **Click the Submit button and the check is in the mail!** (Although you won't receive it until 7 to 14 days from now.)

Electronic funds transfer

Although it sounds like an electronic transfer should be completed within seconds of clicking the mouse, it actually takes three to four business days before the funds show up in your account. PayPal does not charge a fee to transfer the funds. Here's how to transfer your money:

1. **Click the <u>My Account</u> link.**

2. **Click the <u>Withdraw</u> link.**

3. **On the Withdraw Funds page (see Figure 5-4), click the <u>Transfer funds to your bank account</u> link.**

   The Withdraw Funds by Electronic Transfer page shows the amount of money in your PayPal account available for transfer. (If you haven't completed the verification process, there is a $500 monthly limit on the amount you can transfer.)

4. **Enter the transferred amount in the Amount field.**

   You need to transfer a minimum account of $10.00 USD. (Other currencies have different limits.) Even if you have a credit card linked to your account, the amount of money you can transfer must be less than the amount of money in your PayPal account.

5. **PayPal shows a list of bank accounts that are linked to your PayPal account; you can choose from one of these, or click the <u>Add Bank Account</u> link to add a new bank to the list.**

   If your bank account information is incorrect, the money will be returned to your account, but you are charged a fee.

6. **After filling out the form, click the Continue button.**

   PayPal shows you a confirmation page containing a warning about what will happen if your bank account information is not correct.

7. **If you're feeling confident, click the Submit button to make the transfer.**

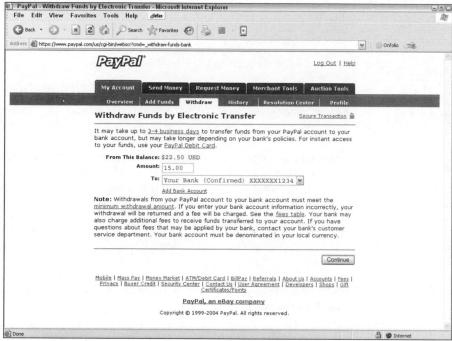

Figure 5-4:
Compared
to receiving
a check,
transferring
funds
electroni-
cally is a
faster
process,
taking only
three to
four days.

Instant transfer

Instant transfer is the process of sending money to another PayPal member via e-mail. (Basically the same process that was described in Chapter 2.) With an instant transfer, if there aren't enough funds in your PayPal account to cover the transfer, funds are taken from the bank account that you've linked to your PayPal account. Before you can use instant transfer, you also need to link a credit card to your PayPal account. This credit card account is used as backup financing in the event that your bank refuses the transfer.

Not all banks permit instant transfers.

To initiate an instant transfer, follow these steps:

1. **Log on to PayPal, click the <u>Send Money</u> link.**

2. **Fill out the form with the details of the transfer (who the money is going to, the amount, and so on) and click the Continue button.**

   On the Check Payment Details page, in addition to seeing who the money is going to and the amount, you also see the source of funds: First PayPal pulls from the PayPal balance, then from your bank account, and finally from your credit card.

   3. **Confirm the shipping information and click the <u>Send Money</u> link.**
      Voila! You've just made an instant transfer!

   You can look at the transaction details of the transfer to see how much
   money was used from each of your funding sources.

Using ATMs

If you've had a bank account in the last quarter century, I'm going to assume
you know how to use an ATM. (Sadly, the *ATM For Dummies* book refers to a
high-speed networking technology, but if you need help, you can always ask
the local branch of your bank.)

If you want access to your PayPal account when you're offline, you can apply
for a PayPal ATM/debit card. To qualify for the card, you need to meet a few
criteria:

   ✔ **You have to have a U.S. PayPal account and be a PayPal member for
      at least 60 days.**

   ✔ **You need to have linked a credit card to your PayPal account.**

   ✔ **You need to be verified.**

   ✔ **You need to have a Premier or Business account.**

   ✔ **You have to be a PayPal member in good standing.** In other words, if
      the funds in your PayPal account have been frozen while a dispute is
      being worked out, this is not the time to apply for the debit card.

If you meet the criteria for getting a card, here's the process of applying
for one:

   1. **Click the <u>ATM/Debit Card</u> link, which you find on the bottom of every
      PayPal page.**

   2. **Click the Continue button after reading the page that describes how
      the Debit Card plan works.**

      The Apply for the PayPal ATM/Debit Card screen shows you which cri-
      teria you've met and any that you still need to achieve, before applying
      for the card.

   3. **After you meet all the criteria, click the Request Debit Card button.**

      PayPal displays a Debit Card Request Information screen that shows
      your name and primary credit card billing address.

   4. **Select the "I have read and agree to the PayPal MasterCard Debit
      Card User Agreement" option (after reading the user agreement, of
      course) and click the Submit button.**

Your debit card should arrive in two to four weeks. You can withdraw money from any ATM that displays the Cirrus/Maestro logo; the funds are withdrawn from your PayPal account. In the event that the ATM asks whether your card is a checking, savings, or credit card, select the "Checking Account" option.

There are daily limits on the debit card; you can charge up to $1,000 USD for purchases and withdraw up to $300 from ATMs. Although there's no fee to apply for the Debit Card, a $1.00 fee will be charged each time you withdraw money at an ATM.

The bank that owns the ATM may also charge an additional fee.

You can have up to two debit cards per PayPal account. To apply for a second card, click the <u>Profile</u> link and then click the <u>PayPal Debit Card</u> link. In addition to applying for a second card, you can use this page to change your PIN number, or to report a lost or stolen card.

PayPal also offers a "Cash-back" program (more information can be found in PayPal Help at `www.paypal.com/us/cgi-bin/webscr?cmd=_help&leafid=494&answer_id=9571777`). PayPal's Cash-back program is designed primarily for eBay sellers. If you list at least one auction every three weeks, activate the "PayPal Preferred" log on all your eBay auctions, and make PayPal the only online payment option for your auctions, you can qualify to get 1.5 percent cash back for every item you purchase with your PayPal Debit Card. Purchases must be those where you do not use your PIN number.

Writing eChecks

When you make an Instant Payment, PayPal lets you finance the payment through your bank account (unless there are enough funds in your PayPal account). The payment is sent instantly, even though PayPal doesn't receive the actual payment from your bank for several days.

An alternative method of payment is to use an eCheck (especially in cases when you need to send a large amount). An eCheck allows you to send money that is withdrawn directly from your bank account, instead of using a credit card to fund a payment.

Writing an eCheck is much like writing a paper check from your bank (although there is a $5.00 fee per eCheck). When you write an eCheck, the transaction status is shown as "Pending" until your bank has cleared the electronic transfer. (Generally, this takes three to four business days.)

To send an eCheck, follow these steps:

1. **Click the <u>Send Money</u> link.**

2. **Fill out the form with the details of the transfer (who the money is going to, the amount, and so on) and click the Continue button.**

3. **Click the <u>More funding options</u> link.**

4. **Select the eCheck option and pick the bank that you are using to fund the payment.**

5. **Click the <u>Continue</u> link.**

6. **On the confirmation page, verify that the payment details are correct and click the Send Money button to send the eCheck.**

Non-U.S. PayPal members can't send an eCheck from a U.S. bank account. This restriction affects PayPal members in Austria, Belgium, Denmark, Finland, France, Germany, Greece, Ireland, Italy, Luxembourg, Monaco, The Netherlands, Portugal, Spain, Sweden, and The United Kingdom.

Chapter 6

PayPal Credit

*I*t happens sometimes . . . you want to purchase an item and there's not enough money in your PayPal account. But if you have a PayPal line of credit, you can purchase either to your heart's content or until you hit your credit limit, whichever comes first.

To be able to use your PayPal Buyer line of credit, you have to use PayPal to pay for the item. When it's time to make the payment, PayPal Buyer shows as one of the funding options available to you to finance your purchase. If you're approved for the line of credit, you won't get a standard plastic credit card in the mail. Instead you receive a paper "card," which shows your Credit Line number.

You have some advantages to using your line of credit instead of paying for merchandise with a credit card. Unlike many credit cards, there are no activation or annual fees for your PayPal Buyer Credit. PayPal's Buyer Protection program covers merchandise purchased with Buyer's credit, assuming the other criteria required by the Buyer's Protection program has been met. (See Chapter 2 for additional details.) Payments made with your line of credit do not count against your total spending limit (for unverified PayPal members).

Applying for Credit

You need a U.S. PayPal account before you can sign up for a line of credit. To apply, start by logging on to your PayPal account. Then, follow these steps:

1. **Click the <u>Buyer Credit</u> link found at the bottom of the PayPal screen.**

   You see a screen that gives you more information about the line of credit.

2. **Click the <u>Continue</u> link.**

   PayPal shows you the terms and conditions covering the line of credit.

3. **Click the I Accept button to continue.**

   This brings you to the PayPal Buyer Credit Application page. (Figure 6-1 shows you the form to be filled out.) You need to provide the following information:

   - **Your first and last name.** PayPal fills these fields out for you, but you can change the information.

   - **The e-mail address you want to use during the application process.** PayPal uses your default PayPal account e-mail but you can change this to a different e-mail account by clicking on the <u>Change Email</u> link and selecting another email address associated with your PayPal account.

   - **Your street address.** You can use the address that is shown, select a different address from the list, or add an address to the list by clicking on the <u>Add Address</u> link.

   - **Phone numbers where you can be contacted.** You must provide your home phone number, but you can also add your business number and a third number, if you want.

   - **The length of time you've lived at your current address.** If this is less than two years, you need to give information about your previous place(s) of residence.

   - **Your date of birth.**

   - **The number of your driver's license, or state-issued I.D., and the date when the license or I.D. expires.**

   - **Your Social Security number.**

   - **Your mother's maiden name.**

You have the option of buying Account Security insurance. The insurance will pay off debt that you've accumulated by using your line of credit (up to $10,000) in the event of certain catastrophic events. These include involuntary unemployment, leave of absence, disability, hospitalization, nursing home care, or your death. If you sign up for the plan, you'll pay $1.50 per month for every $100 of debt. The program can be expensive if you owe a large amount, so think carefully about whether you really need the insurance.

4. **Click the Accept and Submit button to apply.**

Usually, you receive an immediate response, letting you know if you are approved for the line of credit. (If not, PayPal mails you the information, which can take seven to ten days to arrive.) If you are approved, you are given your Credit Line Number and the amount of credit for which you're approved. If you want to, you can start using your line of credit right away.

In a week or two, you receive a letter from PayPal Buyer Credit containing a printed copy of the Credit Card agreement and Privacy Policy. You also receive a paper card with your name, credit line number, and credit limit. The card has a Web address you can go to when you need customer service for credit-related issues.

If you ever close your PayPal account, your PayPal Buyer's Credit account remains open. If you want to close this account as well, you can call the Buyer's Credit Service Center at 866-571-3012 or send a letter to

PayPal Buyer Credit
P.O. Box 981064
El Paso, TX 79998-1064

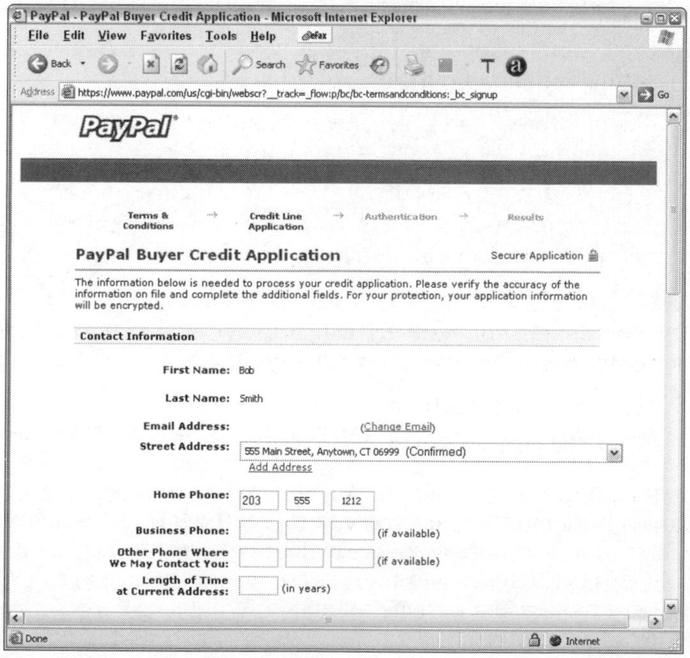

Figure 6-1: Some of the information you have to provide when applying for a line of credit.

Terms and Conditions

I hope you at least scanned the PayPal Buyer Credit agreement before clicking to indicate you accept the terms. If you didn't — and you probably only read the Cliffs Notes version of *Hamlet,* didn't you? — this section of the chapter will fill you in on the highlights.

I try my best to paraphrase the terms and conditions, but please remember that I'm not a lawyer. The chance is always there that I may have misinterpreted something. You should also be aware that these terms may have changed by the time you read this . . . for this reason, I urge you to read the latest version of the PayPal User Agreement and check with your lawyer if you have any questions.

- ✔ **General:** This just states that agreement is between you and GE Capital Consumer Card Company. The agreement goes into effect as soon as you're approved for the line of credit.

- ✔ **Use of Credit Line:** You can use your line of credit when you use PayPal to purchase goods and services. GE Capital Consumer Card Company can refuse to give you access to the credit line at any time and they can change the amount of your credit limit. The credit line can only be used for personal, family, or household items (in other words, you can't use the credit to finance your start-up company).

- ✔ **Promise to Pay:** You have to promise you'll pay back the money you borrow, plus any fees or interest that result from using the account.

- ✔ **Finance Charges:** You are charged interest for each day you owe money, and there is a minimum finance charge of $1.00.

The rate of interest can vary. Check under the section of this chapter called "Calculate Your Monthly Payments and Interest" to read more about the interest rates you are charged.

- ✔ **Finance Charges, continued:** If you're late on your payments, you are charged a delinquency rate (so keep up with your payments!).

- ✔ **Balance Subject to Finance Charge:** This covers how GE Capital Consumer Card Company calculates the amount of interest you owe. It also says that if you don't owe any money, you can't be subjected to finance charges.

- ✔ **When Finance Charges Begin to Accrue:** Basically, this says that in month one you owe money, so you get a finance charge. In month two, the finance charge is calculated against what you owe, plus the finance charges from month one. In month three, the interest is calculated against what you borrow, plus the finance charges of month one and two. (This is the beauty of compound interest, which is so great when you have money in a savings account and *not so great* when you owe money to a creditor.)

✔ **Payments:** You need to pay the minimum balance by the date shown on your statement. The minimum balance is at least $10.00.

✔ **PayPal Account:** You need to be a PayPal member in good standing if you want to use PayPal credit.

✔ **Assignment of Rights in Certain Funds Held by PayPal:** This covers the scenario where you get an advance from your line of credit and, for some reason, the money gets deposited in your PayPal account (maybe because the seller refused payment). If you start to earn interest on that money, through PayPal's money market, the interest payments belong to GE Capital Consumer Card Company.

✔ **Entire Agreement:** The latest and greatest version of the agreement supersedes any previous version of the agreement.

How to Use Your Credit Account

You can use your line of credit anytime you pay for a service or goods with your PayPal account. After selecting the item(s) you want to purchase, click the checkout button or link. Different vendors will have different versions of the same steps (getting your name, contact information, shipping information, and so on). When you are presented with payment options, click the PayPal icon and follow these steps:

1. **Log on to your PayPal account.**

   You can review the payment and shipping details of the transaction.

2. **Click the <u>More Funding Options</u> link, select the PayPal Buyer Credit option, and then click the <u>Continue</u> link.**

   If there are funds in your PayPal account, these funds are used for payment first and the remainder of the payment is charged to your PayPal credit account.

3. **Click the Pay button to complete the transaction and see the Payment Complete page.**

   The item is paid, and you financed at least part of the payment with your line of credit.

If you find yourself wondering whether you should use your line of credit to purchase something, PayPal helpfully lets you know what it will cost you in payments each month. On the Check Payment Details page, look at the right-hand side of the page, under the Source of Funds section, to see what your monthly payments will be. See Figure 6-2 for an example of how the PayPal Buyer Credit tip looks.

Figure 6-2:
For this transaction, my payments are $125 a month if I borrow $2,982.11 USD from my PayPal line of credit. It doesn't tell me how many months I'll be paying, however!

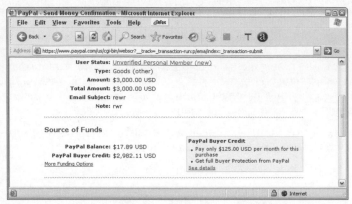

If you want to take advantage of any promotional financing offers (that is, no interest payments for six months, or no payments for the first three months, and so forth), you need to pay for the purchase entirely with your PayPal line of credit.

If you start using your line of credit, you have to start making monthly payments. Although the bulk of your credit line information is actually on the GE Consumer Credit Web site, you can get there from within PayPal. Here's how:

1. **Log on to your PayPal account and click the __Profile__ link.**

2. **Click the __PayPal Buyer Credit__ link.**

   There are two options on the PayPal Buyer Credit page:

   • **The first option lets you deactivate your line of credit account by clicking the __Deactivate Account__ link.** When you deactivate, your Buyer's Credit no longer shows as a payment option when you are purchasing an item with PayPal.

   • **Deactivating your account is not the same as closing your account.** You need to close your line of credit with GE Capital Consumer Card Company by writing to them at:

PayPal Buyer Credit
P.O. Box 981064
El Paso, TX 79998-1064

TIP

- **You need to click the second option: For More PayPal Credit information, click here.** This brings you to a page where you can log out of your PayPal account and be redirected to the GE Capital Consumer Card Company Web site. Make sure to write down your Credit Line number before your log out as you will need it on the next page, especially if you haven't received your PayPal Buyer Credit card in the mail.

3. **Click the <u>Log out and continue</u> link.**

   You are redirected to the GE site and prompted to enter your PayPal Credit Line number. You can see the logon screen by looking at Figure 6-3.

4. **If this is your first time accessing the site, click the <u>Register now for a passcode</u> link.**

   When you're creating an account on the GE Web site, you are asked to review the Paypal User Agreement and Privacy Policy, which cover your Buyer Credit account.

5. **Click the Continue button.**

   You are asked to enter the following information: credit line number, zip code, mother's maiden name, your Social Security number, your phone number, and the passcode you want to use when you access the account. Your passcode must be between 6 and 15 characters and has to include both letters and numbers.

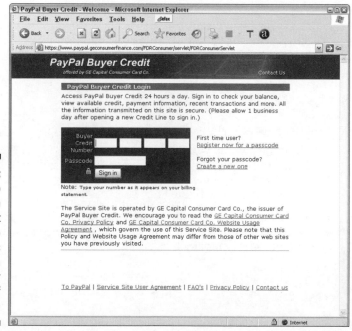

Figure 6-3:
You need to create an account here to access information about your line of credit.

6. **Click the Continue button.**

   After filling out the form, you are logged into your PayPal Buyer Credit account. From this Web site, you can see an account overview, information about specific transactions, any promotional financing deals you took advantage of, and your billing statement.

7. **From the Self Service page (which you see when you first log on), you can click the <u>Buyer Credit Overview</u> link.**

   This takes you to a page that explains how to change your address and also has a link to let you close your account.

Even if you close your browser window when you're at the GE Web site, you are not logged out of their system. You need to remember to click the <u>Sign Out</u> link before closing your browser.

If you're click-happy (like I am) and you try to go back and forth between the GE and PayPal Web sites using your browser's Back button, after leaving the GE Web site, you'll be locked out for ten minutes. GE does this for security reasons (so someone can't access your account after you leave your desk), but it can be a drag if you're trying to look something up quickly.

Calculate Your Monthly Payments and Interest

After you start using your line of credit, GE sends a monthly bill in the mail (meaning snail mail, not e-mail). To make a payment, make the check payable to PayPal Buyer Credit/GECCCC. The check needs to be mailed to

PayPal Buyer Credit
P.O. Box 960080
Orlando, FL 32896-0080

GE will also accept electronic transfers from your bank. Oddly enough, you can't use PayPal to pay your PayPal Buyer Credit bill. (Go figure.)

As with any credit bill, you need to make the minimum monthly payment to avoid getting penalty charges. The bill shows you the amount to pay, of course, but here's how GE Capital Consumer Card Company calculates the interest rate you have to pay.

The rate can be determined in one of two ways. GE Capital Consumer Card Company charges you according to which amount is higher. (You're not surprised, are you?)

```
An annual percentage rate of 20.8%. Ouch! -or-
```

```
(The prime rate + 15.5%) X 1/365
(In other words, the prime rate plus 15.5% divided by the
          number of days in the year. The prime rate is an
          interest rate charged by banks to their most
          credit-worthy customers [usually other banks]. You
          can look the prime rate up in the Wall Street
          Journal.)
```

Of course it's always easiest just to look the payment up online by logging on to the GE Capital Consumer Web site. If you don't want to go through the bother of logging on to PayPal, only to be logged out again before being redirected, you can go straight to the source and type **www.paypal.geconsumerfinance.com** into your Web browser.

Know Your Limits

Anytime you apply for credit (credit card, line of credit, car loan, whatever . . .), you receive a credit limit, based on your credit history and ability to pay the loan back. Knowing the limits you have on your Buyer Credit is important because PayPal's Check Payment Details screen can be a little misleading.

If you look at Figure 6-2, I'm trying to make a payment of $3,000. I have only $17.89 USD in my PayPal account, so I need to finance the rest from an alternate funding source. PayPal suggests using $2,982.11 from my line of credit. Unfortunately, GE Capital Consumer Card Company only saw fit to give me $2,500 of credit.

Even if PayPal wants you to spend freely from your line of credit, it helps to know your limits!

Keeping Your Contact Info Current

If you move, you need to update PayPal of your new address. To make the change, follow these steps:

1. **Click the <u>Profile</u> link under My Account.**

2. **Click the <u>Credit Cards</u> link.**

3. **If you have more than one credit card listed, select the address for the card to be changed and click the Edit button.**

4. On the Edit Credit Card page, enter the expiration date for your credit card and the card verification number.

This is the three- or four-digit code that you find on the back of the card.

5. Click the Save button.

PayPal verifies that the new address matches where the credit card bill is sent.

You may have to repeat the process for each credit card that you linked to your PayPal account.

Just because you updated your address on the PayPal site does not mean that the information is updated with GE Capital Consumer Card Company (the people who mail your Buyer Credit bills — remember?).

Unfortunately, there's no online way to change your contact information on the GE Web site. If you move, you need to inform them by filling in the new address information on your monthly billing statement.

You can also make the change by calling their customer service line (866-571-3012) or by writing to

PayPal Buyer Credit
P.O. Box 981064
El Paso, TX 79998-1064

You need to mail information to GE Capital Consumer Card Company if you need to change your name. GE requires legal documents as proof of the name change, so you may want to call their customer service number first to find out what you need to send.

Part III
Selling with PayPal

The 5th Wave   By Rich Tennant

"Oh, we're doing just great. Philip and I are selling decorative jelly jars on the Web. I run the Web site and Philip sort of controls the inventory."

In this part . . .

Here I show you how to make money by selling goods and services. I also show you how to set up your preferences as a seller, including how to set up your payment preferences. I show you how to list an item on eBay and how to customize the PayPal logo associated with your auction. You learn how to organize your auctions through PayPal's Selling Manager and even how to earn cash back when making purchases yourself! I explain how to send an invoice through e-mail, and how to create an invoice template to speed up your billing process. PayPal can even be used to organize your shipping; you can select a shipper and print a shipping label, without ever leaving the PayPal Web site. Finally, I show you how to download information about your transactions, review your sales, and analyze your transaction data.

Chapter 7

Getting Ready to Sell

. . . .

. . . .

*A*s a seller who accepts PayPal, you have tremendous flexibility when it comes to choosing how you want to accept payments from buyers and how you want to sell your goods or services. In this chapter, I show you how to set up your selling preferences and decide which of PayPal's many options is right for you and your business. (Even if your so-called "business" is just occasionally selling stuff on eBay.)

Setting Up Your Selling Preferences

You can find your selling preference options by logging into your PayPal account and clicking the Profile link. Under the Selling Preferences column, you see the options that are available to you, depending upon the type of account you have.

Non-U.S. accounts do not have the same options as U.S. accounts. Table 7-1 shows the selling preferences available by account type.

Table 7-1	Selling Preferences Offered by PayPal
Personal Accounts	*Premier or Business Accounts*
Auctions	Auctions
	Sales Tax
	Shipping Calculations

(continued)

Table 7-1 *(continued)*

Personal Accounts	Premier or Business Accounts
Shipping Preferences	Shipping Preferences
USPS Preferences	USPS Preferences
UPS Preferences	UPS Preferences
	Payment Receiving Preferences
	Instant Payment Notification Preferences
PayPal Shops	PayPal Shops
	Reputation
Seller Eligibility for PayPal Buyer Protection	Seller Eligibility for PayPal Buyer Protection
	Website Payment Preferences
	Encrypted Payment Settings
	Custom Payment Pages
Invoice Templates	Invoice Templates

The following sections of this chapter give a short overview of each of the options and provide in-depth information for a few. The other options are described in detail in different chapters of this book. Figure 7-1 shows the PayPal selling preferences on the Profile page.

Auctions

On the Auction Accounts page, you can set three different options when selling items on eBay: whether to have PayPal logos inserted automatically when you list an item; whether you want the buyer to receive a notification from PayPal as soon as the auction ends; and whether you want to add the PayPal Preferred logo to your eBay auction. I discuss these options in detail in Chapter 8.

If you're really interested in all the options available to you when you sell items at auction, don't bother clicking the Auctions link under Selling Preferences. You get these and many more options if you click the Auction Tools tab, which you find on the top-level PayPal navigation bar.

Sales Tax

The options under the Sales Tax link apply only to holders of Premier or Business accounts.

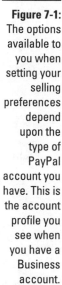

Figure 7-1:
The options
available to
you when
setting your
selling
preferences
depend
upon the
type of
PayPal
account you
have. This is
the account
profile you
see when
you have a
Business
account.

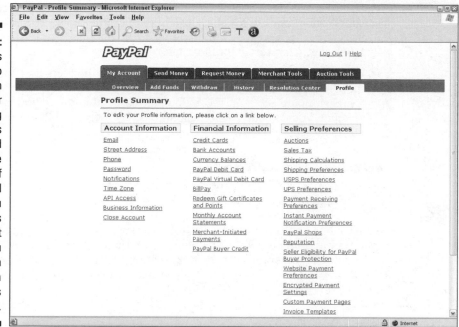

If you have a Premier or Business account, you can collect sales tax for items you sell with the PayPal Shopping Cart, Buy Now buttons, or PayPal Donations. You can opt to have the tax payment displayed in Winning Buyer Notifications and the PayPal Smart Logos. See Chapter 17 for more information on calculating and configuring PayPal to accept taxes.

Shipping Calculations

The options under the Shipping Calculations link apply only to holders of Premier or Business accounts.

If you sell an item and collect payment through the PayPal Shopping Cart, Buy Now buttons, or Donation buttons, you can calculate shipping costs and pass these on to the person purchasing the item from you. Shipping calculations can be set at a flat rate or based upon the value of the item. You find more information about shipping calculations in Chapter 10.

Shipping Preferences

You can decide whether you want to see the Shipping Carrier Selection page when you're ready to ship a package. If you decide not to show the page, you must choose either the U.S. Postal Office or UPS as a default shipping option. The page also lets you change your shipping address and decide whether to see a Ship button (shown to you, not to buyers) for items you're selling. Chapter 10 gives you information about using PayPal shipping, so jump ahead if you want to read more.

✔ **USPS Preferences:** Even though PayPal shows a separate link for setting USPS preferences, it's just another way of setting up shipping options. This page lets you set printing options, so you can print USPS shipping labels. See Chapter 10 for more information.

✔ **UPS Preferences:** Like USPS Preferences, this option lets you choose from more shipping preferences. This page has a button to let you register for a UPS shipping account (if you don't have one already). If you have an account, you can enter your account number here. See Chapter 10 for more information.

Payment Receiving Preferences

The options under the <u>Payment Receiving Preferences</u> link apply only to holders of Premier or Business accounts.

This page lets you block payments from users who don't meet your criteria. Examples might include blocking buyers who don't have a U.S. account, or aren't verified, and so on. See the next section, "Setting Up Your Payment Receiving Preferences," to read how you can set up your payment receiving preferences.

Instant Payment Notification Preferences

The options under the <u>Instant Payment Notification Preferences</u> link apply only to holders of Premier or Business accounts who have developer experience. Only Webmasters or developers should try to integrate PayPal transactions into an existing Web site; see Chapter 17 for more information.

This option lets you set the options for integrating PayPal Instant Payment Notification into your existing Web site.

PayPal Shops

If you want to use PayPal as a vehicle for driving traffic (and hopefully sales) to your existing e-commerce Web site, you can take advantage of the PayPal Shops option, which is free to PayPal members. There are certain criteria you need to meet before you can list your site with PayPal Shops. These include

✔ Link a credit card or debit card to your PayPal account.

✔ Link and confirm a bank account (checking or savings) to your PayPal account.

✔ Invest in PayPal's Money Market account.

When you apply to have your Web site listed in PayPal Shops, you give PayPal permission to run a credit check on you or your business. (They do this to ensure that only valid shops are listed.)

To list your Web site with PayPal Shops, follow these steps:

1. **Log on to your PayPal account and then click the <u>Profile</u> link.**

2. **Click the <u>PayPal Shops</u> link, which you find under Selling Preferences.**

3. **Register your Web site by entering a title for your Web site, the Web address, and a brief description of your Web site.**

4. **Select up to two categories that describe your Web site (clothing, coins, and so on).**

5. **Enter up to ten keywords that describe your Web site and click the Continue button.**

6. **If you submit the form correctly, a Website Registration Successful page appears.**

You can see the sites that have already been listed by clicking the <u>Shops</u> link, which you find at the bottom of every PayPal page. Figure 7-2 shows the PayPal Shops page.

Figure 7-2:
The Shops page shows shops promoted by PayPal, along with links to let you browse through the shops or search for something specific.

Reputation

The options under the <u>Reputation</u> link apply only to holders of Premier or Business accounts.

Everybody cares about their reputation . . . especially power sellers. If you sell to more than 1,000 verified PayPal members, PayPal lets you cap your reputation at the 1,000 mark. (If you sell to more than 1,000 people and are still in business, I think we can assume that you're okay to buy from.)

Seller Eligibility for PayPal Buyer Protection

If you want to see whether the goods you sell on eBay are eligible for PayPal Buyer Protection, you can submit your eBay user ID here and PayPal tells you whether you qualify. If your eBay ID has already been registered with PayPal, it will be displayed, along with an <u>Add</u> link if you want to add more IDs. If you haven't registered your eBay user ID, you can fill in a form with the ID and your eBay password. After filling in the form, click the Submit button. On the Seller Eligibility Details page (see Figure 7-3 for an example), PayPal shows you a checklist of the criteria you've met and any that you still need to achieve. A button is also there to let you see a demo that gives more information about the Buyer Protection plan.

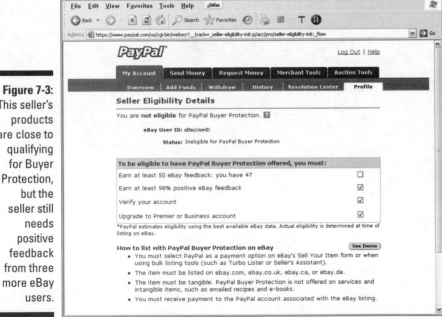

Figure 7-3: This seller's products are close to qualifying for Buyer Protection, but the seller still needs positive feedback from three more eBay users.

Website Payment Preferences

The options under the Website Payment Preferences link apply only to holders of Premier or Business accounts who have developer experience.

There are a number of options to choose when you're integrating PayPal into a Web site. (You can find detailed information about integrating PayPal into your Web site in Part V, "Integrating PayPal into Web Sites and Applications.") You can change the settings for any of the following features:

- ✔ Whether you want the user to return to your Web site after they pay through PayPal. You need to provide your Web address to use this feature.

- ✔ If you integrated PayPal into your Web site, you can receive instant payment notification after a buyer pays for an item.

- ✔ You can opt whether to block payments from buyers who don't use encrypted payment buttons. To ensure your Web site has encrypted buttons, you must encrypt them yourself or create secure buttons using the PayPal Button Factory. (See Chapter 14 for more details about creating and integrating payment buttons.)

- ✔ You can determine whether buyers are required to sign up for a PayPal account (assuming they don't already have one) when purchasing an item from your Web site. You must be using Buy Now, Donations, or Shopping Cart buttons to take advantage of this feature.

- ✔ You can decide whether customers must provide a telephone number when they provide information during the checkout process.

Encrypted Payment Settings

The options under the Encrypted Payment Settings link apply only to holders of Premier or Business accounts who have Web developer experience.

When you accept online payments, it's important that you secure credit card numbers and other buyer information so hackers can't get access to the data. Secure Sockets Layer (SSL) is an encryption technology used by most e-commerce Web sites. I won't go into a lengthy explanation here, but to implement SSL, you need a certificate that has been issued by a trusted authority, such as GeoTrust, an organization that verifies you really are who you say you are. PayPal gives you the option of using their certificate or entering a certificate that you already obtained for your Web site.

Custom Payment Pages

The options under the Custom Payment Pages link apply only to holders of Premier or Business accounts.

PayPal lets you customize the style of payment pages to match the look of the rest of your Web site. You can create different styles if you need more than one. Each style lets you specify the page title, the header image, the header border color, and the background color of the Web pages.

Invoice Templates

PayPal lets you create and save invoice templates, which can speed up the process of sending out an invoice. You can choose from any templates previously created from this page. If you haven't created any invoice templates, I discuss how to do so in Chapter 9.

Setting Up Your Payment Receiving Preferences

You can set up your payment receiving preferences so that you won't accept payments from users who don't meet your criteria. Follow these steps:

1. **After logging on to your PayPal account, click the <u>Profile</u> link, which you find under the My Account navigation bar.**

2. **Select the <u>Payment Receiving Preferences</u> link, which you find under Selling Preferences.**

   You can choose from the following options:

   - **You can block payments from U.S. users who have not confirmed their address with PayPal.** You have the choice to accept these buyers, not accept these buyers, or get asked by PayPal whether you want to accept on a case-by-case basis.

   - **You can block payments from buyers who want to send payment in a currency that you don't currently have in your PayPal account.** You have the option of blocking the payment entirely, accepting the payment and having it converted to U.S. dollars (there is a currency conversion fee for selecting this option), or getting asked by PayPal whether you want to accept on a case-by-case basis.

   - **You can block payments from users who do not have U.S. PayPal accounts.**

   - **You can block payments from people who want to pay you using the Pay Anyone options (found under the Send Money section of the PayPal site).** The Pay Anyone option is a payment initiated by the buyer, who can select the type of payment to be made (eBay items, other auction items, goods not purchased at auctions, payment for services, or Quasi-cash). These payments are less secure because they were not made in response to one of PayPal's standard payment methods, and they include Buy Now buttons, Donation buttons, a PayPal Shopping Cart, subscription payments, requests for money, invoices, Smart logos, or eBay checkout payments.

If you want to redirect the buyer to use a more secure method of payment, rather than Pay Anyone, PayPal gives you the options of entering the Web address of your Web site, where buyers are redirected to complete the purchase. Using the Alternate Payment URL (Web address) method only makes sense if you have a secure e-commerce Web site where the checkout process can be completed.

- **You can block payments from buyers who try to pay with a credit card, when they have their bank account linked to their PayPal account.** This blocking option protects you in two ways — buyers won't be able to use stolen credit cards to make a payment, and the buyer can't choose to use the Charge Back option offered by their credit card company in the event that they choose not to pay.

- **You can block eCheck payments, which take three to four days to clear, before the money is transferred from the buyer's bank account to your PayPal account.**

- **The last option on the Payment Receiving Preferences page is a box where you can enter the name that appears on the credit card purchases made by your sellers.** The Credit Card Statement name can't be longer than 11 characters, and can use letters, numbers, and spaces.

In addition to setting up your Payment Preferences, as you get ready to sell, you may also want to set up access for multiple users.

Setting up Multi-User Access for Your Business

If you have a small company and different people in your organization need to work with your PayPal account, you can set up multiple users to be able to access the account. Setting up multiple users is a pretty fast process and you have the option of giving your employees as much (or as little) access to the features in your account.

Upgrading from a Personal account

Multi-user access requires a Business account. If you don't have a business account, you can follow these steps to upgrade from a Personal or Premier account:

1. **Log on to your PayPal account and go to the Overview page, which you find under the My Account tab.**

   This page is generally the first page you see after logging on to your PayPal account.

2. **Click the Upgrade Account link, which you find in the column on the left side of the page.**

3. **Click the Upgrade Now button.**

4. **Select one of the options (do business under your company's name or under a group name) and click the Continue button.**

5. **You are asked to provide information about your business or organization.**

   This information includes

   • **The name of your business or organization.**

   • **Your business address.**

   • **The telephone number of your business.**

   • **A customer service e-mail address.**

   • **A customer service phone number.** This is optional.

   • **The category into which your business or organization fits.** These are mostly business-oriented, so if you are setting up a Business account for a charitable organization, select the Other category.

   • **The subcategory in which your business belongs.** If you picked the Other category, your subcategory is General.

   • **The average price of the transactions you expect to make using your Business account.**

   • **The average volume of business you expect to do each month with your Business account.**

   • **The place where you anticipate most transactions to take place.** Options include eBay, other marketplaces, your business Web site, or some other place.

   • **The Web address of your business or organization.**

6. **Click the Save button.**

   You are redirected to a page that confirms that your account has been upgraded to a Business account.

Upgrading from a Premier account

If you already have a Premier account, you can easily upgrade to a Business account. Try this:

1. **Click the <u>Profile</u> link.**

2. **Click the <u>Business Information</u> link, which you find under the Account Information column.**

3. **Click the Edit button.**

   The Edit Business Information page appears.

4. **Provide the requested business information.**

   This information includes the category and subcategory that your business falls under. You're asked to estimate your average price of the transactions and your average monthly sales volume. You're also asked where you sell from and your business Web address.

5. **Click the Save button, and you're upgraded to a Business account.**

Downgrading an account

Although it's not promoted on the PayPal Web site, you do have the option of downgrading from a Business/Premier account to a Personal account (but only one time!). You lose all the advantages of a Premier or Business account, for example, the ability to accept credit cards, make shopping cart buttons, and so on. To downgrade, you must send a question to customer service and follow the steps shown below:

1. **Go to** `www.paypal.com/us/cgi-bin/webscr?cmd=_contact-submit&flow=default&opt1=def`.

2. **Select the My Account Profile topic from the first list.**

3. **Select Downgrade account from the second list.**

4. **Summarize the reason you want to downgrade in the text box and click the Continue button.**

5. **You can provide more detailed information on the next page; click the Continue button.**

You'll receive a confirmation e-mail from PayPal customer support.

Having a Business account is useful for a number of reasons, especially if you want to protect your privacy when conducting online transactions (when selling on eBay, for example). With a Business account, people who conduct transactions with you have access only to your business information — not your personal information.

Setting up multiple accounts

After you have a Business account, you can start the process of setting up multiple users. Here's how:

1. **Log on to your Business account and click the <u>Profile</u> link.**

2. **Click the <u>Multi-User Access</u> link, which you find under the Account Information column.**

3. **Before you can begin adding additional users, PayPal requires you to have at least two e-mail addresses linked to your Business account.**

   - **The person who opens the PayPal account is the account owner.** This person can add other users to the account and set the level of permissions for these users.

   - **You have to link at least one other e-mail address to your business account, so you can designate someone as the Administrative Contact.** The Administrative Contact cannot be the account owner. This person gets an e-mail whenever other users conduct transactions with the Business account. The Administrative Contact is meant to serve as a supervisor of account activity and cannot receive payments as transactions are conducted with the account.

   - **If you have only the account owner e-mail associated with the Business account, click the <u>Add an E-mail Address</u> link, shown at the bottom of the Multi-User Access – Current Users page.**

   - **Fill in the E-mail Address text box and click the Save button.** You're allowed to have up to eight e-mail addresses added to your Business account. (Please note that this is different from adding "users" to your Business account; you can add up to 200 separate users.)

When you add e-mail accounts to your Business account, you're not allowed to use an e-mail address that already has PayPal accounts. This means that if you have an employee who used their corporate e-mail address to open a personal PayPal account, this e-mail address cannot be added to your Business account.

• **After you add a second e-mail address to the Business account, a confirmation e-mail is sent by PayPal to the e-mail address entered.** As with any PayPal account, the owner of the second e-mail address needs to click the confirmation link contained in the PayPal e-mail.

4. **After you add at least one other user to your Business account, designate your Administrative contact by selecting the e-mail address from the list and clicking the Continue button.**

5. **Only the Business account owner (also called the Primary Login) is able to add multiple users to the account and set permissions.** Click the Add User button to add a new user. Figure 7-4 shows an example of the page that lets you add users to your Business account.

Figure 7-4:
To add a new user to a Business account, start by entering the user's name and then assigning that person a user ID and password.

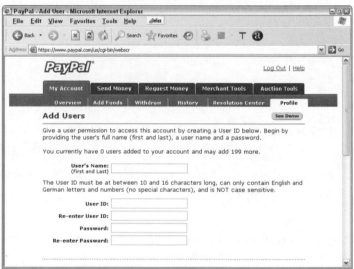

Start the process of adding a new user by entering the name of the person and then assigning that person a username and password. The username must be between 10 and 16 characters in length and can only contain English (or German) letters or numbers (that is, no special characters). The password must be at least eight characters long and unique to that user — you can't assign everyone the same account password.

Setting levels of access for each user

You don't need to assign any privileges when you first create the new user account. If you've created the account but want to add or change the privileges, you can do so by going to your Account Profile and clicking the

Multi-User Access link. PayPal lists the user accounts associated with the Business account. Select a username and click the Edit button. This takes you to the Multi-User Access page.

1. **Click in the box next to each of the activities that you want to allow this user to participate in.**

   Figure 7-5 shows the list of permissions you can assign to each user who can access your Business account.

Figure 7-5:
You can customize the level of access you give to each user account by selecting the options you want to allow.

2. **After clicking next to the permissions you want to give the user, click the Save button to create the account.**

   PayPal lists all the users associated with the Business account. You can click the Add button to continue adding users or to update a user's information by selecting a user and clicking the Edit button. You also have the option of changing a user's password or removing a user.

Logging into a Business account as a multiple user

If you're one of multiple users with access to the same Business account, you log on as you would if you were logging on to your own account, with just a few differences. Here's how:

1. **Direct your Web browser to** `https://www.paypal.com`.

2. **Under the Member Log In section of the home page, type your assigned username into the E-mail Address text box.**

3. **Type your assigned password into the Password text box.**

4. **Click the Log In button.**

Don't enter an e-mail address, even though the logon page prompts you for one. When you click the Log In button, you'll be rejected faster than the losing contestant on a dating game show.

PayPal logs you into the Business account. All of the Business account options appear to be available, but if you try to access information or a feature that you haven't been given permission for, the following message appears:

```
We're sorry. You do not have permission to this area of the
          site. Please contact the Account Administrator to
          obtain the necessary permissions.
```

The Account Optional feature enables you, as a seller, to accept payments from buyers who do not have a PayPal account. This feature is useful because it lets you sell to a larger group of people than if you restricted sales just to PayPal members (although a universe of 50 million PayPal members is pretty large!).

On the down side, you have a greater risk of credit card fraud with the Account Optional feature. The buyer may be using a stolen credit card, or you risk having an unscrupulous buyer issue a chargeback after you deliver the purchased item.

The Account Optional feature is only available to Premier or Business accounts. Additionally, the option is only available when the PayPal payment is initiated through a Buy Now, Donation, or Shopping Cart button. You can find more information about these types of buttons in Chapter 14.

Setting up the Account Optional feature is simple. If you have a Premier or Business account, follow these directions:

1. **Log on to your PayPal account and click the <u>Profile</u> link.**

2. **Click the <u>Website Payment Preferences</u> link, which you find under the Selling Preferences column.**

3. **The first option lets you decide whether the buyer should be redirected back to your Web site after purchasing the item through the PayPal interface.**

If you have the Account Optional feature turned on, but you leave this option off, the buyer is able to decide whether to return to your Web site after completing a purchase. If you want to take advantage of the Auto Return feature, you need to provide the Web address of your e-commerce site. The Web address you enter here is used for all Auto Return payments (certain other types of payments also Auto-Return the user to your Web site) unless you specify a different Web address within the code of your Web site.

4. **The second option lets you determine whether you get notification of successful payment after the transaction completes.**

   The notification here refers to programmatic notification back to your Web site — not an e-mail notification to you. Unless you worked on the development of your Web site, leave this option off.

5. **The third option lets you determine whether to block nonencrypted Web site payments if you have a secure Web site or are using encrypted buttons.**

   If you are not sure about whether you have security implemented for your site or your buttons, leave this option off.

6. **The fourth option lets you set the Account Optional feature if you are selling through Buy Now, Donations, or Shopping Cart buttons.**

7. **The fifth and final option lets you decide whether you require the buyer to include a telephone number when paying for a purchase.**

   PayPal recommends leaving this option off because you don't want to turn off a buyer just when the purchase is almost final!

After changing your Website Payment settings, click the Save button to save your preferences.

Chapter 8

Listing an Item on eBay

*N*ow that you know all about buying with PayPal, and you have set up your selling preferences, it's time for the main event — auctioning an item on eBay. Offering bidders the chance to pay with PayPal is a smart move if you want more bidders — and who doesn't? According to a survey of random eBay buyers, three out of four prefer PayPal over other payment methods. (Hey — the survey was cited on the PayPal Web site . . . it wasn't just me asking friends for their opinions.)

This chapter shows you how to list an item on eBay and set up PayPal as the payment method. For obvious reasons, the information given in this chapter has a PayPal-centric view of the process. If you want more detailed information about selling on eBay, I recommend getting your hands on a copy of Marsha Collier's excellent *eBay For Dummies*. It gives you insider experience on bidding, selling, and everything in between!

Unlike a garage sale, selling on eBay isn't free . . . you pay a fee to list and sell items. The higher the value of the item, the higher the fee. Table 8-1 shows the eBay fees at the time this book was written.

Table 8-1	eBay Listing Fees
Starting or Reserve Price for Your Item	*Fee to Auction Item on eBay*
0.01–$0.99	$0.30
$1.00–$9.99	$0.35
$10.00–$24.99	$0.60
$25.00–$49.99	$1.20
$50.00–$199.99	$2.40
$200.00–$499.99	$3.60
$500.00 or more	$4.80

eBay also has a fee for setting a *reserve price* (the lowest amount of money you're willing to accept), but this fee is refunded if the item sells. If the reserve price is less that $50, there's a $1 fee. If the reserve price is between $50 and $199, there's a $2 fee. If the reserve price is $200 and over, the fee is 1 percent of the reserve price, up to a cap of $100.

In addition to the fees for listing an item, you also pay fees when the item sells. Table 8-2 shows the Final Value fees.

Table 8-2	eBay Fees When Someone Buys Your Item
Price of the Winning Bid	*Final Value Fee Charged by eBay*
If the item doesn't sell	No fee
If the price was between $0.01 and $25.00	You pay eBay 5.25% of the winning bid
If the price was between $25.01 and $1,000.00	You pay eBay: 5.25% of the first $25.00 ($1.31) + 2.75% of the remaining amount
If the price was over $1,000.00	5.25% of the first $25.00 ($1.31)+ 2.75% of the amount between $25.00 and $1,000 ($26.81)+ 1.50% of the remaining amount

Additional fees may be charged by eBay, depending on how aggressively you want to promote your product. To see the other fees that may apply to your listing, go to `pages.ebay.com/help/sell/fees.html`. Under Optional Feature Fees, click the <u>Show</u> link, which is shown to the right of Listing Upgrade Fees.

Select a Category

Selling on eBay always starts with a single step — figuring out what to sell. I can't help you dig around in the garage for hidden auction gold, so I'll jump ahead to the next step, which is what to do after you find the item to list.

You found Grandma's old silver nut dish, the one that's been hidden in the attic since the last spring house cleaning. It's pretty, but it's pretty useless to you, and you decide to list it on eBay. The first thing you need to do is a little research to see which category your item should be listed in and to determine the reserve price for the auction.

Often, it's obvious which category an item belongs in — Cell Phones, for example. Other times an item can fit in multiple categories. My son is passionate about Yu-Gi-Oh! Cards, for example. Yu-Gi-Oh! Cards can be found under multiple categories, including Toys and Hobbies and Collectibles. These are just the top-level categories. Subcategories would include Trading Card Games; TV, Movie, Character Toys; Games; Trading Cards; Animation Art, Characters; and Fantasy, Mythical & Magic.

If you're not sure which categories your item would belong in, you can do a search for similar items. Even though you may think your item is completely unique, it's a large eBay world out there and chances are that someone is listing something similar. To select a category for your item, follow these steps:

1. **Look closely at the item you want to list and try to think of words or phrases that best describe the item.**

2. **Type** www.eBay.com **into your Web browser.**

3. **Type your descriptive words into the search box, located in the upper-right corner of the page.**

4. **Click the Search button.**

   eBay displays a list of similar items like the one shown in Figure 8-1. The column to the left of the item list shows the categories in which similar items are listed. The list of items appears in the middle of the page. Here you can compare prices, see the number of bids (which tell you how popular certain items are at a specific price point), and read descriptions that may help you when it comes time to describing your item.

You can also research possible categories for your item, right from the Sell Your Item: Select Category page. Type some keywords describing your item into the "Enter keywords to find a category" text box and click the Search button. You'll see a list of suggested categories and the percent of time your keywords are used in the category listing.

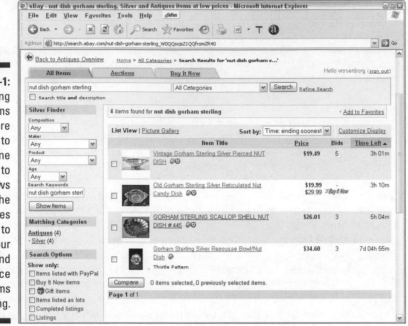

Figure 8-1:
Searching
for items
that are
similar to
the one
you want to
list shows
you the
categories
in which to
list your
item, and
the price
these items
are getting.

Adding a Title and Description

Now that you figured out which categories your item belongs in, you're all ready to list, right? Wrong! You need to put some time and thought into your item's title and a description, which should be both enticing and truthful. Being as accurate as possible is important; if the item doesn't meet the buyer's expectations because you "enhanced" the item in your description, you risk getting negative feedback.

If you get too much negative feedback, not only can it hurt your ratings on eBay (making it less likely that buyers will bid for your items), but it can also affect your status as a PayPal member.

A rose by any other name

"What's in a name? That which we call a rose by any other name would smell as sweet." Shakespeare definitely wasn't selling items on eBay when he wrote these words. When it comes to listing an item successfully, the title (or name) really does matter. You need to think of a title that's provocative enough for a potential buyer to click your item in a list of similar items.

Which of these items sounds more saleable to you?

- ✓ **Silver Nut Dish**
- ✓ **Vintage Gorham Sterling Silver Pierced NUT DISH.** This description was for the first item listed in Figure 8-1.

The second one is a better choice because it gives more detailed information about the item and highlights *four pluses* of the item:

- ✓ **The dish is vintage, which means if it's not an antique, at least it's somewhat old.** For a collector, the age of the piece is an important part of the value.

- ✓ **The dish was made by an important silver company (Gorham).**

- ✓ **The dish is sterling silver (not silver-plated).**

- ✓ **The silver is pierced, which means the lacelike design was made by punching holes in the silver to form a pleasing pattern.** This is another bit of information that would interest a collector.

In addition to making the item sound more enticing, giving a detailed description makes it more likely that your item comes up when buyers use the eBay search function. With the strong title shown previously, searching on the terms *Vintage, Sterling, Gorham,* or *pierced* would show this nut dish in the list of items that meet the search criteria.

eBay allows you to have 55 characters in your title. To come up with a short but powerful title, examine your item closely and try to think of five words that describe it. These words can describe the manufacturer, the condition, the age, and any unique aspects of the item. After you come up with the words, try to incorporate them into your title.

For an additional 50 cents, you can also enter a subtitle, which is searchable when the user does a search on both the title and description. (You should note that over 90 percent of searches are for the title only.) If you can't fit all the descriptive words into the 55-character limit, you can split the title in two and add the second group of words or phrases into the subtitle. Make sure that your strongest words are in the title, because these words are what the potential buyer focuses on when scanning a list of items quickly.

Coming up with a great description

After thinking up the title and subtitle you want to use, now you have to write a more detailed description of the product you want to sell. You could probably come up with a paragraph or two of descriptive text, but you need to remember that this is an advertisement. When the potential bidder reads about your item, they should be enticed enough to want to win the item during bidding.

Take a moment to expand upon the list of five descriptive words that you came up with for the title. Then see if you can use these words in a sentence. (It's starting to sound like grammar class, isn't it?) If I add to the list I created for the title, I come up with the following:

Vintage: I'm not really sure how old Grandma's dish is, so I should say "Vintage-Style" instead.

Gorham: The maker.

Sterling Silver: The quality of the silver.

Lightweight: This is actually a disadvantage when it comes to silver items, where the heavier the weight, the better the piece. But I can turn this negative into a positive, if I describe the dish as "dainty," making the dish sound charming, instead of too light.

Pierced: A design style used when making silver items.

Nut Dish: The type of item.

Footed: Three small, round balls are at the bottom of the dish, which serve as feet.

Heart-shaped: The shape of the nut dish.

Lacy: What the dish looks like to me.

Great Condition: No scratches or dents.

If you need more ideas, take a look at the description of similar items listed on eBay, but please don't plagiarize someone else's description; just use it for inspiration and ideas. You should also add information about the size and/or weight of the article if this helps sell the item or gives the buyer a better idea of what he or she is buying. When your auction terms state that the buyer must pay shipping costs, weight is also an important factor. A heavy item dramatically increases the total amount the buyer must pay.

Using my list of descriptive terms, I come up with the following title, subtitle, and description:

Title: Beautiful heart-shaped Gorham Sterling Silver Nut Dish.

Subtitle: Pierced and footed, in great condition.

Description: This heart-shaped Gorham sterling nut dish would make the perfect gift for a loved one! Vintage-style, this dainty dish features lacy piercing and three small round balls, which serve as feet for the base of the dish. A ribbon design is around the edges and "bows" are in the inside of the dish.

The nut dish is 3½" long, by 3¾" in width and stands nearly 1" at the highest point. The dish is in great condition with no scratches or dings. On the bottom of the dish are the words: Gorham, Sterling, and 956. I don't know the age of this nut dish, but maybe the marks will mean something to collectors of fine silver.

A very pretty nut dish . . . don't let this one get away!

Now that I have my description, I'm ready to take some pictures of the item. You can use a digital camera, or use a regular camera and scan the prints. I won't go into the details of how to produce great pictures for an auction, but I recommend *eBay For Dummies* by Marsha Collier and *Digital Photography For Dummies* by Julie Adair King.

 If you plan on using the eBay Picture Service to add pictures to your item listing (you can find more information on this later in the chapter), reduce your pictures to 400 pixels wide by 300 pixels long because this is the standard size for eBay pictures. If you plan on showing enlarged versions of your pictures (an extra fee applies), you may also want to create 800 pixel by 600 pixel versions.

With title, description, and photos, I'm *now* ready to list my item!

Getting Detailed

Now you're ready to get to the good stuff . . . setting a price for your item and determining how long you want your auction to run. To get started:

1. **Type** www.eBay.com **into your Web browser and click the <u>Sign In</u> link, which you find at the top of the page.**

2. **Enter your eBay user ID and password.**

   You must create an eBay user ID and password when you first sign up for the service, but you can then use a Microsoft Passport account (if you have one) to log on to eBay in the future.

3. **Click the <u>Sell</u> link, which you can find at the top of the page to the right of the eBay logo.**

4. **Click the Start a New Listing button.**

   eBay gives you a number of different ways to sell an item: auction it, sell at a fixed price, advertise your real estate, or sell through an eBay store.

5. **For now, select the Sell Item at Online Auction option and click the Continue button.**

6. **Pick the categories where you want your item to be featured.**

   If you haven't determined the best category yet, enter some descriptive words in the Enter Keywords box to find a category, and click the Search button. If you know which category to pick, select the top-level category from the list on the left, then pick an option from the list to the right of the first. Continue selecting from each list of subcategories until eBay stops offering you options.

7. **If you want to, you can opt to be featured in a second category.**

   According to eBay, this ensures approximately 18 percent more people will see your item, but the cost doubles the insertion fee. Any upgrades you opt for (such as showing the title in bold) also double in cost.

8. **After selecting your category, click the Continue button.**

9. **Enter the title and optional subtitle you came up with to describe your product.**

10. **You may also be asked to provide specific information that relates to your item's category.**

    For the silver nut dish, I can provide the composition, maker, product, and age. See Figure 8-2 for an example of the specialized information requested by eBay.

    On this page, you also enter the product description that you wrote. After pasting your text into the box, you can use the formatting buttons if you want to bold some of your text or change colors, sizes, and fonts. If you want, you can click the "Enter your own HTML" tab at the top of the box and enter your own HTML, formatted any way you like.

11. **After you finish entering your description, click the Continue button.**

The next page is where you add pictures and make choices about how your auction is to be run.

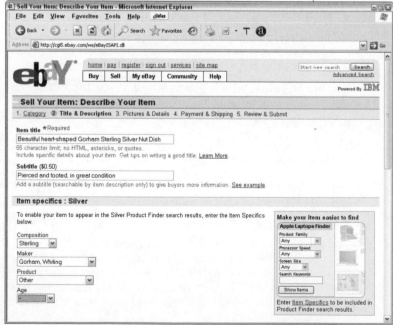

Figure 8-2:
Providing eBay with additional information about your product makes it more likely that your product can be found in response to a search.

The Enter Pictures & Item Details Page

On the Enter Pictures & Item Details page, you can determine the lowest price you're willing to accept for your item, the duration of the auction, and the quantity of items you're selling. You can also add pictures to your listing to let buyers see what they're bidding on. You can select a theme for your listing, to jazz it up a bit, and specify additional features to add to your listing to help it stand out from the competition. Figure 8-3 shows what the Enter Pictures & Item Details page looks like.

Figure 8-3:
The Enter Pictures & Item Details page is where you set up the main components of your auction: the starting price, the reserve price, and the length of the auction. You can also add pictures to your listing and take advantage of special eBay features, such as themes and enhanced listings.

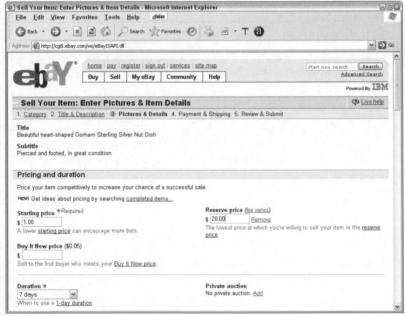

1. **Under the Pricing and Duration section of the page, enter the auction starting price.**

   If you set $5.00, then bidding cannot start any lower than $5.00.

    By clicking the Completed Items link, shown under Pricing and Duration, eBay displays a list of similar items, along with the price of the winning bid. This helps you determine the reserve price to set for your item.

2. **You can also set the reserve price for your item.**

   Regardless of the starting price, the reserve is the lowest price you'll accept for the item. Bidders won't see the reserve price, but are told if their bid has not met the reserve price. It works like this: You start the bidding at $5 but you have a reserve price of $20. If the highest bid is $15, the bidder does not win the item because your $20 reserve price has not been met.

3. **If you want, you can set a Buy It Now price.**

   When you set this price, a bidder can halt the bidding by buying the item outright, at the price you set.

4. **Select the length of time you want your auction to run (between one day and ten days).**

   The longer the auction, the more time you have to get bids for your item, but the longer you have to wait for your money. The default length of time is seven days. If you want a ten-day auction, eBay charges a $0.20 fee.

5. **Select whether the auction should start as soon as the listing is submitted, or pick the day you want your auction to start.**

6. **Pick the quantity of items you're selling (usually one).**

7. **eBay has you confirm the city and state where you're located (for U.S. bidders).**

8. **You can add pictures to your listing.**

   - If you have a Web site where the pictures are featured, you can enter the Web address and eBay links to your images.

   - If you don't already have a picture posted on a Web site, you can use eBay Picture Services to add pictures to your item listing. Click the Add Picture button to add your picture. You can add up to 12 pictures, but there is a $0.15 fee for each picture you add, after the first one, which is free. See Figure 8-4, which shows eBay Picture Services.

   - eBay also offers options, such as adding supersized pictures and a slide show to your listing.

Figure 8-4:
You can use
the eBay
Picture
Service to
easily add
pictures to
your listing.
There's a
$0.15 fee
for every
picture after
the first one,
so having
a listing
with four
pictures
costs me
$0.45.

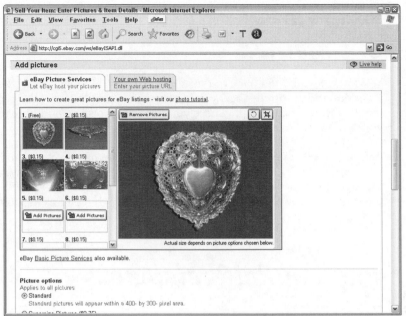

9. **For a $0.10 fee, you can add a theme.**

   A background image can be added to your listing and you can choose the placement of your pictures. Click the Preview Listing link to see how a particular theme looks with your listing.

10. **The last section of the page shows different promotional options you can choose for your listing.**

    I recommend adding a gallery image to the listing because it helps your item stand out in a list of items. Other options (for example, putting a border around your listing, highlighting your listing, and so on) may or may not be useful to you, depending on what you are trying to sell.

11. **After making all your choices on the Enter Pictures & Item Details page, click the Continue button.**

For the silver nut dish, I set a starting price of $1 and a reserve price of $20. I chose seven days as the duration of the auction and a quantity of one. I used eBay Picture Services to add four pictures to be shown on my item listing and chose the standard (400 x 300 pixels) option. I selected the Stores – Metallic Silver Theme, with the photo displayed on top. I chose to add a Gallery picture to my listing (at a price of $0.25) and decided not to put a page counter on the page. A page counter shows how many people are looking at your listing. It helps you determine if the title and category for your listing are working well, or if you need to tweak them in future auctions.

Choosing PayPal as Your Payment Method

You knew I would get back to the subject of PayPal — right? On the Enter Payment and Shipping page, you get to make choices about the type of payments you want to accept, where you're willing to ship, and how to price your shipping costs.

Before you click your way through the rest of the page, you should take a moment to think about whether you want to set your default PayPal options through the eBay Web site or the PayPal Web site. Doing it the eBay way is the quickest way to get your item listed, but you have more options if you go through the PayPal Web site.

Changing PayPal Preferences through eBay

If you decide that listing quickly is more important to you, you can set many PayPal options without ever leaving the eBay Web site. Here's how:

1. **From the eBay Enter Payment and Shipping page, make sure that PayPal is selected as one of the payment methods you accept.**

   Confirm that your PayPal user account is correctly displayed in the payment notification box. If not, you can type in the correct e-mail address.

2. **Click the Edit Preferences link, shown to the right of your e-mail address.**

   This brings you to the Payment & Shipping Preferences page. Figure 8-5 shows you the PayPal options that can be configured.

3. **You can opt to have a Buy It Now button displayed in all of your eBay listings.**

   This button displays on the listing page when the auction has ended, and on e-mail invoices sent by eBay. If the buyer looks at the Items I've Won page, the Pay Now button is also displayed. If you select the top Pay Now option, the buyer payment goes through eBay for payment processing.

4. **If you choose the "Show the Pay Now Button only in listings where I offer PayPal" button, the Pay Now option appears in all listings where you accept PayPal.**

   When the buyer clicks the Pay Now button, the payment goes through PayPal for processing.

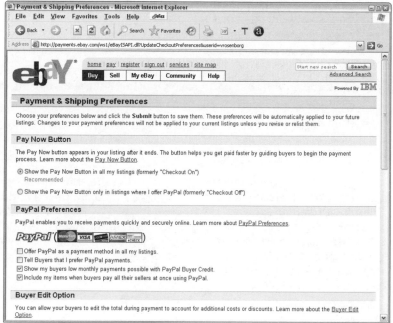

Figure 8-5:
On the eBay
Payment &
Shipping
Preferences
page, you
can set
many of
your PayPal
account
options
without ever
leaving the
eBay site.

5. **In the next section of the page, you can click the PayPal Preferences options that you want to take advantage of.**

   Your options include the following:

   - Ensure PayPal is offered as a payment option in all your listings.

   - Let buyers know that you would prefer payment through PayPal.

   - Show buyers how they can use PayPal Credit to make monthly payments to purchase the item (of course, this only makes sense for items with a high start or reserve price).

   - Combine your items into a single invoice, if the buyer buys multiple items from you.

6. **You can update your payment address, if necessary.**

   This address is where buyers send checks and money orders if they don't want to use an alternative payment method.

7. **If you provide UPS shipping to your buyers, you can select the type of shipping rate to offer to your buyers.**

   If you don't have a Daily Pick Up account with UPS, select the first option so the shipping cost is calculated for your buyers. If you do have a Daily Pick Up account, select the second option and the shipping price calculates accordingly.

Although you are required to pick one of the two UPS options on this page, you don't have to offer UPS as a shipping option to your buyers. You select the shipping carriers you want to use on the eBay Payment and Shipping page. To read more, see the section "eBay's Payment and Shipping Page," later in this chapter.

8. **Click the Submit button to save your PayPal payment and shipping preferences.**

   eBay displays a page confirming your preferences and letting you know that your selections will be applied to all of the items you've listed for auctions.

Going back to the silver nut dish example, from the eBay Enter Payment and Shipping page, I clicked the <u>Edit Preferences</u> link to go the PayPal Payment & Shipping Preferences page. I opted to show the Pay Now button in all my listings and decided to use PayPal as a payment option in all my listings. I won't allow the buyer to edit the total payment amount. I confirmed my address (even though I won't accept checks as payment) and opted to offer UPS On-demand rates to my buyers.

eBay's Payment and Shipping Page

After you set your PayPal preferences, you're ready to fill out the rest of the Payment and Shipping page to ensure that bidders have all the information they need to make an informed bid. Here's how:

1. **Select whether you want to accept any other methods, in addition to PayPal.**

   You can also opt to accept money orders, cashiers checks, or personal checks. If you have a merchant account with a credit card processor, you can also accept credit card payments.

2. **Decide whether to let the buyer change the amount sent to you when paying for an item.**

3. **You can pick the locations that you are willing to ship merchandise to.**

   Your shipping options include sending packages Worldwide, or to the Americas, Canada, Mexico, Europe, the United Kingdom, Germany, Asia, Australia, or Japan.

   You can also decide not to ship anywhere; buyers need to pick up the item from your location. Unless your item is very large, this is not a good option to select because very few bidders are willing to pick up merchandise because of travel time and expenses.

4. **You can choose whether to set a flat rate for shipping the item, or cal-culate the shipping costs based on the carrier used, the weight of the item, the distance to be shipped, the type of package or container, and so on.**

   For a detailed explanation of the shipping options available to you, see Chapter 10.

5. **By clicking the <u>change</u> link shown under each option, you can opt whether to add a packaging and handling fee, offer shipping insur-ance, add sales tax to the cost of your item, and change the shipping zip code, if necessary.**

6. **Your last option is to send the buyer payment instructions and return policy information by typing a message into a text box.**

   This message can contain instructions about shipping, your return policy, and so forth. It is included in the invoice that is sent to the winning bidder.

7. **After setting these options, click the Continue button.**

Back on the eBay Enter Payment and Shipping page, I selected PayPal as my only payment option. For my Ship-to locations, I decided to ship only to the United States. For Shipping Costs, I selected a calculated fee, based on the weight of my item (under a pound) and the size of the package (in my case, a package or thick envelope). I selected U.S. Postal Service Parcel Post as my domestic shipping carrier. I also gave the buyer the option of buying shipping insurance.

Submit Your Listing

On the Review and Submit Listing page, you have a chance to review all the options you selected and preview how your listing looks. Before you review the listing details, eBay provides you with a Listing Analysis. This is a list of suggestions that helps improve your chances of having a successful and profitable auction. The only recommendation for the silver nut dish is that I remove the reserve price of $20. According to the analysis, your listing is likely to get more bids and sell at a higher price if you list without a reserve price. I decide to take the advice of eBay and click the Edit button to remove the reserve price.

The first step in reviewing your listing is to confirm that the title, subtitle, description, category, subcategory (if you have one), item specifics, pictures, details, payment, and shipping information are correct. You can also click a link to preview how your listing will look to potential bidders.

The second step is to review the fees that you are charged for placing the listing. Table 8-3 contains the fees I accumulated in listing the silver nut dish. In addition to the listing fees, I pay a Final Value Fee if my nut dish sells. Table 8-2 shows the Final Value Fees, based on the price of the winning bid.

eBay also shows your current account balance. Please note: Your eBay balance is not the same as your PayPal balance! If you have any money in this account, the cost of the fees are deducted from this account. If no money is in the account, you have the option of paying for the listing with a credit card.

Table 8-3 Sample Listing Fees (Listing the Silver Nut Dish)	
Fee Description	*Cost*
Fee for placing the listing (Insertion Fee)	$0.35
Adding a subtitle to the listing	$0.50
Adding three additional pictures to the listing through the eBay Picture Service	$0.45
Adding a gallery image (which will be seen when this item is shown in a list of listings)	$0.25
Using one of the themed backgrounds and page layout templates (Listing Designer)	$0.10
Total listing fee	$1.65

If you are satisfied with the listing and the fees, clicking the Submit Listing button lists your auction. eBay displays a confirmation page, along with a link to your listing. Figure 8-6 shows what the final listing looks like.

The confirmation page also has a link to your My eBay page, where you can track the information about your auction, including the current price, number of bids, the ID of the current highest bidder, the number of people watching your item, the number of questions asked about your item, and the time left before the auction ends. You can also click a link to list a similar item.

Figure 8-7 shows the newly listed nut dish. Notice that all of the competitive products have gallery pictures, so it's a good thing that I spent the extra $0.25 for my gallery picture. The other detail to notice is the little "double P" logo to the right of the item title. This logo shows that I accept PayPal payments for this item.

Pay your eBay fees with your PayPal account

You can pay your eBay fees through your PayPal account. After logging on to your eBay account, click the My eBay link, which you find at the top of the page. This page summarizes all the items you're selling, bidding on, have won, and if applicable, are watching.

In the column at the left of the page, under the My Account heading, click the Seller Account link. This page shows the total amount of fees you owe to eBay. On the right side of the page is a "Pay your eBay Seller fees" section. In the blue box with the PayPal logo is the amount you owe, with a Pay button.

Click the Pay button to pay the fees with your PayPal account. You are redirected to the PayPal Web site, where the payment details are shown and you're asked for your password to log on to PayPal.

Enter your password and click the Continue button. PayPal then asks you to confirm the payment.

Click the Pay button. You see the payment confirmation screen with a Click here to continue link. Click the link. You're returned to the eBay home page, not the My Account page.

Figure 8-6: The listing shows the title and picture of the item, along with the starting price, the number of bids (if any), and the amount of time left before the auction closes.

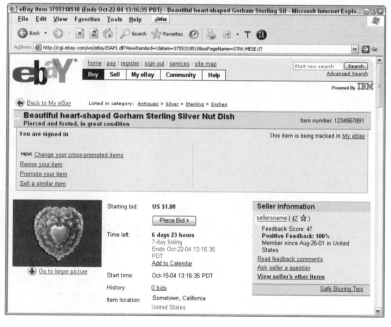

Figure 8-7:
You can find
the nut
dish by
searching
on the terms
Sterling,
Gorham,
and nut
dish. The
item just
listed is at
the top
of the list,
but five
competitive
items are
also for
sale.

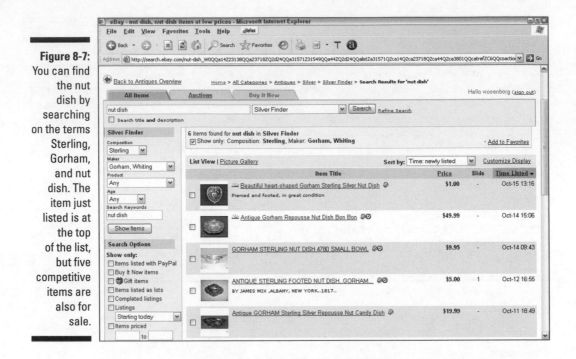

Some of the competitive listings have a shield logo, shown to the right of the
"double P" logo. This logo shows that the item qualifies for the PayPal Buyer
Protection plan, which can be reassuring to a nervous bidder. To find out
how your item can qualify for the Buyer Protection program, see Chapter 7.

For those of you who want to know the end of the story about the silver nut
dish, seven people bid on the dish. At the end of the auction, the dish was
sold for $31.44.

Adding an Automatic PayPal Logo

Earlier in this chapter, I showed you how to set PayPal Seller Preferences
through the eBay interface. Now it's time to show you how to set preferences
through the PayPal Web site, where you have more options from which to
choose.

One of the reasons that the "double P" logo was shown next to my eBay listing is because I had that option set through PayPal. It's easy to set up an
automatic logo insertion in PayPal. Just follow these steps:

1. **Click the <u>Profile</u> link, found under the My Account section of the site.**

2. **Under the Selling Preferences column, click the <u>Auctions</u> link.**

   The Auction Accounts page shows your eBay user ID, on or off settings for Automatic Logo Insertion, Winning Buyer Notification, and whether to show a PayPal Preferred logo on eBay.

3. **If you have no auction accounts registered with PayPal, click the Add button to add an account, as shown in Figure 8-8.**

   Enter your eBay user ID and password into the text boxes on the page and click the Add button.

   You cannot add an eBay user ID that has already been linked to another PayPal account, but you can add multiple eBay user IDs to a single PayPal account. To remove an eBay account, select the account and click the Remove button.

   If you update your eBay user ID on the eBay Web site, you need to remember to update it on PayPal as well — the update does not happen automatically.

4. **Click the <u>Off</u> link, shown under the Automatic Logo Insertion column.**

   On the Insertion page, select the On choice and click the Update button.

Figure 8-8:
You can link your eBay account to your PayPal account, which will allow you to set auction preferences through the Account Profile.

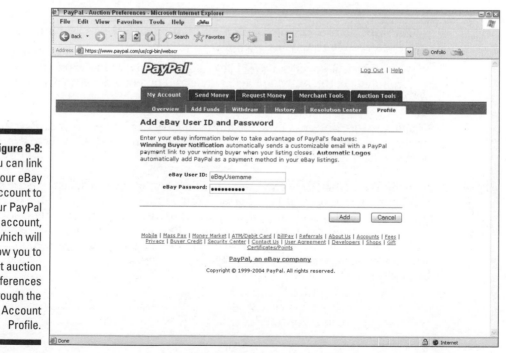

5. **You can change the Winning Buyer Notification option in the same way.**

   When you turn this option on, PayPal sends an e-mail invoice to the winning bidder within an hour after the auction closes.

   - **PayPal includes a default message that will be included in the e-mail.** You can also choose to customize this message by changing the text displayed in the message text box. You have up to 2,000 characters for the entire message. PayPal recommends that you include specific shipping information targeted towards international buyers if you sell items to buyers outside of the United States.

   - **You can also include a logo, which is featured in the e-mail.** The logo must be 150 pixels in width and 100 pixels high. The logo must be stored on a Web server and you need to know its location to include it in the e-mail. An example of a logo location is `http://www.mywebsite.com/images/mylogo.jpg`. You can click a link to test your logo to make sure it is displaying correctly.

   - **If you have more than one e-mail address linked to your PayPal account, you can choose from which e-mail address to send.** In fact, PayPal is sending the e-mail, but your e-mail address appears in the "From" field when the e-mail is sent.

   - **You can also opt to have a duplicate of the Buyer Notification e-mail sent to your e-mail address.**

6. **A third option, on the Auction Account page, lets you add the PayPal Preferred logo to your auctions.**

   To add the logo, click the <u>Off</u> link under the PayPal Preferred on eBay column. On the Activate PayPal Preferred on eBay page, select the On option and click the Update button.

Changing these options automatically is an easy way to set up your PayPal preferences and then forget about them, knowing that they'll apply to every item you list on eBay.

Remembering that the eBay and PayPal sites work together when you are setting your auction options is important. You'll notice this if you use the PayPal Auction Account page to turn Automatic Logo Insertion on. If you then edit your PayPal preferences on the eBay Enter Payment and Shipping page and turn off the "Offer PayPal as a payment method in all my listings" option, you'll notice that when you log back into your PayPal account, Automatic Logo Insertion has been turned off.

Adding a PayPal Logo Manually

Although it's not obvious from looking at the logo shown on the Auction Account page, when you automatically add a PayPal logo to an eBay listing, you're really adding a Smart Logo. Smart Logos are only available on eBay auctions.

A Smart Logo detects whether your auction listing is still open (that is, people can still place bids for your item) or closed, when the auction ends. As soon as the auction closes, the Smart Logo changes to a Pay Now logo. When returning to the item description, the winner can pay for the item by clicking on the Pay Now logo. Because it's so easy for the winner to pay, the chances are high that you get paid more quickly for the item you auctioned.

For most auctions, Smart Logos are the right choice, but you may want to display a different PayPal logo under specialized circumstances. You can choose from a variety of different logos when you opt to add a logo manually. With a manually added logo, you copy the code from the PayPal Web site and paste it into the description of the item you're listing on the eBay Web site.

Unless you want the Smart Logo to show in auctions where you decide a manual logo would be better, you need to remember to turn the Smart Logo option off on the PayPal Auction Account page.

Manual logos that can be added to your auctions include:

- ✔ **The Standard (static) PayPal logo.** This looks just like the Smart Logo — it has the PayPal logo, followed by credit card icons: Visa, MasterCard, Discover, American Express, and eCheck. Unlike the Smart logo, the Standard logo does not change after the auction ends.

- ✔ **The No Surcharge Logo.** Sellers in the U.K. who do not add a surcharge (additional fee) to items purchased with PayPal can use this logo.

- ✔ **The (other) Standard Logo.** This version is identical to the Standard logo but doesn't include the credit card icons shown to the right of the PayPal logo.

- ✔ **The Globe Logo.** You use this logo to indicate that you accept international bidders for items you list on eBay.

- ✔ **The Pounds Sterling Logo.** You use this logo to indicate that you accept payment in pounds sterling, even if the item has been listed in U.S. dollars.

- ✔ **The Euros Logo.** You use this logo to indicate that you accept payment in euros, even if the item has been listed in U.S. dollars.

✔ **The 234 x 60 Logo.** This logo is a larger version of the PayPal logo that is compliant with many non-eBay auctions.

If you try to use this logo in one of your eBay listings, eBay won't allow you to list the item.

✔ **The 468 x 60 Logo.** This logo is an even larger version of the PayPal logo that is compliant with many non-eBay auctions.

If you try to use this logo in one of your eBay listings, eBay won't allow you to list the item.

To add a logo to your auction listing, start by logging on to your PayPal account and then follow these steps:

1. **Click the Auction Tools tab and then click the <u>Manual Logos</u> link.**

2. **Choose the logo you want to add to your listing.**

   Each logo shows a text box containing HTML code.

3. **Right-click in the text box containing the code and click Select All.**

   After the text is highlighted, copy the text.

4. **In a new browser window, go to eBay.com and sign in.**

   If you are creating a new item listing, follow the directions given earlier in this chapter. If you are adding to a listing you were working on, click the <u>Sell</u> link at the top of the eBay page.

5. **Click the <u>Finish Your Last Listing</u> link and then click the <u>Title & Description</u> link.**

   Scroll down to the Item Description section of the page.

6. **With the Standard tab selected, type in the description of your item and click the "Enter your own HTML" tab.**

   The text you enter displays in the text box, formatted with HTML tags.

7. **Move the cursor under the text already entered and paste the HTML code you copied from the PayPal Web site.**

8. **Click the <u>Preview Description</u> link.**

   The description you entered appears and the manual logo displays below your text. Figure 8-9 shows a preview of the item description with the manual logo inserted at the bottom.

If you know how to edit HTML, you can change the text of the manual logo, which is displayed before the logo image. If you don't know how to edit HTML, click the Standard tab and change the text, as you would any text in the description.

Figure 8-9:
This preview shows what the manual Globe logo looks like when added to an item description. The text that reads "PayPal— eBay's service to make fast, easy, and secure payments for your eBay pur- chases!" comes from PayPal's HTML code, as does the logo that shows the words "PayPal" displayed over a world map.

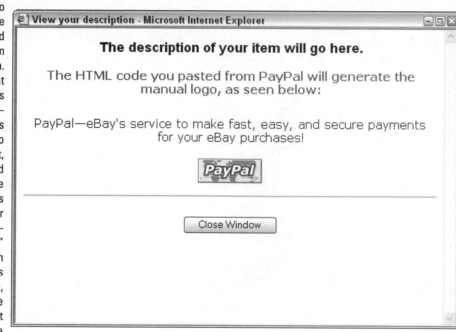

Figure 8-9:
This preview shows what the manual Globe logo looks like when added to an item description. The text that reads "PayPal— eBay's service to make fast, easy, and secure payments for your eBay pur- chases!" comes from PayPal's HTML code, as does the logo that shows the words "PayPal" displayed over a world map.

Bulk Up: eBay's Selling Manager

If you're an eBayer who sells multiple items on eBay, you may want to sign up for the eBay Selling Manager service. The service can help you organize multiple listings by showing a summary of all your auctions: open, closed, (both sold and unsold), and ones that are scheduled. Through the Selling Manager interface, you can send e-mails to buyers, leave feedback, print ship- ping labels, and send invoices. See Figure 8-10, which displays the Selling Manager page that replaces the Sell page when you sign up for the service. The Selling Manager is a very useful tool for people who sell in volume, but if you sell less than 75 items a month, it's probably overkill.

Figure 8-10:
The eBay
Selling
Manager
helps
organize
items you
listed for
sale on
eBay. The
service lets
you look at
your items
in multiple
ways and
makes it
easy to
relist items
that haven't
sold.

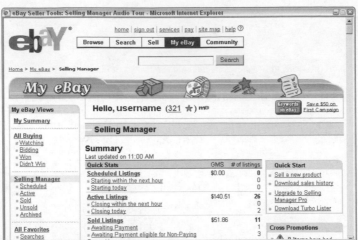

Selling Manager helps you manage existing listings, but does not help you list items. For that you need Selling Manager Pro. Alternatively, you can use Selling Manager in conjunction with another eBay service — Turbo Lister. Together, the two services provide some, but not all, of the features available in Selling Manager Pro. Selling Manager Pro costs $15.99 per month, but Turbo Lister is free.

The Selling Manager service, while invaluable to power sellers, costs $4.99 a month (the subscription is automatically added to your eBay account monthly invoice). You find a table comparing the features offered by each service, along with two additional services (Seller's Assistant Basic and Seller's Assistant Pro), by going to http://pages.ebay.com/selling_manager/comparison.html.

If you sell items only occasionally on eBay, you probably don't need the features and cost of eBay's Selling Manager. But you can get some of the Selling Manager features by using the PayPal Post-Sale Manager. This tool won't give you information on pending or current auctions, but it lets you organize information for auctions that have ended in the past 30 days and helps you send invoices. See Chapter 9 for more information about the Post-Sale Manager.

Cash-Back: PayPal's Preferred Rewards

PayPal has a cash-back rewards program, where you can get back 1.5 percent of every purchase you make with the card. Before you rush out and start putting all your purchases on your debit card, you need to make sure you meet the criteria for the rewards program. The following criteria apply:

✔ **You need to have a Premier or Business PayPal account.**

✔ **You must have applied and activated your PayPal Debit Card.**

✔ **You need to have a valid eBay user ID registered with PayPal.**

✔ **You have to enroll in the rewards program:**

1. **From the Account Overview page, click the <u>PayPal Preferred</u> link.** PayPal displays a box with a check next to each of the program criteria you already met.

2. **Click the <u>Confirm that you sell on eBay</u> link.** If you have an eBay user ID linked to your PayPal account, you can click the Submit button to be enrolled in the program. If your eBay user ID has not been linked, you have the opportunity to add it here.

✔ **You need to list an item in an eBay auction at least every three weeks.**

✔ **You need to activate the PayPal Preferred option for all of your eBay listings.** Click the <u>Profile</u> link; then click the <u>Auction</u> link and click the <u>off</u> link under the PayPal Preferred column.

✔ **Select PayPal as the only payment option shown in your listing (except for checks and money orders).** You can mention alternative payment options at the end of listing e-mail you send to winning bidders.

Although the criteria is pretty stringent, the rewards can add up, so it's good to enroll if you sell a lot of items on eBay and you don't mind showing PayPal as your only payment option.

Selling in PayPal Shops

If you have a Web site that accepts PayPal as a payment option, you can list your site in PayPal Shops, a directory of more than 42,000 online storefronts.

If you don't have a Web site, but you want to be listed on the PayPal Shops, go to the Shop page (by clicking on the <u>Shops</u> link shown at the bottom of every PayPal page), then click the <u>Need a Website</u> link, shown at the bottom of the right column of the page. PayPal lists a number of shopping cart and storefront solutions vendors. You can select one of these to help build your online store.

To see these stores, click the <u>Shops</u> link found at the bottom of every page. Featured shops are shown in the middle of the page; shop categories appear on the left. Shops are listed by the amount of sales, so the top sellers are always shown first. You can search the shops for specific items or just browse.

There are no fees to enroll in the PayPal Shops program. To meet the qualifications for the program, you must meet the following criteria:

✔ You need a Premier or Business account.

✔ You need a bank account linked to your PayPal account.

✔ You need a credit card linked to your PayPal account.

✔ Your PayPal funds need to be invested in the PayPal Money Market Fund.

Chapter 9

Sending an Invoice

....

....

*B*efore your auction ends, you should take the time to customize the buyer notification e-mail, or invoices, that you'll send to winning bidders. Personalizing your communications helps to set a more professional image and may mean repeat business in the future, because the buyer remembers who you are, or your business.

PayPal offers a variety of tools that let you customize these e-mails. In this chapter, I show you the tools and explain when to use one tool, as opposed to another.

Customizing Your Buyer Notification Message

The PayPal Winning Buyer Notification service automatically sends an e-mail to the winner of your eBay auction, an hour after the auction ends. This service is very convenient, especially if you're running a number of auctions simultaneously. Sending instant notification saves you the tedium of writing the same set of instructions to each winning bidder and saves you from remembering to send an e-mail the day the auction closes.

The e-mail that the buyer receives contains a Pay Now With PayPal button. Clicking this button opens eBay in a browser window. The buyer can review the details of the listed item, select PayPal as a payment option, and click the Continue button. The buyer is then redirected to PayPal's Web site, where he or she logs on to complete the payment process. The Buyer Notification feature is very useful, but unfortunately is available only with eBay sales.

Setting up Buyer Notification only requires you to fill in a single form: PayPal and eBay do the rest. Here's your part:

1. **Log on to your PayPal account and click the Auction Tools tab.**

2. **Under the Receiving and Managing Payments section of the page, click the <u>Winning Buyer Notification</u> link.**

3. **If you have more than one eBay user ID linked to your PayPal account, select the account from which you are selling.**

   If you want to add an additional eBay user ID, click the <u>Add</u> link. (If you haven't linked an eBay account to your PayPal account, you see a short form where you can enter your eBay user ID and password.)

4. **A message box displays the text that will be sent in the e-mail to your buyer; click anywhere in the box if you want to customize or change the default message text.**

   Remember to keep your message in the 2,000 character limit! PayPal suggests that you provide shipping and handling information if you are shipping items internationally.

5. **If you have a logo, you can add it to the e-mail that is sent from PayPal.**

   The logo needs to be 150 pixels wide by 100 pixels in height, less than 10 kilobytes (KB) in size, and saved on a Web server. If you know the Web address of the location of your logo image (an example would be `http://www.yourwebsite.com/yourlogo.jpg`), you can type it into the box and click the <u>Click here to test your logo</u> link. Figure 9-1 shows what the Test Your Logo page looks like, after you've successfully added your logo image. Image files must be formatted as a GIF, JPEG, or PNG file. (Table 9-1 tells you how to find out the Web address of your logo, if you're unsure.)

   If the logo image is hosted on a secure server (one that starts with `https://` instead of `http://`), you won't have any problems with the image. If your image is hosted on a nonsecure Web server (which most of them are), then users may see a warning message, depending on their browser's security setting. The message warns users that the page contains both secure and insecure (that's your image) items. Users won't experience any problems when looking at the page, but it might make some buyers a little nervous.

6. **Select the e-mail address that the notification comes from.**

   The e-mail address should match the address that you use with your eBay account.

7. **Check the box if you want to receive a copy of the e-mail that is sent to the buyer.**

   I recommend you always do this, just to make sure it looks the way you intend it to look.

Figure 9-1:
If your
logo is the
correct size
and you
enter its
Web
address
correctly,
the Test Your
Logo page
shows you
what your
logo looks
like when it
is added to
the Buyer
Notification
e-mail.

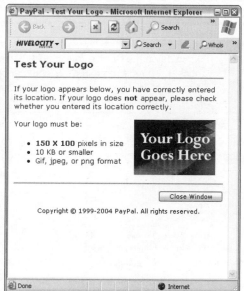

8. **Click the Submit button and you're finished setting up the Winning Buyer Notification options.**

Figure 9-2 shows an example of what the notification looks like after the buyer receives it.

Table 9-1	Finding the Address of Your Logo Image
Browser	*Get the Web Address*
Internet Explorer (on Windows PC)	Place your mouse cursor over the image and click the right-mouse button. From the menu, select Properties. The address (URL) of the image displays; copy this address and paste into the PayPal Display Your Logo box.
Netscape (on Windows PC)	Place your mouse cursor over the image and click the right-mouse button. From the menu, select the Copy Image Location option. Click in the image text box on the PayPal Winning Buyer Notification Registration page and click the right-mouse button. Select Paste from the options. The correct Web address for the image file pastes in the text box.

(continued)

Table 9-1 *(continued)*

Browser	Get the Web Address
Safari (on the Mac)	Holding down the Control key, click the image and choose the Open Image in New Window option. The image opens in a new window that displays the Web address of the logo image.

Figure 9-2:
The Buyer
Notification
e-mail
includes a
Pay Now
with PayPal
button,
which
makes it
easy for the
buyer to
start the
payment
process
from the
e-mail itself.

After you set up Buyer Notification and the auction has ended, you're ready to manage your auction(s) with the PayPal Post-Sale Manager.

Manage End-of-Listing Activities with the Post-Sale Manager

If you don't use an eBay service such as the Selling Manager for tracking your eBay auctions, you can use the PayPal Post-Sale Manager (see Figure 9-3), which has the advantage of being free. But the Post-Sale Manager has a few limitations when compared to the eBay Selling Manager:

✔ **The Post-Sale Manager doesn't track an item until after the auction has ended (and only if the item was sold).**

✔ **The Post-Sale Manager only tracks auctions listed on the U.S. version of the PayPal Web site.**

✔ **The Post-Sale Manager doesn't show listings unless the currency used in the listing was U.S. dollars.** If you want to see summary information for sales in other currencies, you need to download the PayPal Merchant Sales Report (you can find more information about this report in Chapter 13).

✔ **Items are only shown for a 30-day period.** You can still view the transactions by using the PayPal History feature. See Chapter 11 for more information about your Account History.

Figure 9-3:
The Post-Sale Manager lets you see all eBay sales that have ended in the last 30 days and lets you filter the sales by different criteria so you can see who has sent payment, which buyers still need their packages shipped, and so forth.

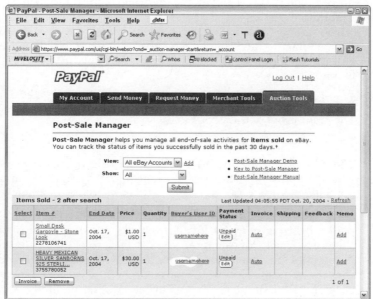

After your auction has ended, you can get to the Post-Sale Manager one of two ways:

✔ By going to your Account Overview and clicking the <u>Items Sold</u> link (with the eBay logo shown to the right of the words), which you find at the end of the row that starts with the Recent Activity heading.

✔ You can also get to the Post-Sale Manager by clicking the Auction Tools tab and then clicking the <u>Post-Sale Manager</u> link (which you find under the Receiving and Managing Payments section of the page).

Seeing what sold

The Post-Sale Manager shows all eBay items you sold in the last 30 days. You can view sales activity for any eBay accounts you linked to your PayPal account by selecting your eBay username from a list.

For each auction that has ended, the Post-Sale Manager displays the following information:

✔ **At least part of the title you gave the item when you listed it on eBay and the item number.** Clicking the partial name brings up your eBay listing.

✔ **The date that the auction ended.**

✔ **The final price of the item.**

✔ **The number of items listed in the auction.**

✔ **The eBay user ID of the buyer.** Clicking the ID opens a new e-mail in your mail program. The buyer's e-mail address and the item number are filled in for you (all you have to do is write the message!).

✔ **The payment status of the item, showing whether the item has been paid for through PayPal.** If you received some other type of payment (personal check, for example), you can click the Edit button, shown to the right of the payment status. In the Post-Sale Manager Payment Status window, you can select which payment method was used (personal check, cashiers check or money order, PayPal, or other method). If PayPal was used, you must fill in the PayPal transaction ID so PayPal can track the payment for you. Figure 9-4, shows the Payment Status window.

✔ **The invoice status of the item.**

 • If this field is blank, an invoice has not yet been sent.

 • If you have Winning Buyer Notification turned on as a default, the invoice was sent automatically when the auction ended and Auto shows as the status.

- If you haven't sent an invoice yet, an Invoice button displays; clicking the button lets you send an invoice to the buyer.

- If an invoice has been sent, then the word Sent appears.

- If you had to resend an invoice, as a gentle reminder to the buyer, you see a Re-Sent status.

- If this invoice has been combined with others into a single invoice sent to a buyer who has purchased multiple items, a status of Consolidated is shown.

✔ **The shipping status of the item.**

- If the item is not marked as paid, the Shipping Status is blank, because PayPal recommends you don't send an item until after you receive payment.

- After the item is paid for, a Ship button displays. Clicking this button lets you use PayPal Shipping to purchase and generate a shipping label from UPS.

- If you don't use PayPal Shipping (you decide to use the eBay Shipping interface instead, for example), you can mark this item as Shipped.

- If you do use PayPal Shipping, you can Track your package by clicking the Track button.

✔ **The feedback status of the item.**

- If the item is not marked as paid, the Feedback Status is blank because PayPal recommends you don't leave feedback for a buyer until after you receive payment.

- If you want to leave feedback, clicking the Leave button opens a form where you can post your eBay feedback about the buyer.

- If you were selling multiple items through a Dutch Auction, a status of Multiple shows. Clicking this link opens a Post-Sale Manager page, especially designed for Dutch Auctions.

- If you already left eBay feedback, the status shows as Done.

✔ **Whether you leave yourself a memo about the item.** You can add a short (up to 2,000 characters) memo to yourself about the transactions by clicking the Add link. After you leave a memo, you can read it by clicking the View link. Memos expire after 30 days.

Figure 9-4:
You can change the Payment Status of an eBay sale by specifying how the item was paid for if PayPal was not used. If PayPal was used, but payment was sent through a different PayPal account, you can fill in the transaction ID to track the payment.

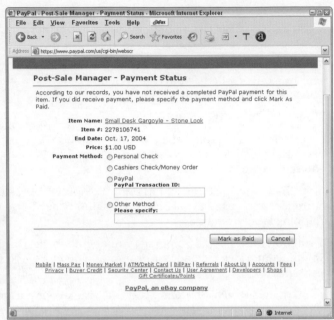

Getting organized with the Post-Sale Manager

If you sold a large number of items in the past 30 days — such as your entire collection of original Star Wars action figures, including Jabba the Hutt — it may be difficult to find specific transactions within a long list. The Post-Sale Manager lets you organize the listings by different criteria. To filter your items, pick one of the Show options and click the Submit button:

✔ **All auction items sold in the last 30 days.**

✔ **Items that are unpaid.** You can refine this list further by choosing to see items that have not been invoiced, items sold to a single buyer that can be consolidated into a single invoice, and items for which you already sent invoices.

✔ **Items that have been paid for. (Although you won't see items that have been paid for without PayPal. You need to find these in the Unvoiced items and change the Payment Status to paid.)** You can refine the Paid Items listing by seeing items that still need feedback, need to be shipped, and those that are Done. (No, the item hasn't been cooked to perfection. "Done" means you left feedback for the buyer.)

✔ **You can also see items you already removed from the list, as long as they were sold within the 30-day period.**

In addition to filtering how the items are displayed, you can select an item (by clicking the box shown to the left of the item number) and send an invoice, or remove the item from the list.

Sending an Invoice

PayPal has a free service called the Invoice Manager that can speed up the process of sending invoices for items you recently sold on eBay. The Invoice Manager prepopulates the item fields, based on the auction information. You have no limit to the number of invoices you can send at a single time with the Invoice Manager.

You access the Invoice Manager through the Post-Sale Manager:

1. **Click the Auction Tools tab.**

2. **Under the Receiving and Managing Payments heading, click the** <u>Post-Sale Manager</u> **link.**

3. **Select your eBay username from the list, or select the All eBay Accounts option.**

   You can add your eBay username and password if you haven't yet linked your eBay account to your PayPal account.

4. **Select the Uninvoiced option from the Show list and click the Submit button.**

5. **Place a check next to each of the items you want to create an invoice for and click the Invoice button.**

   This brings up the Item Invoice Details page (also known as the Invoice Manager).

Each item is in a separate section of the page, displayed as a mini-invoice. If you sold more than one item to the same buyer, the items are grouped into a single invoice. The invoices include a Pay Now with PayPal button or link to make it easy for the buyer to send payment immediately.

Most of the fields on the invoice are already filled out for you. These include

- The item name (clicking this shows the eBay listing in a new window)
- The item number
- The date the auction ended
- The quantity of items sold
- The price of the final bid
- The total price

Figure 9-5 shows what the Invoice Manager looks like. Note that two items are combined into a single invoice for the second invoice that is being generated.

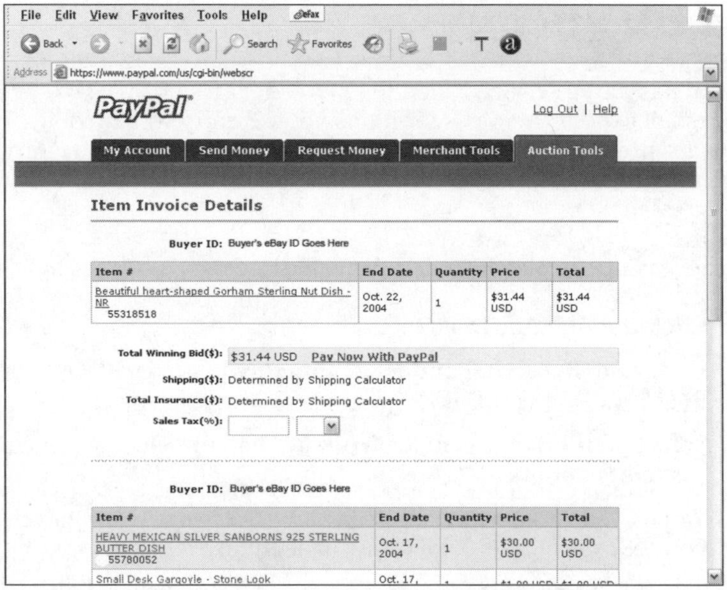

Figure 9-5:
For eBay items, the Invoice Manager lets you create invoices quickly with most of the fields already populated with auction information.

Shipping, insurance, and taxes

If the buyer's address is known, the price of shipping the item is determined by the eBay shipping calculator. (For more information about eBay and PayPal shipping, see the next chapter.) If the shipping price is filled in, you can enter the amount you plan on charging the buyer.

eBay can also calculate the cost of providing the buyer with shipping insurance. If you don't know the buyer's address, you have a place on the page where you can enter the cost of shipping insurance yourself; adding insurance is optional, so don't feel like you have to offer it if you don't want to.

Estimating how much to charge for insurance

Shipping insurance is provided automatically if you ship with UPS; the item is insured up to a value of $100. If the item you're sending is more valuable, you can purchase additional insurance at a cost of $0.35 for each additional $100 of coverage. The maximum value of insurance is $500.

Insurance can be purchased online when you're purchasing shipping from the U.S. Postal service. The maximum value of insurance is up to $200. As I'm writing this book, to insure items for $50 or less costs $1.30. Items between $50.01 and $100 in value cost $2.20, and items from $100.01 to $200 cost $3.20.

If you want additional insurance, you need to buy it directly from the post office. You can get insurance up to $5,000 for regular mail, and up to $25,000 if the item is sent via registered mail.

The last field on the Item Invoice Details page is where you add sales tax to the price of the item. Enter the tax rate, as a percentage, in the box and select your state from the list shown to the right. Sales tax is charged when you are selling to a buyer who is located in the same state you are.

The Sales Tax Clearinghouse has a nifty little online tool to help you calculate what percentage to use for sales tax. The tool is available at `http://thestc.com/RateCalc.stm`. All you do is enter your state, the address of the buyer, and click the Lookup button.

Formatting your invoices

After filling in any fields that haven't been filled in already, you can choose to customize your invoice by clicking the <u>Edit Formatting Options</u> link at the bottom of the page. You can select an alternate e-mail address, if you have more than one linked to your PayPal account. You can also edit the message to be sent to the buyer.

You can also add a logo to the invoice. See Chapter 8 for more information about how to add a logo or other image to an invoice. After entering the Web address for the image, make sure to try the <u>Click here to test your logo</u> link to make sure the image is the right size and looks professional.

You can opt to have a copy of the invoice sent to yourself and can save the formatting settings as a default to use with all the invoices you send. Click the Save button to save the settings.

Sending out the invoices

After formatting the invoice, click the Send button on the Item Invoice Details page. You return to the Post-Sale Manager page. At the top of the page, PayPal shows confirmation that the invoice has been sent and displays an order number. The items shown in the Invoice column show a status of "Sent." If multiple items are combined into a single invoice, the status shows as "Consolidated."

A gentle reminder

After sending an invoice, when you look at your Account Overview, you may notice a Remind button. You don't get the chance to customize this message before it is sent, so make sure you're really ready to send it before clicking. Figure 9-6 shows what the reminder looks like when it arrives in your buyer's mailbox.

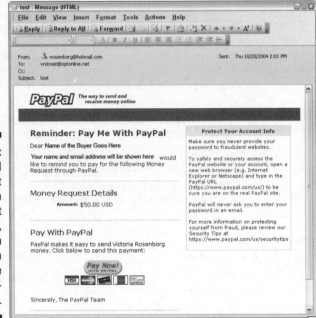

Figure 9-6:
The e-mail reads like it comes from PayPal, not from you, which makes it a little more authoritative.

Creating an Invoice Template

Creating an individual invoice is easy, but it can become tedious if you have to send the same invoice to a specific client or buyer on a regular basis. Instead of typing the same message five months in a row, you can use an invoice template, where you can save the message once and have it repeated on all five invoices. PayPal lets you save up to ten different templates. Here's how:

1. **Select the Create an Invoice option from the Request Money tab.**

   If you already created invoice templates, you can choose which one to use by selecting it from the list and clicking the Continue button. If you don't have any invoices saved, you can create one (see Step 3, below).

2. **Click the <u>Saved Invoice Templates</u> link, which you find in the middle of the page.**

   You see a list of templates, if you created any. For each template, you can view, edit, or remove it.

3. **To create a new template, click the Add button.**

   On the Create Invoice Template page, you can select an existing template (if you have one) as the basis of a new template.

4. **Select New Invoice from the list and click the Continue button.**

   On the Create Invoice Template page (see Figure 9-7), you start by giving a name to your template.

   Try to give a more descriptive name to your template, rather than Template 1, Template 2, and the like. When you create a number of templates that are slightly similar, forgetting which one is the one you want to use is easy. A name, such as _Goods Invoice – message for eBay buyers_ is a better choice.

5. **Your name is already filled in, but you can choose to add an address, add an optional phone number, and enter the recipient's e-mail address by typing it in the box or picking it from a list of people with whom you recently had transactions.**

   If you're creating a template for an invoice that will be sent to multiple people, you can separate the e-mail addresses with commas or press the Enter button after each address.

6. **Under the Invoice Details area of the template form, you can select which currency to use and the type of invoice (whether it is sent to buyers of goods or services).**

   You can enter an optional e-mail subject header and add that note you don't want to keep retyping. (The note is also optional.)

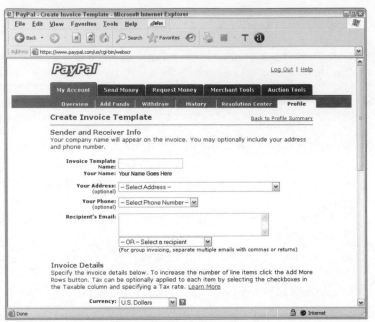

Figure 9-7:
By creating
an invoice
template,
you can
save those
fields that
are always
the same to
avoid having
to retype
them each
time you
want to
send an
invoice.

7. **You need to fill in at least one row of the table that is shown on the Invoice Template page.**

   The table lets you add the following fields to your invoice template:

   - Quantity of items

   - Item ID (this can be a tracking number that you assign to a specific item)

   - A brief description of the item

   - The unit price of the item — the currency shown depends on which currency you selected earlier

   - PayPal calculates the amount for you by multiplying the quantity by the price

   - Whether the items being sold are taxable

   - The shipping cost

   - The tax rate you want to use, if the item is taxable

8. **Although you need to add at least one row, you only need to specify the item description and unit price.**

   Whether you fill in the other fields depends upon how specific you want your invoice template to be. If you need additional rows, you can click the Add More Rows button. PayPal calculates the amounts, subtotal, and total cost for you.

9. **After filling in the table, click the Continue button.**

   PayPal lets you preview the template before you save it (see Figure 9-8 for an example). If there are any fields that need to be changed, just click the Edit button.

10. **Using an invoice template is easy.** When you're ready to send an invoice, click the Request Money tab and then click the Create an Invoice link, found at the top of the page.

11. **Click the down arrow to the right of the Select Template list, select a template, and click the Continue button.**

12. **The Create an Invoice page appears with the fields you saved in the template already filled in for you.**

    All you have to do is fill in the additional information and click the Continue button.

13. **PayPal displays a preview of the invoice that will be sent.**

    Unless there is something you need to edit, you can click the Send Invoice button and you're done!

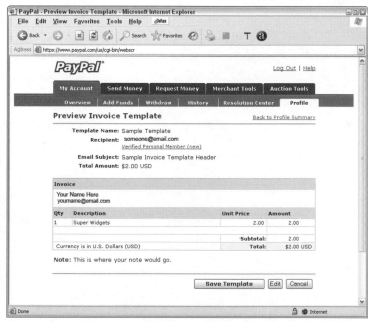

Figure 9-8:
You can preview your invoice template before saving it and edit it if necessary.

Chapter 10

PayPal Shipping

*Y*ou have two components to shipping items: First you need to figure out how much to charge a buyer; after the item is sold, you pay the shipping company to ship the item for you. You want to make sure that what you charge is pretty close to what you'll be charged. Charge the buyer too much and you risk getting negative feedback, and risk being in violation of eBay's rules. Charge too little and the buyer may be grateful, but your wallet won't be.

The cost of the shipment is calculated by how big the package is, how heavy the package is, the shipping distance, and how quickly it needs to get there. Using the shipping tools offered by eBay and PayPal, you can calculate how much it costs to ship the package, purchase and print your shipping labels online, and track the package as it makes its way to the seller.

Shipping Items Sold on eBay

If you are selling an item on eBay, figuring out shipping costs is made easier because you can use the eBay Shipping Calculator. When you list an item for auction, you can determine whether to use a flat or calculated shipping rate, which the buyer pays when paying for the item.

If you choose the flat rate, you can select a carrier (USPS or UPS) and charge a fee that is the same for all buyers, regardless of where they live. This method is easy, but you run a greater chance of overcharging or undercharging.

If you select calculated shipping, the eBay Shipping Calculator estimates the most accurate shipping cost, based on the weight and size of your package, the distance of the delivery, and the shipping service you select.

The first step is to determine how big and how heavy your package is. You can use eBay's Shipping Calculator to help you estimate the weight. You can find the Shipping Calculator listed on eBay's site map; look under the Selling Tools section.

The first page gives rough estimates of 1 pound, 3 pound, and 10 pound items. By comparing your item to these benchmarks, you can guess how heavy the item is. (If the item is more than 10 pounds, then go for the bathroom scale.) See Figure 10-1 to determine the estimated weight of your item.

Figure 10-1:
If your bathroom scale is not accurate, the eBay Shipping Center demo offers examples of 1 pound, 3 pound, and 10 pound items. This can help you guesstimate how much your item weighs.

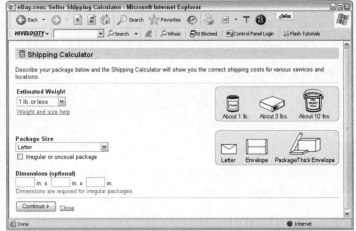

 Make sure you weigh or guesstimate your item *after* packing it in the shipping materials and box. It's no good getting a shipping estimate if your item weights mere ounces, but you're packing it in a pound's worth of protective material. You also need the dimensions of the final box before you can determine the correct postage.

After estimating the weight, measure the length, width, and height of your package.

eBay is a great resource when you want to figure out how big your package is. For a comparison of package size options and the shipping carriers that accept them, see the eBay Package Sizes chart, which you find at `http://pages.ebay.com/help/sell/ship-calc-package.html`. For more information about oversized packages, check out `http://pages.ebay.com/help/sell/irregular-package.html`.

1. **In the Shipping Calculator, enter the estimated weight of the item.**

2. **Select the type of package you are sending (large envelope, package, and so on).**

3. **Check the "Irregular or unusual package" check box if your package does not conform to the sizes described on the Package Sizes page.**

   If you have an irregularly sized package, you need to provide the dimensions of the package (measured in inches).

4. **Click the Continue button.** If you know the zip code of the place to where you are mailing, enter it in the ZIP Code box.

   If you don't know the zip code, select the closest location from the Domestic Rates list. If you're shipping internationally, select the country from the International Rates list.

5. **Click the Show Rates button.**

6. **The Shipping Calculator returns the rates if you shipped by USPS or UPS.**

   See Figure 10-2 for an example of the rates that are returned when I want to ship a 1 pound package from Connecticut to New York.

7. **You can select up to three domestic and three international shipping services and click the Offer Services button**.

   The rates you selected apply to your listing.

8. **Click the Close button.**

   You can also choose to add packaging and handling charges and shipping insurance.

After the auction has ended, eBay calculates the shipping cost and adds it to the final cost of the item, if the buyer uses one of the following PayPal processes to make payment: eBay Checkout, Winning Buyer Notification, End of Auction Notification, Post-Sale Manager Invoicing, or Smart Logos. Any package specifications you enter into the Shipping Calculator prepopulate the fields on the form you fill out to generate the shipping label, saving you time and extra effort.

If you are using the PayPal Post-Sale Manager to track your eBay auctions, you can access the shipping tools described in this chapter, directly from the Post-Sale interface. For more information about the Post-Sale interface, see Chapter 9.

Figure 10-2:
You can
compare
the costs of
shipping
with the
postal
service
versus UPS
and see
how the
prices vary,
depending
upon how
quickly you
want your
package
delivered.

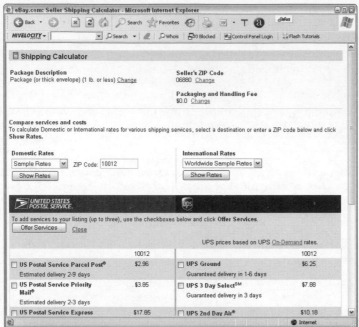

Calculating Shipping for a Non-eBay Item

If you want to sell a non-eBay item and accept PayPal as the form of payment, you can estimate and apply shipping costs to the invoice or money request you send to the buyer. (See Chapter 9 for more information about invoicing.) You can add shipping costs as a percentage of the total cost or as a flat dollar amount. You can add the shipping cost when you're creating the invoice, or you can set your shipping calculations and preferences in advance, as described in the "Setting Shipping Preferences" section of this chapter.

If you're unsure about how much to add when estimating shipping costs on a specific invoice, you can still use the eBay Shipping Calculator for help, even if you're not selling the item through eBay! On the eBay Web site, click the Site Map link, which you find at the bottom of every page. Click the Shipping Calculator link, which you find in the middle of the Services column under Selling Tools. Go through the Calculator steps, filling out the weight and size of the package, the zip codes for the seller and the buyer, and opt to see sample domestic or international rates. You see approximate rates to charge your buyer, depending upon the type of shipping service(s) you plan to offer.

Choosing Which Shipping Service to Use

PayPal offers domestic shipping services, only. You have a choice between two carriers: UPS or the U.S. Postal Service.

Both services have advantages and disadvantages. Shipping via the U.S. Postal Service is usually the less expensive option, but UPS makes it much easier to track a missing package. Table 10-1 compares the advantages and disadvantages of using each service.

Table 10-1	Advantages and Disadvantages of USPS versus UPS	
Advantages	**USPS**	**UPS**
	The cost is usually lower than the equivalent service from UPS.	UPS offers more domestic options for getting your package delivered quickly (in less than three days).
	The USPS provides free boxes if you're shipping with Priority Mail Service. You can order free boxes through eBay at `http://ebay supplies.usps.com` and arrange to have the boxes delivered right to your doorstep!	You get up to $100 of insurance when you ship with UPS; adding additional insurance is less expensive, compared to USPS insurance.
	You get a tracking number, which lets you know when your package has been delivered.	The tracking number you get from UPS gives you the ability to go online and track your package wherever it is, en route.
	You can have USPS do a free pick-up on the next postal delivery day; or you can drop off at the nearest post office.	Pick-up service available, but you are charged for the service; or you can ship the package from a drop-off location.
Disadvantages	**USPS**	**UPS**
	Unlike UPS, where you get up to $100 insurance included in the base price, you need to pay extra to insure the contents of your package.	UPS is considerably more expensive than shipping with USPS.

If you can't decide which service to use, look at the value of your item. If the item is very expensive, you should use UPS because the cost of insurance is less expensive. eBay's Standard Purchase Protection Program offers $200 worth of coverage, minus a $25 processing fee. PayPal's Buyer Protection program offers $1,000 worth of coverage. But if you're selling Aunt Nellie's sterling silver tea service, worth $2,500, you may want to buy extra insurance and peace of mind through UPS.

If you have a relatively inexpensive item, which doesn't require a lot of insurance, you may want to take advantage of the cheaper USPS rates. If you want to ship outside of the United States, you need to use USPS because the UPS integration with PayPal only lets you ship if the addresses for both the sender and the receiver are located in the United States. Using USPS is also necessary if the shipping address you are given is to a P.O. box. Unfortunately, UPS does not ship to P.O. boxes.

Setting Shipping Calculations

If you have a Web site that you set up to accept PayPal payments for goods and services you sell online, you can set up default shipping options that automatically add to the costs of the items you sell. These shipping options work when an item is paid for through a PayPal Shopping Cart purchase, Buy It Now button, or a Donation button. To set up your shipping options:

1. **Click the <u>Profile</u> link (under the My Account section of the PayPal Web site).**

2. **Under the Selling Preferences column, click the <u>Shipping Calculations</u> link.**

3. **Select the currency to use for the shipping rate.**

   The default is U.S. dollars, but if you previously added shipping rates for a different currency, select the currency and click the Select button. You see the current settings and have the ability to modify them, if desired.

4. **Select whether you want to calculate shipping amounts based on a sliding flat rate or on a sliding percentage basis.**

5. **You can set up to five shipping rates (flat or percentage) based on the value of the item(s) you are shipping.**

   With a flat rate, you can charge $2.00 for shipping if the value of the item is less than $10.00. You can charge $4.00 for shipping if the item is worth more than $10.00, but less than $50.00, and so on. Percentages work the same way, except you charge a percentage of the value, instead of a specific dollar amount. You can change the price ranges shown by clicking the Edit button. See Figure 10-3 for an example of the Shipping Calculations page.

6. **Click the Save button to save your Shipping Calculations settings.**

Figure 10-3:
You can set
shipping
rates based
upon a flat
dollar value
or a per-
centage of
the value of
the item.
You also
have the
option to
change the
shipping
amount, as
the dollar
value of
the item
increases.

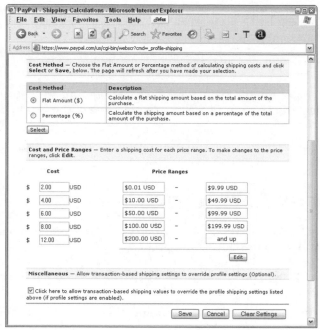

If you set up the code or PayPal buttons used on your e-commerce Web site to charge specific shipping amounts based on individual products or services, making changes to the shipping calculations overrides your settings. To avoid this, select the option that says "Click here to allow transaction-based shipping values to override the profile shipping settings listed previously," and then click the Clear Settings button. The shipping values that you set up programmatically will be maintained.

Setting Shipping Preferences

You can set up default shipping information for your address, the types of transactions to incorporate shipping, and a selection of USPS or UPS as a carrier from the PayPal Shipping Information page.

1. **Click the <u>Profile</u> link (under the My Account section of the PayPal Web site).**

2. **Under the Selling Preferences column, click the <u>Shipping Preferences</u> link.**

3. **PayPal shows the shipping name and address that are used when printing shipping labels.**

   You can update the address information by clicking the <u>Modify this Address</u> link.

4. **You can select which types of payments should show the Ship button on your Account Overview or Post-Sale Manager pages, after the buyer has paid you.**

   Options include eBay items and other auctioned goods, goods that have not been sold through an auction, services, and Quasi-cash.

5. **When you're ready to ship your package, you can opt between choosing from both USPS or UPS and selecting one of the two to be your default choice.**

6. **After making any changes to your preferences, click the Save button.**

Setting up USPS preferences

Before you can print a USPS shipping label, you need to set up your printer and paper source, so the labels print properly.

1. **Click the <u>Profile</u> link (under the My Account section of the PayPal Web site).**

2. **Under the Selling Preferences column, click the <u>USPS Preferences</u> link.**

3. **Select whether you plan on using a standard laser or inkjet printer, or a special Zebra LP2844-Z label printer, for printing labels.**

4. **If using a standard printer, you can also choose to print a receipt along with the label.**

5. **If you're using a label printer, select the Zebra LP2844-Z from the list and choose the 4.0 x 6.0 paper size (the size for the sticky label paper).**

   You also need to download the Java 2 Runtime Environment (basically, special code that the label printing program needs to work properly). Click the link to start the download process and follow the instructions given to download and install the software.

6. **Click the Save button to save your preferences.**

Setting up UPS preferences

In order to be able to print UPS labels, you need to have an account with UPS; you can either enter your existing UPS account information or apply for an account.

1. **Click on the <u>UPS Preferences</u> link (which can be found on the Account Profile page).**

2. **Click the Open UPS Account button.**

If you don't have an account, select the New UPS Shipping Account option. If you do have an existing account, select the Existing UPS Shipping Account option and enter your UPS account number.

3. **Enter an estimate as to how many ground packages you expect to ship a week and how many packages are to ship by air.**

   You also are asked to declare if you ship hazardous materials, high-value or breakable goods, and if you act as a shipping outlet.

4. **PayPal shows your default account information for the company name, contact name, address, and phone number.**

   If you already have an existing UPS account, you need to make sure the information shown is the same as that associated with your UPS account.

5. **You can opt to pay for your shipping labels with your PayPal account or have your UPS account billed.**

6. **Click the Continue button.**

   You are asked confirm your account information; if everything's correct, click the second Continue button. You need to agree with the UPS shipping agreement to finish opening your UPS account.

If you opt to use your PayPal account to pay for your UPS shipping labels, the funds will be taken from your account balance. As with other PayPal payments, if there isn't enough money in your account, funds are transferred from your bank account, or you can opt to directly bill your UPS account.

A nice benefit to opening your UPS shipping account is that you are sent a complimentary UPS package containing shipping labels and envelopes. The sign-up package is sent to the address used when you signed up for your UPS account.

Printing Shipping Labels

You can print a shipping label after you receive payment through PayPal for an item. Items that are ready for shipping show a Ship button under the Action column of the Account Overview or Post-Sale Manager page.

To get started with shipping, click the Ship button. Unless you already picked a default carrier from the Shipping Preferences page, select either USPS or UPS as the shipping carrier.

Shipping with USPS

1. **Click the Continue button.**

   You must be using a Windows system to be able to print USPS labels from the PayPal Web site; Macs are not supported. Additionally, you need to be using Internet Explorer 5.0 or above, or Netscape 6.2 or above. Your browser needs to be JavaScript-enabled and you cannot be blocking pop-ups, or you won't be able to use the interface.

2. **Click the Continue button.**

   On the U.S. Postal Service - Print Your Label page, confirm your address and the address to which you are shipping. (See Figure 10-4.)

3. **You also select a service: Priority Mail, Express Mail, Parcel Post, Media Mail, or First-Class Mail.**

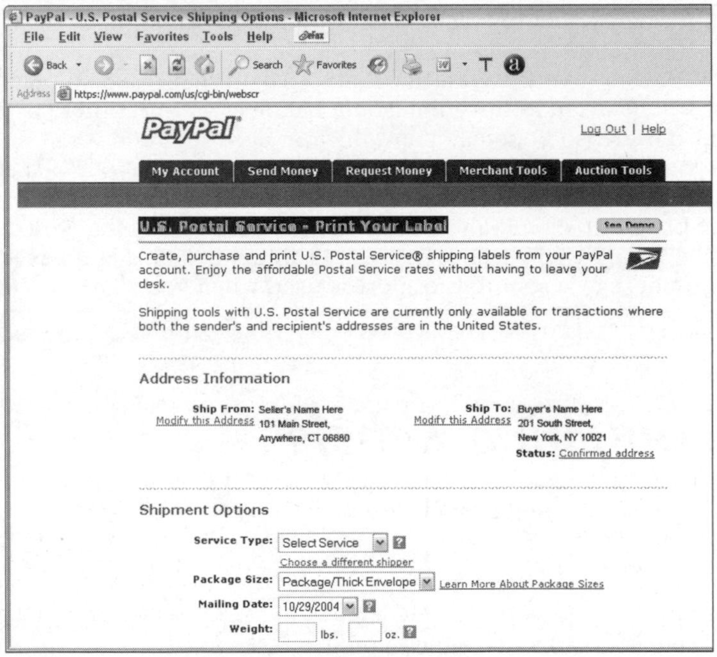

Figure 10-4:
On the Print Your Label page, you select the type of shipping service you want, and enter information about the weight of your package and where it is going. The correct postage is calculated for you and a label is generated for you to place on your package.

 4. **Select the package size: Package/Thick Envelope, Large Package, Very Large Package, or Flat Rate Envelope.**

 5. **Select the mailing date and specify the weight of the package in pounds and ounces.**

    Depending on the service type selected, delivery confirmation (you receive notice when the package gets to its destination) and label processing (a fee charged by PayPal for printing the label) may be free. If these options are not free, the cost for delivery confirmation is between $0.13 and $0.55. The cost for label processing is normally $0.20.

 6. **You can opt to get a confirmation signature from the recipient when the package arrives.**

    This confirmation costs an additional $1.30.

 7. **If desired, you can choose to have the cost of the shipping printed on the label itself.**

    You can send an optional e-mail to the buyer.

 8. **Unlike UPS, you cannot purchase additional insurance online; if you want insurance, you need to buy it from a post office.**

 9. **You can also change or update your printer settings.**

10. **Click the Continue button.**

    You see a confirmation page; unless you want to change some of the information, click the Pay and Continue button. On the Print Postage page (see Figure 10-5), you receive confirmation that you successfully created your postage shipping label.

11. **Click the Print Sample Label button to preview how the label will look when printed from your printer.**

12. **When you're ready to print the actual shipping label, click the Print Label button.**

    It's important to make sure that you use the original label printed from your computer — you cannot use a photocopy or reproduction.

13. **Affix the label to your package (using tape or glue), but be careful not to tape over the bar code label.**

    You're now ready to arrange to have your package picked up, take it to a post office, or drop it in a post office collection box. Under the window with the label to be printed is the U.S. Postal Service Shipping Label Completed page. This page contains links to let you

    • Request to have the package picked up from your location.

    • Order free shipping supplies.

Figure 10-5:
The Print
Postage
page shows
you a
sample label
that you can
print out to
make sure
all of the
information
is correct
and your
printer is
printing
the label
correctly.
After
ensuring the
sample is
correct,
click the
Print Label
button.

- Create a packing slip, which you can include in the package. This slip contains the details of your transaction and includes a message, which you can customize for your buyer.

- The page also gives instructions on how you can void the transaction (request a refund for the money you spent to purchase the shipping label) as long as you request the refund within 48 hours of generating the printing label. (Of course, if you already used it to ship the package, it cannot be voided.) The void request is sent to the USPS for confirmation; if they approve it, the funds are redeposited in your PayPal account within 15 days. (If you used Parcel Post or Media Mail service, the refund may take up to 21 days.) After the original label is voided, you can generate another label, if necessary, with corrected information.

- You can void the label from the Transaction Details page by clicking the Void Label link. A link to let you void the transaction is also available in the label confirmation e-mail you receive after ordering the label.

14. **After printing the label, you receive a confirmation e-mail, which serves as a receipt for your purchase of the mailing label.**

    The e-mail contains multiple links to let you

    - Track the package as it is shipped.

    - Request a free pickup of the package. Your package will be picked up the next postal service day, at your location.

    - Void the shipping label transaction (good only for 48 hours after the label has been generated).

    - Reprint the label (good only for 24 hours after the label has been generated).

15. **The buyer also receives an e-mail with information about how the package is being shipped.**

    This e-mail contains a link to track the package as it is shipped, and a link to let the buyer view the details about the PayPal transaction.

16. **The options that are available on the U.S. Postal Service Shipping Label Completed page are also available on the Transaction Details page. Options include**

    - **You can get to the transaction details by going to the Account Overview or History pages and clicking the <u>Details</u> link.** Two items let you view the shipping details. You can see the details for the original transaction (when the buyer paid for the goods) or look at the transaction for the purchase of the shipping label (when you paid the USPS for the label generation).

    - **On either Transaction Details page are links to let you track the package, see the details of the related PayPal transaction, reprint the label (24 hours only), or void the label (48 hours only).**

Shipping with UPS

If you and the buyer of your item are both located in the United States, you have the option of using UPS for shipping your package. To use UPS as your carrier, click the Ship button, shown in the transaction record for the item.

1. **Click the Continue button after selecting UPS as the shipping carrier.**

   You can preview the process of buying a UPS label before getting started; click the See Demo button shown at the top of the page. (See Figure 10-6 for the UPS – Print Your Label page.)

2. **You can update the Ship To address, if necessary, and you need to select whether the address is residential or business.**

Figure 10-6:
On the Print
Your Label
page, you
select the
type of UPS
shipping
service you
want to use
and enter
information
about the
weight
of your
package
and where it
is going. If
you don't
have a UPS
account yet,
you can sign
up for one
by clicking
the link
shown at
the bottom
of the page.

3. **Select the type of service you want to use for shipping.**

   Your options include Next Day Air, Next Day Air Saver, 2nd Day Air A.M., 2nd Day Air, or 3 Day Select. You can also choose whether you want Saturday delivery.

4. **Select the type of packaging you are using.**

   Choices include UPS Letter, UPS PAK, UPS Tube, or UPS Express Box.

5. **If you're not shipping a UPS Letter package, enter the weight of your package. If you are using your own packaging (instead of UPS standard packaging), enter the dimensions of your package, as measured in inches.**

6. **Enter the value of your item (for insurance purposes).**

7. **You can also personalize the e-mail message that is sent to the buyer, after you generate the UPS shipping label.** (Figure 10-7 shows sample shipping labels for UPS and USPS.)

Figure 10-7:
Click the
See Demo
button at the
top of the
UPS – Print
Your Label
page to
preview the
steps you go
through
when
generating
your
shipping
label. This
figure
shows what
the label
looks like
after it's
printed.

8. **If you have not previously registered with UPS, you need to click the Register with UPS button at the bottom of the page.**

   You need to complete the UPS registration form. See the "Setting up UPS preferences" section of this chapter for more information.

9. **If you already have a UPS account linked to your PayPal account, click the Continue button.**

10. **Confirm the shipping information to be used on the label and then click the Complete Shipping Order button.**

    Depending on how you configured your UPS account, the fee for the shipping label is deducted from your PayPal balance or charged to the credit card you registered when you signed up for a UPS account.

11. **On the next page, select the option to print your label.** After the label has been printed, click the Continue button.

    • **You can print the label on plain paper from your regular printer.** After printing, fold the label on the line, as directed.

    • **The label is ready to be placed in a standard UPS shipping pouch.** If you don't have a pouch, you can also fold and place the label on your package, covering the entire label with clear plastic shipping tape.

• **If you are shipping items in multiple packages, you can click the Create Additional Labels button to print as many labels as you need for additional packages.** Additional labels can also be printed from the Transaction Details page by clicking the Ship Another button, which you find at the bottom of the page.

12. **You can track the package as it is shipped by clicking the <u>Track Package</u> link on the Transaction Details page.**

If you make a mistake when printing the label, you can void the transaction and get your payment back, as long as you do so within 24 hours of generating the label. In your Account History, find the item created when you paid for the UPS label and click to see the transaction details. At the bottom of the page, click the <u>Void Label</u> link and then click the Void Shipment button to cancel the shipment.

Chapter 11

Managing Your PayPal Payments

*T*he first page you generally see after logging on to your PayPal account (sometimes PayPal displays a promotional page) is your Account Overview. Unless you already filed selected items, you can see a list of all transactions conducted in the past seven days.

In the Account Overview, you get the file type for each item whether the payment was from you or to you, the name or e-mail of the person/entity the transaction was with, the date and status of the transaction, a link for more details, a button for any actions that can be performed for that item (for example, shipping), the amount of the transaction, and any fees charged by PayPal. The Account Overview is useful, but what if you want to see older transaction data? For that, you need to review your Account History.

The Account Overview provides a lot of information, which can make it hard to quickly scan your recent transactions. If you want to see a quick summary of the recent items (the overview of the Account Overview, so to speak), click the Help link at the top of the PayPal page and type the word **history** in the search box. PayPal then displays a condensed version of the account activity for the past seven days. See Figure 11-1 for an example of the condensed recent activity table.

Figure 11-1:
The
shortened
version of
the recent
account
activity
shows the
date, name
or e-mail,
and amount
of each
transaction,
along with a
link to let
you view the
transaction
details.

History Class

To see your Account History, click the History link, shown under the Account tab. Alternatively, you can also click the All Activity link, shown on the Account Overview page. Your Account History has data on every transaction you conducted since becoming a PayPal member. Because the Account History covers so many transactions (especially if you've been an active PayPal member for a year or more), knowing how to sift through the data and learn about the different details and what you can do with the data is important.

To see how long you've been a member, click your Account Overview. At the top of the page, under your name and e-mail information, is a Status line (which reads "Verified" or "Unverified"). Click the number or word shown to the right of the status (which reads either "Verified" or "Unverified"). This displays your Member Information Box, which gives the date your PayPal account was created and how long you've been a member.

A trip down memory lane

A number of reasons why you need to access your account's history are

✔ You need information about a transaction that is more than seven days old and is no longer accessible through the Account Overview page.

✔ You need information about a transaction that is less than seven days old, but you chose to file the item, so it's no longer accessible from the Account Overview page.

✔ You want to see a running balance for transactions conducted over a certain time period.

✔ You want information about a non-eBay transaction. (Only eBay transactions are shown in the Post-Sale Manager or Pay for eBay Items Won pages.)

✔ You want to filter and view specific types of transactions over a specific period of time.

✔ You want to see monthly data collected in a single report.

✔ You want to download data and analyze the data offline by importing it into other applications, such as Microsoft Excel, Quicken, or QuickBooks.

✔ You want to view summary information about sales transactions.

✔ You want to search all transactions for specific, specialized criteria (for example, a type of currency, transactions conducted with a specific person, and so forth).

✔ You want to see all transaction disputes.

No matter how you filter the data, items in the History report display in reverse chronological order (that is, the newest transaction is on top). (See Figure 11-2 for an example.) For each item, the following information is shown:

✔ **Date:** When the transaction took place.

✔ **Type.** Types of transactions include

- **ATM Withdrawals:** Any ATM withdrawals done using your PayPal Debit Card.

- **BillPay:** When you send a payment using the PayPal BillPay feature.

- **Bills:** When you send a money request.

- **Bonus:** Any bonuses you accrue (for example, merchant referrals, new account bonuses, and so on).

- **Cash Back Bonuses:** The 1.5 percent cash-back you earn when using your Debit Card and meeting the other Cash Back criteria.

- **Currency Conversion:** Any money in your account converted from one currency to another as the result of conducting a type of transaction.

- **Debit Card Purchase:** Any purchases made using your PayPal debit card.

- **Dividend:** The monthly dividend paid if you chose to invest your balance in the PayPal Money Market Fund.

- **Mass Payment Sent:** Any mass payments you sent from your account.

- **Payment:** Any payment that has been sent to your account as the result of a standard transaction.

- **PayPal Services:** A payment for the generation of a UPS shipping label.

- **Subscription Cancellation:** An item shows when a buyer cancels a subscription.

- **Subscription Creation:** An item shows when a buyer starts a subscription.

- **Temporary Hold Placed:** If you send an Instant Transfer payment that gets cancelled or returned, a hold is placed on the transfer amount in your account until your bank clears the returned payment.

- **Temporary Hold Released:** After the hold (described previously) is released because of clearance from your bank, a transaction shows the returned funds.

- **Transfer:** Any money transferred from your bank account or to your back account, as the result of a transaction.

✔ **To/From:** Whether the payment was to you or from you.

✔ **Name/E-mail:** Address of the person or organization with whom you conduct the transaction.

✔ **Status:** The current state of the transaction (which depends upon the type of transaction conducted). Valid statuses include Completed, Paid, Pending, Denied, Processed, Charge, Cancelled, Cleared, Uncleared, Denied, Reversed, Unclaimed, Rewarded, and Active.

✔ **Details:** A link that you can click to see specific transaction details.

✔ **Action:** Buttons appear in this column if there are any actions (for example, Shipping) you can take to complete or continue processing the transaction.

✔ **Gross:** The amount of money sent or received as a result of the transaction.

✔ **Fee:** Any fees or charges that PayPal applies to the transaction.

✔ **Net Amount:** This amount is a running total of the amount of money in your account, obtained by adding money that is credited to your account, subtracting debits from your account, and subtracting any PayPal fees.

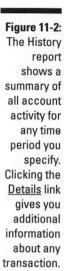

Figure 11-2:
The History
report
shows a
summary of
all account
activity for
any time
period you
specify.
Clicking the
Details link
gives you
additional
information
about any
transaction.

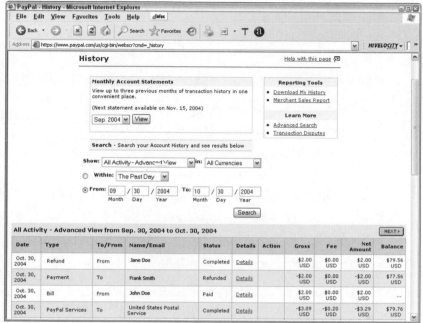

Two main ways to filter the data in your Account History are by looking at
the monthly account statements generated by PayPal or by searching for specific criteria (transaction type, currency, and/or date).

Monthly account statements

If you have a Premier or Business account, you can get all of your transaction
data summarized into a monthly report. This report is posted on the 15th day
following the month's end. In other words, if you want to see the monthly
data for October, you'll need to wait until November 15. Up to three months'
worth of data is stored for you to look at and analyze.

You need to sign up for the monthly account statement:

1. **Go to your Profile Summary page (which can be found under the
   My Account tab).**

2. **Click on the <u>Monthly Account Statements</u> link, under the Financial
   Information column.**

3. **Select the Yes option and click on the Save button.**

To see the Monthly Account, select the month from a list of three, which you find at the top of the History page, and click the View button. The report shows the balance at the beginning of the month and the balance you had at the end of the month. Check out Figure 11-3.

For each day in the month, the report shows

- The number of payments received
- The total value of the payments
- The number of payments sent from your account
- The total value of payments sent
- The total amount of PayPal fees incurred during the day
- Other credits added to the account during the day
- Other debits withdrawn from the account during the day
- The net profit or loss for the days

To see a summary report of all transactions conducted on a certain day, click the date link. In addition to viewing the report online, you can click the Get Printable Version button to see a version of the page, optimized for printing. Clicking the Print button prints the report. Click the Close Window button after you finish printing.

You can click the Download button to download a copy of the report as a Comma Separated Values (CSV) file. You can open CSV files in spreadsheets or you can import them into databases. The File Download window appears, giving you the option of opening or saving the downloaded CSV file. You can also press the Cancel button. Click the Save button and choose the folder where you want the file saved. Double-click the file after it has downloaded to open it in Excel, where you can manipulate the data.

After viewing the daily data, click the Done button to return to the History page.

Filtering the transactions

Unless you just opened a PayPal account, chances are you don't want to see all of your transactions since the dawn of time. To make the History page meaningful, you need to filter the transactions to show transactions of a certain type, transactions conducted in a specific currency, transactions in a certain time period, or some combination of the three.

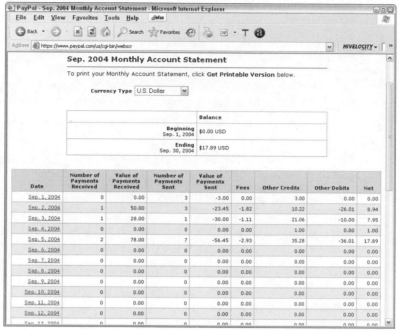

Figure 11-3:
The Monthly
Account
Statement
shows the
transactions
in your
account,
ordered by
each day of
the month.

The Search section of the History page lets you filter the transaction records in a variety of ways. You start by selecting one of the options in the Show list. Your options include

- ✔ **All Activity - Advanced View:** This view provides all available transaction data. Transactions that involve multiple steps are broken out separately.

- ✔ **All Activity - Simple View:** This view provides all available transaction data. Transactions involving multiple steps are grouped together.

- ✔ **Payments (both Payments Sent and Payments Received):** You can see payment data in one of three ways: all payments, payments you sent, or payments you received from other PayPal members.

- ✔ **Mass Payments:** You can see all the Mass Payments you sent; these are payments made to multiple people through a single transaction.

- ✔ **Money Requests:** Any requests for money (including bills and invoices) sent from your account.

- ✔ **Funds Added:** Any transactions that added funds to your PayPal account, including bank transfers, transfers from other PayPal accounts, cash-back bonuses, and so on.

✔ **Funds Withdrawn:** Any funds withdrawn from your bank account to pay for an item.

✔ **PayPal Debit Card Transactions (both a Primary Debit Card and a Secondary Debit Card):** If you have a PayPal debit card, you can also see purchases made with the card. If you have more than one debit card linked to your account, you can choose to see the transactions for the individual cards broken out separately, or combined into a single report.

✔ **Referrals:** If you make any PayPal referrals, you can see a report with the status of each.

✔ **Fee:** Any transaction fees charged against your PayPal account.

✔ **Subscriptions:** Any transactions involving subscriptions (whether you're the one paying for the subscription or the person receiving the subscription payments).

✔ **Dividends:** Any dividends paid as a result of having your PayPal funds invested in the PayPal Money Market Account.

✔ **BillPay Transactions:** Any payments you make using the PayPal BillPay services.

✔ **Refunds:** Any payments deposited into your account as the result of a refund.

✔ **Currency Conversions:** Any transactions in which PayPal converts payment from one currency to another currency.

✔ **Balance Transfer:** Any transfers of money in your PayPal account from one currency to another.

✔ **Reversals:** Any time PayPal customer support has to reverse payment, as the result of a dispute.

✔ **Shipping:** Any payments made for the purchase of UPS or USPS shipping labels.

✔ **Balance-Affecting Transactions:** Any transactions that alter the balance of your account. This includes payments, dividends, and so forth.

✔ **eChecks:** Any eCheck payments you send or receive.

✔ **Gift Certificate Reporting:** If you've sold any gift certificates, you can use these as a filter for the account history information.

✔ **Merchant-Initiated Payments:** Payments where a merchant requests and receives funds directly from your PayPal account. (This requires an agreement between you and the merchant.)

After selecting the type of transactions to show in the report, you can narrow down the list of items by choosing to look only at items made in a specific currency. Only those currencies you had transactions in show in the currency list.

Finally, you can select a date range for the transactions you want to see. PayPal lets you see records from the past day, week, month, or year. You can also choose a range of dates by picking a start and end date and clicking the Search button.

If you need more advanced search options, click the <u>Advanced Search</u> link. Like a regular history search, you can specify a date range, but you can also search by:

- ✔ E-mail address
- ✔ Transaction ID
- ✔ Last name of the person involved in the transaction
- ✔ Last name and first name of the person involved in the transaction (enter the last name, a comma, and then the first name of the person)
- ✔ Receipt ID
- ✔ Item number

After selecting your search criteria, PayPal displays a report showing you the results. Twenty transaction records display per page. To see the other records, click the Next button shown at the end of the list.

Downloading Your Account History

If the search of your PayPal History returns a lot of transaction records, it can be tedious to use the Next and Previous buttons to see the entire list. You may want to download your PayPal History and view the list of your transactions offline.

1. **To download your History, click the <u>Download My History</u> link, which you find in the upper-right corner of the History page.**

2. **On the Download History page (see Figure 11-4), you start by selecting a date range for the records you want to download.**

3. **You can choose to download the information formatted in one of four ways:**

    • **Comma-delimited file:** Also called a CSV file. Commas separate the data in the columns of the report. Because Excel recognizes the CSV format, you are able to open your account history in a spreadsheet after downloading the file.

    • **Tab-delimited file:** This is another common format used when structured data (such as a table of information) is saved as a text file. The columns are separated by tab characters. Many database programs recognize the tab-delimited format.

Figure 11-4:
Instead of viewing multiple transaction records online, you can choose to download a file that contains all the records. Clicking the Customize My History Download link lets you decide which columns to include in the report.

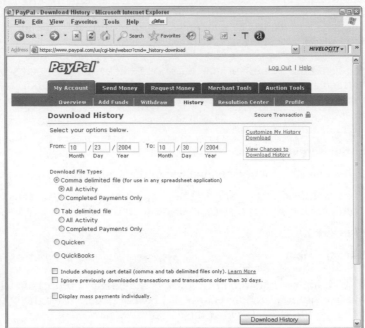

- **Quicken:** You can import the saved file directly into your Quicken program.

- **QuickBooks:** You can import the history file directly into QuickBooks.

4. **If you plan on saving the file in CSV or tab-delimited format, you can opt to have shopping cart information broken out into separate items.**

   For example, one row per item is placed in the shopping cart instead of a single shopping cart transaction. If you choose this option, "Quantity" information is included with the History report.

5. **You can choose not to download transactions previously downloaded or any that are more than 30 days old.**

   Picking this option is useful if you download the data on a regular basis and don't want to spend time downloading records that have already been added to your spreadsheet, database, Quicken, or QuickBooks files.

6. **If you made any mass payments, you can choose to display a single payment or break the payments out individually.**

   Also, a link is on the page (View Changes to Download History) that gives you a list of changes that PayPal has made to the Download History feature.

7. **Before downloading the file, click the <u>Customize My History Download</u> link.**

   • The Customize My History Download page lets you decide which columns should be included in the report you download.

   • By default, the report includes columns for Date, Time, Time Zone, Name, Type, Status, Currency, Gross, Fee, Net, From E-mail Address, To E-mail Address, Transaction ID, Reference Transaction ID, Receipt ID, and Balance.

   • Additionally, you can add specialized columns containing information for Website Payments, Auction Payments, and Other Fields.

   • After selecting the columns you want, click the Save button to return to the Download History page.

8. **Click the Download History button.**

9. **In the File Download window, click the Save button.**

   • Click Open to open the file in Excel, Notepad, or Quicken (depending on the format you opted to save the file in). If you picked QuickBooks, you need to enter the name of the PayPal account, the name of the other Expenses Account, and the name of the other Income Account before you can download the Log file with the records.

   • If you want to save the file, click the Save button and choose the folder where you want to save the file.

   • You can also click the Cancel button, if you decide not to proceed with the download.

10. **After downloading the file, click the History tab to return to the Account History page.**

Reviewing the Merchant Sales Report

The Merchant Sales Report, as shown in Figure 11-5, provides summary information about any sales transactions you had in the last week. You access the report by clicking the <u>Merchant Sales Report</u> link, accessible from the History page.

The report provides information about the number of sales transactions, the currency used, the total amount of revenue, and the average transaction amount. The report also provides channel information, showing you where your sales are coming from.

Figure 11-5:
The
Merchant
Sales
Report
provides a
weekly
summary of
all your
sales from
the previous
week.

To download the report, click the Download button shown at the bottom of the page. The report is only available in CSV or tab delimited formats. After downloading or reviewing the report, click the Done button to return to the History page.

The report has a couple of drawbacks. You can't get report information for weeks prior to the current week. If you want to keep historical records, you must remember to download the report every week. The other drawback to the report is that it's only useful if you have a large number of sales transactions.

Looking at Your Transaction Disputes

Hopefully, you won't have many transaction disputes over the life of your PayPal membership, but the History page gives you an easy way to look up any disputes you had. Here's how:

1. **Click the Transaction Disputes link, shown on the upper-right corner of the History page.**

2. **On the Resolution Center page (see Figure 11-6), you can select whether to see open disputes, closed disputes, or all disputes.**

For each dispute, the page displays the type of dispute, the name of the other involved party, the transaction ID, the date of the transaction, the amount of money involved, the reason the dispute was filed, the date of the filing, the status of the case, a link to the details, and a button if any additional action can be taken.

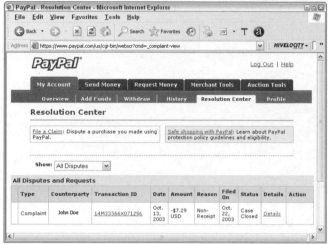

Figure 11-6: On the Resolution Center page, you can quickly see any disputes and the status of each.

3. **Click the Transaction ID link to view information about the original transaction.**

   You can also click the Details link to see a page with the details about the original complaint and the status of the dispute.

   To file a new claim, click the File a Claim link at the top of the Resolution Center page.

Downloading a Transaction Log

If you have a Business or Premier account and do a large amount of transactions, you can request automated scheduling of your daily transaction log. After you are set up, you can schedule what time you want the tracking to start each day.

Unfortunately, you have to contact PayPal's customer service to turn on the automated download service. To contact customer service, call 402-935-2050 and ask for automated downloading of your log file. You can reach customer service from 4:00 a.m. to 10:00 p.m. PST, Monday through Friday. They are also open from 6:00 a.m. to 8:00 p.m. PST, on Saturday, and 8:00 a.m. to 6:00 p.m. PST, on Sunday.

After the service is set up, you receive an e-mail notification whenever the new log is available. The e-mail contains a link to let you download the file. After retrieving the log, you can upload the file into a database, spreadsheet, Quicken, or QuickBooks, depending on the format you select for the download.

You can also set up automated retrieval of the files, if desired, but this requires a Business account. You need to set up a secondary logon account, which is used only for the scheduled download of the files. After setting up the account, you need to write a short script (or have your Web developer write a script) to post a request for the log. PayPal gives the following example of a Web form that downloads the file for you:

```
<FORM ACTION="https://www.paypal.com/us/HISTORY-SCHED-LOGIN"
          METHOD="post">
<INPUT TYPE="hidden" NAME="day" VALUE="dd">
<INPUT TYPE="hidden" NAME="month" VALUE="mm">
<INPUT TYPE="hidden" NAME="year" VALUE="yyyy">
<INPUT TYPE="hidden" NAME="uname" VALUE="uuuuuuu">
<INPUT TYPE="hidden" NAME="pword" VALUE="pppppppp">
<INPUT TYPE="submit" VALUE="Submit">
</FORM>
```

In the previous form:

> dd = day of desired log file
>
> mm = month of desired log file
>
> yyyy = year of desired log file
>
> uuuuuuu = secondary logon username
>
> pppppppp = secondary logon password

Part IV
Getting Money in the (e)Mail

The 5th Wave   By Rich Tennant

"So, someone's using your credit card info to buy stylish clothes, opera tickets and exercise equipment. In what way would this qualify as 'identity theft'?"

In this part . . .

In Part IV, I explain the difference between requesting money and sending an invoice. I introduce you to eChecks and show you the difference between eChecks and instant transfers. I show you how to accept payment in the form of eChecks and how to block eChecks, when necessary. I also show you how to work with different currencies, if you plan on selling to buyers outside of the United States. Finally, I help you understand the currency conversion process, and help you avoid unnecessary conversion fees.

Chapter 12

Asking for Money

*W*hen requesting payment for a good or a service, you can use PayPal to send an invoice, but if you're requesting money for some other reason, you should send a Money Request instead. The differences between the two transactions are pretty subtle, but there are reasons when you should pick one over the other. In this chapter, I explain when to use a Money Request instead of an invoice and tell you about different types of PayPal "money" — including Quasi-cash and eChecks.

Invoicing versus Requesting Money

Sending a PayPal Money Request is a lot like sending an invoice, but the process of creating a request is quicker. Use invoices only when you sell a good or a service and are asking for payment. With an invoice, individual line items are broken out for each type of product or service and shipping and tax get added to the total bill. Figure 12-1 shows an example of the fields that get filled out when creating an invoice.

When you send a Money Request, you enter the total amount of the request and select the type of payment that is being requested. If you're sending the Money Request to ask for payment of an auction item, you have the opportunity to provide information about the auction item; but if you're requesting money for a non-auction good or service, the only way you can track what the payment is for is by entering a descriptive e-mail subject and note.

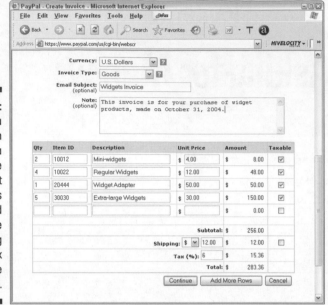

Figure 12-1:
When you
send an
invoice, you
itemize the
different
products
being sold
and add the
shipping
and tax
costs to the
total.

When a recipient of an invoice opens the e-mail, the line items are displayed individually, the way you entered them into the table on the Create Invoice page. The recipient of a non-auction Money Request gets significantly less information about why they're being asked to send money. Figure 12-2 shows the difference in the types of e-mails that are generated when you send an invoice versus a Money Request for the sale of some widgets.

So when is it useful to send a Money Request? You can send Money Requests under the following circumstances:

- ✓ **When asking for payment for an eBay item:** If you haven't turned on Winning Buyer Notification, you can send a Money Request when the auction has ended to ask for payment. (See "Creating a Money Request" to read more on how to do this.)

- ✓ **When asking for payment for goods sold through a non-eBay auction.**

- ✓ **When asking for payment for goods that have not been sold through an auction** (although an invoice would be a better choice because you can ask the buyer to pay tax and shipping).

- ✓ **When asking for payment for a service** (although an invoice would be a better choice because you can ask the buyer to pay sales tax, if appropriate).

- ✓ **When requesting Quasi-cash** (more on this in the section "Quasi-Cash").

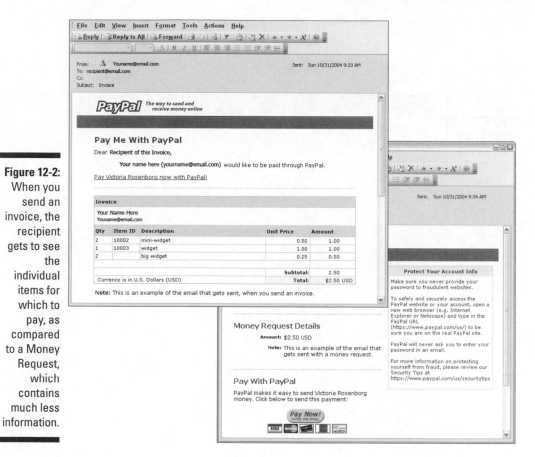

Figure 12-2:
When you send an invoice, the recipient gets to see the individual items for which to pay, as compared to a Money Request, which contains much less information.

Creating a Money Request

Creating a Money Request is quick and easy. See Figure 12-3 for an example of the Request Money page.

1. **Start by logging on to your PayPal account and then click the Request Money tab, which you find at the top of the page.**

2. **Enter the e-mail address of the person from whom you're requesting money.** (Or you can select an e-mail address from the recipient list, if you had transactions with this person or entity in the past.) If you want to send the Money Request to multiple people, separate the e-mail addresses with commas or press the Enter key after adding each address. (Don't worry, the recipients of these e-mails can't see the other people you sent the Money Request to!)

3. **Enter the amount of money you're requesting.**

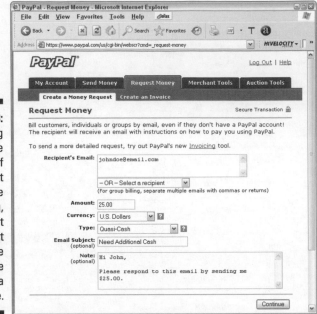

Figure 12-3: Depending upon the type of payment you're requesting, filling out the Request Money page can take less than a minute.

4. **Select the currency in which you want to be paid.**

5. **Select the type of payment you're requesting.**

   Payment for eBay items, payment for auction items not sold through eBay, payment for goods, payment for service, or Quasi-cash.

6. **Enter an e-mail subject header.**

   Try to make this header as descriptive as possible so that the recipient knows why you're requesting money.

7. **You can add a note to the e-mail to be sent.**

   Again, try to add a couple of sentences about why you're asking the recipient for a payment.

8. **Click the Continue button.**

   The page that displays next depends upon which type of payment you're requesting.

   eBay Items:

   • **If you have a Dutch auction and you sell items to multiple winners, enter the number of winners in the box and click the refresh button.** You are asked to enter the e-mail addresses of the other winners. If you enter the e-mail addresses separated by commas on the previous page, you won't need to fill out multiple e-mail addresses on this page.

- If you request money from multiple people for non-auction sales (for example, Goods, Services or Quasi-Cash), you'll see a Request Money Group page, where you can enter the name of an event, if appropriate, and modify the amount you're asking from each person.

- **Because you already entered the amount of payment you're requesting, you won't need to enter it on this page, but you can modify the price, if necessary.** You can also add shipping and handling, sales tax, and insurance costs, if desired. The currency you previously selected displays, but you have the opportunity to change it here.

- **Enter the auction item number in the box shown.** If you're sending a Money Request to a buyer who has purchased more than one auction item from you, separate item numbers by commas.

- **Your eBay user ID shows.** You can change the ID if necessary.

- **Enter the closing date of the auction.**

- **Enter the URL of the item.** To get the URL, log on to eBay and go to your My eBay page. Locate the item that you're sending the Money Request for and click the item name link; this brings you to the item description page. Copy the URL shown in the address bar of your browser and paste it into the box on your PayPal Request Money page.

- **Enter the title of the item.**

- **Add an optional message to the buyer and click the Continue button.**

- **You can confirm the details of the Money Request and edit or cancel, if necessary.** If you're satisfied with the request, click the Request Money link.

Auction Goods (non-eBay):

- **If you sell items to multiple winners, enter the number of winners in the box and click the Refresh button.** You are asked to enter the e-mail addresses of the other winners.

- **Because you already entered the amount of payment you're requesting, you won't need to enter it on this page, but you can add shipping and handling, sales tax, and insurance costs.** You can change the currency, if necessary.

- **Enter the auction item number in the box shown.**

- **Select the site where you auctioned the item.** Choices include Yahoo! Auctions, uBid.com, Amazon.com Auctions, MSN Auctions, BidVille, or other (an unspecified) auction.

- **Enter you auction user ID.**

- **Enter the closing date of the auction.**

- **Enter the Web address (URL) of the item, if desired.** Go to the auction page where your item is displayed, copy the Web address, and paste it into this box.

- **Enter the title of the item, if desired.**

- **Add an optional message to the buyer and click the Continue button.**

- **You can confirm the details of the Money Request and edit or cancel, if necessary.** If you're satisfied with the request, click the Request Money link.

Goods (items not sold at auction): After entering the fields on the Request Money page, click the Continue button. You are asked to confirm the information entered for your Money Request. If everything is fine, click the Request Money link to send the request e-mail.

Payment for a Service: After entering the fields on the Request Money page, click the Continue button. You are asked to confirm the information; click the Request Money link to generate the request.

Quasi-Cash: After entering the fields on the Request Money page, click the Continue button. You are asked to confirm the information; click the Request Money link to generate the request.

After the Money Request is sent, you can opt to view the details of the request, go to your Account Overview, or issue another Money Request.

Quasi-Cash

Most of the payment types listed on the Request Money page are pretty self-explanatory, except for Quasi-cash. (Actually, Quasi-cash is pretty self-explanatory, too, when you think about it.) Sending a $5.00 bill via e-mail is hard but you can request (or send) Quasi-cash and accomplish the same feat.

From the standpoint of the recipient, there's very little difference between receiving payment from an invoice, a Money Request, or getting a Quasi-cash payment. The money is deposited in the recipient's PayPal account, and if the account is a Premier or Business account, the fee charged by PayPal is the same in all three cases.

If you don't have enough funds in your PayPal account to cover a Quasi-cash payment, you can choose to get funds from a credit card, PayPal credit, or bank account, depending upon which funding options you linked to your account.

Some banks, when you use a credit or debit card to fund a Quasi-cash payment, view the transaction as a cash advance and charge you a fee for the funds transfer. Other banks treat the transaction as a cash withdrawal (just like withdrawing cash from an ATM) and may charge you a fee for the funds transfer.

If you want to avoid additional fees for sending someone Quasi-cash, consider sending money for a service payment, instead of Quasi-cash. The recipient receives the same amount, but you avoid extra fees.

You may be wondering, with the risk of extra fees, why anyone would request or send Quasi-cash payments. In the course of writing this book, I discovered a way in which Quasi-cash can be valuable (but it's a bit obscure and requires two PayPal accounts).

Say there's an item you want to buy, and the retailer only accepts debit cards or cash. You want the item, but don't have enough cash in your PayPal account. You try to buy the item anyway, anticipating that the extra funding will come from a credit card you linked to your account, but your debit card is rejected for lack of insufficient funds.

Now what? You can try to transfer money from your bank account into your PayPal account, but the funds take several days to clear. If you have a second PayPal account, linked to a credit card, you can send a Quasi-cash payment from the second account to the first.

The funds for the payment from the second account pull from the credit card linked to that account. The Quasi-cash payment deposits into your first account and is available immediately. You can now buy the item, using your PayPal debit card!

If you really want to be slick, you can use a Web-enabled cellphone to facilitate the Quasi-cash payment from one account to the other. You don't even need to be near a computer!

Accepting eChecks

You sent a request for money to someone and the payment came back in the form of an eCheck. What is an eCheck, and how does it differ from an instant PayPal payment?

In the same way that Quasi-cash is the equivalent of cash in the physical (as opposed to online) world, eChecks are the digital counterpoints of the pieces of paper found in a checkbook. When someone sends you an eCheck as payment, the funds won't be deposited into your account for three or four days (however long it takes for the eCheck to clear).

eChecks from the buyer's point of view

From the buyer's standpoint, sending an eCheck is advantageous; the funds are left in the buyer's bank account for a few extra days, earning interest, and no credit card debt is incurred. To send an eCheck, in response to an invoice or Money Request, you need to have a bank (checking or savings) account linked to your PayPal account. Here's how:

1. **When you receive a request for money, click the Pay button to make a payment.**

2. **On the Pay Money Request page, click the <u>More Funding Options</u> link under the Funding Options section of the page.**

3. **On the Funding Options page, select the eCheck option and choose which bank account to use (see Figure 12-4).**

   If necessary, you can link a new bank account to your PayPal account by clicking the <u>Add Bank</u> link.

4. **Click the Continue button.**

   Verify the payment details and click the <u>Send Money</u> link.

Figure 12-4:
When you send payment in the form of an eCheck, the funds remain in your bank account for three or four days, until the eCheck clears and payment is deposited into the recipient's PayPal account.

eChecks from the seller's point of view

If you receive an eCheck payment, you get a PayPal e-mail informing you that "Cash is on the Way!" If you hoped for "Cash is Already Here!" you may feel a little disgruntled, but the good news is that you'll get payment in three or four days.

If you look at the transaction in your PayPal Account Overview, you see a status of Uncleared until the funds are transferred from the buyer's bank account. It's important that you don't mail any items to the buyer until after the payment has cleared.

From a buyer's standpoint, there's one big advantage to getting an eCheck. Unlike other PayPal fees, which are charged as a percentage (usually 2.9 percent) of the value of the item, the total fee for an eCheck won't exceed $5.00. If you're selling an item that's valued at over $162, you'll get a break on the transaction fees. If the item is very expensive, you can save a good amount.

Refunding eChecks

A few times when I've purchased an item on eBay, a red-faced seller admitted to me that the item description wasn't an accurate representation of the item, and offered to refund my payment. Had I paid via eCheck, the seller could have issued a refund. Like other PayPal payments, the seller could not have initiated the refund, until the funds had been deposited into their PayPal account.

As with any PayPal payment, the eCheck payment must be refunded within 60 days after the payment was sent. PayPal reimburses the seller for any PayPal fees charged against the transaction.

Blocking eChecks

Some sellers don't want to wait for their money and decide to block eCheck payments. If you decide to block eCheck payments, you can

1. **Log on to your PayPal account and click the <u>Profile</u> link to go to the Profile Summary page.**

2. **Click the <u>Payment Receiving Preferences</u> link, which you find under the Selling Preferences column.**

3. **Check the "eCheck for Web site and Smart Logo payments with PayPal" option.**

4. **Click the Save link.**

Buyers can no longer pay for your items with eChecks.

Canceling Your Money Request

If you issue a Money Request and then receive a check in the mail (we're talking paper check and snail mail), what should you do about the Money Request? It's no problem — you can just cancel the Money Request.

1. **To cancel a request, find the transaction in your Account Overview or History and click the Details link.**

2. **At the bottom of the page is a Cancel Money Request button.** Click the button.

3. **The Cancel Money Request page shows the details of the transaction.**

   You can choose whether to send an e-mail to the buyer to announce the cancelled payment.

4. **If you want to cancel the payment, click the Yes button.**

   Your Money Request is cancelled.

Making a Refund

You can also refund money, when necessary (see Figure 12-5). If you don't have enough funds in your bank account for the refund, PayPal uses one of the alternate funding sources you linked to your account.

1. **To make a refund, find the transaction in your Account Overview or History and click the Details link.**

2. **At the bottom of the page is a Refund Payment link; click the link.**

3. **The Refund Offer page gives details about the transaction.** You can give a full or partial refund by changing the number shown in the Gross Refund Amount box.

   PayPal shows you the net amount to be refunded, plus any fees that were charged when you originally received the payment.

4. **You can add a note to the buyer (explaining the reason for the refund) and click the Submit button.**

5. **Confirm the details of the refund and click the Process Refund button.**

   The amount refunded is deposited back in the buyer's bank account.

Figure 12-5:
You can opt
to send a
full or partial
refund. The
funds are
deposited
back in the
buyer's
PayPal
account.

Chapter 13

Accepting Payments in Multiple Currencies

. . . .

In This Chapter

▶ Understanding conversion rates

▶ Selecting a currency

▶ Managing currencies in your PayPal account

▶ Organizing your currency conversions

▶ Automating currency conversions

▶ Transferring between currencies

▶ Withdrawing from a currency account

▶ Adding currency information to your Web site

. . . .

*E*ach year we go to England to visit my husband's relatives. After each trip, my daughter comes home with a couple of pounds (leftover pocket money she didn't spend). It's a small amount, so we don't bother converting the pounds back into dollars. The pounds get lost at the bottom of her dresser drawer, useless unless she remembers to look for them before our next trip to England.

When you get paid in a different currency, thanks to the PayPal currency conversion services your money can avoid my daughter's "dresser drawer" fate (and you don't need to drive to the bank to exchange the money!).

Picking a Currency

PayPal lets you pay, or accept payments, in U.S. dollars, Canadian dollars, pounds sterling, euros, and yen, making it easy to buy and sell globally. PayPal has plans to add more currencies, including Australian dollars, in the future. Depending on the settings in your PayPal profile, currency conversions are done automatically, or you can decide which currency to use at the time you're making a payment.

What's the current currency rate?

XE.com has a Universal Currency Converter tool which lets you see the midmarket exchange rate. This rate represents the midpoint between the highest and lowest rates (for both buyers and sellers) "large-value transactions" in the global currency markets. (In other words, the middle range of what banks charge each other for currency conversions.) Unfortunately, when you or I want to exchange money, we won't get nearly as favorable a rate because of the fees that are charged by foreign exchange providers.

To get a sense of how much you're being charged when exchanging money, go to www.xe.com/ucc and enter the amount you want to exchange. Then select the currency you have, the currency you want to convert to, and click the Click Here to Perform Currency Conversion button. When I enter $1.00 as the amount and select U.S. dollars, which I want to convert into euros, the rate is 0.771160 euros for every dollar converted. Good to know, but what does this have to do with the rate that I'll be charged by PayPal? Keep reading and I show you how to see what PayPal charges you.

The XE.com Currency Conversion Tool can give you a general sense of what the exchange rates are, at any given time, but the rate that you receive will be less favorable because of the fee you'll be charged by your foreign exchange provider.

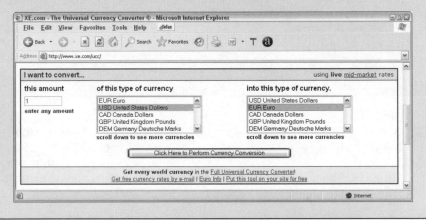

The value of a dollar

You land at the Charles de Gaulle Airport in Paris, and you're ready to take a taxi to your hotel. Without exchanging some of your dollars into euros, you're not going to get very far. Luckily, every international airport has a bank where you can convert your money. The exchange rates are usually prominently displayed, so you can see how many euros your dollars will buy.

At today's rates, one U.S. dollar buys you less than one euro, but how much less depends upon where you're exchanging your money. All foreign exchange providers (the bank or company doing the conversion for you) charge a percentage of the transaction as a fee, which is how they make their money.

PayPal shows you its exchange rates before you complete a transaction, but what if you want to know ahead of time? PayPal has a Currency Converter tool, which you can check before sending or converting money. To access the tool, click the <u>Fees</u> link, found at the bottom of every PayPal page. At the bottom of the Fee page is a <u>View Currency Converter</u> link. Click the link and the tool appears in a second window. Enter the amount you want to convert and the currency from which you want to convert. Then select the currency to which you want to convert, and click the Convert button. Figure 13-1 shows a picture of the Currency Converter. Notice that there is a difference between the buy rate and the sell rate. The difference between the two rates is the fee that is paid to PayPal for the conversion.

At today's rate, I receive €0.75 euros for every dollar I exchange. For those of you that read the sidebar, you see that €0.75 euros isn't quite as good as €0.771160 euros. That's because PayPal charges a 2.5 percent fee every time you convert money from one currency to another. As it turns out, the PayPal fee is comparable to those of standard banks.

Figure 13-1: The PayPal Currency Converter shows you the actual exchange rate you get if you convert money from one currency to another.

According to Bankrate.com, an independent Web site that lists rates for many types of banking transactions, most large banks like Bank of America, Citibank, or Chase charge between 2 and 2.5 percent, depending upon whether you are making a credit or debit card purchase. (If you withdraw money from an ATM, you can pay up to $3.00 in additional fees.) To check the conversion rates for yourself, go to www.bankrate.com/brm/news/cc/20020513c.asp.

Sending payment in a different currency

Sending a payment in a different currency is a lot easier than exchanging money at the airport. Here's how:

1. **Start by logging on to your PayPal account and click the Send Money tab.**

2. **Enter the payment details into the Send Money form.**

   See Chapter 4 if you need help in sending money. The Send Money form gives you a list of the five currencies that PayPal supports:

   - U.S. dollars

   - Pounds sterling

   - Euros (Euros are accepted as currency in Austria, Belgium, Finland, France, Germany, Greece, Ireland, Italy, Luxembourg, Monaco, Netherlands, Portugal, and Spain)

   - Canadian dollars

   - Yen

If your PayPal balance is in one currency (for example, U.S. dollars), PayPal converts the currency for you before sending the payment. On the Check Payment Details page, PayPal shows the currency conversion rate (that is, how much it costs in U.S. dollars to send the payment in a different currency. (See Figure 13-2 for an example of the information displayed on the Check Payment Details page.) The recipient of the payment does not need to have a balance in the currency of the payment.

A conversion fee is charged whenever you

✔ Send a payment in a currency in a nonlocal currency (that is, U.S. dollars to yen). The fee is taken out of the payment sent to the recipient.

✔ Accept payment in a nonlocal currency and convert to your local currency (that is, accept payment in yen and convert to U.S. dollars).

✔ Transfer funds that are held in a nonlocal currency to a local bank (that is, transfer yen to a U.S. bank account that holds the balance in dollars).

✔ Transfer funds between PayPal accounts from a nonlocal currency balance to a local currency balance (that is, transfer funds from your yen PayPal balance to your dollars PayPal balance).

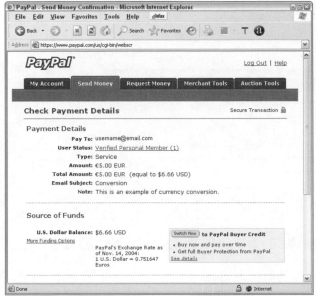

Figure 13-2:
This Check
Payment
Details page
shows that I
pay $6.66 in
U.S. dollars
to send a
payment of
€5.00 euros.

You do not pay a conversion fee when you

✔ Send payment in a nonlocal currency from a nonlocal PayPal account in
the same currency (that is, send a payment in yen from your yen PayPal
balance).

✔ Receive payment in a nonlocal currency if you have a PayPal balance in
the same nonlocal currency (that is, accept payment in yen, if you have
a yen PayPal balance).

✔ Transfer funds from a nonlocal currency to a bank account that holds
funds in the same nonlocal currency (that is, transfer yen from your yen
PayPal account balance to a bank in Japan).

After sending the payment in a nonlocal currency, you can see the transaction
details of the conversion by going to your account history. (See Figure 13-3 for
the details of the conversion.)

After you send a payment, the recipient gets an e-mail notification. If the
recipient has an account in the currency you sent, the money is added to the
currency balance of the account. If a balance in that currency does not exist,
the recipient is given 30 days to decide whether to accept or deny the payment. See Figure 13-4, which shows the Accept or Deny a Payment page.

Figure 13-3:
When you send a payment of €5.00 euros, $6.66 in U.S. dollars transfers out of your PayPal account.

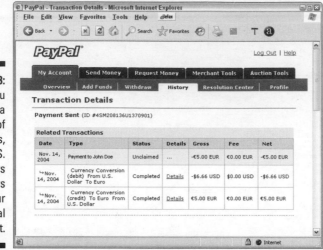

Figure 13-4:
Although you paid $6.66 to send a payment of €5.00 euros, the recipient is paid only $6.32 to convert the euros back to dollars. The $0.34 difference is the fee PayPal earns for converting the funds from one currency to another.

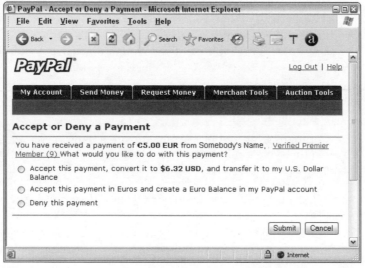

The recipient has the option of accepting the payment and converting to a local currency; accepting the payment in the currency sent and opening a currency balance, if one does not exist; or denying the payment. If the payment is denied, all funds are returned to the sender, including any currency fees that would have been charged had the transaction gone through.

If you issue a refund request within 24 hours of when the transaction took place, the full amount of money is returned to you. If you wait longer, the exchange rate may have changed. Say, for example, you convert $1.00 U.S. dollars and receive £0.52 in pounds. A few days go by and you request a refund. Unfortunately, the dollar has dropped since your original transaction and is now worth only £0.49. You won't be refunded the full dollar because the exchange rate has shifted (and not in your favor!).

Creating a Currency Account

PayPal lets you have account balances in multiple currencies. Maintaining these balances is a good way to avoid paying conversion fees if you do a lot of international transactions. Two ways to open a currency balance are to accept payment in a currency you don't already hold or to open a balance from your account profile.

Accepting a payment and opening a currency balance

The easiest way to open a currency balance is to accept payment in a currency you don't already hold and to choose not to transfer the money to a balance you do hold. Try this:

1. **After receiving a payment notification e-mail (for a payment made in a different currency), click the link in the e-mail and log on to your account.**

2. **On the Accept or Deny Payment page, select the "Accept this payment in *Euros* and create a *Euro* Balance in my PayPal account" option.**

   Please note: The word *Euro* in the previous sentence can be any of the PayPal currencies.

3. **Click the Submit button.**

   PayPal shows a Payment Accepted page. You have the option to view the details of the transaction or go to your account.

4. **Click the <u>Go to My Account</u> link.**

In addition to the transaction details shown at the bottom of the screen, PayPal shows the balance maintained in each currency account and the total value of the account in U.S. dollars. See Figure 13-5 for an example of how the Account Overview page looks when balances are maintained in multiple currencies.

Figure 13-5:
If dollars become stronger against the euro, my account will be worth more. If the dollar weakens, my account will be worth less.

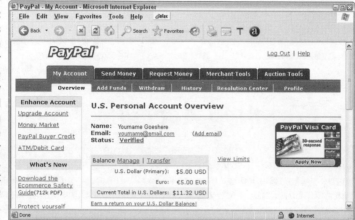

In Figure 13-5, the Account Overview page shows that I have $5.00 U.S. dollars and €5.00 euros in my account (worth $6.32 U.S. dollars at today's conversion rate). The total value of my account is $11.32 in U.S. dollars, but this number can fluctuate depending upon the exchange rate.

Opening a currency balance manually

You don't have to wait until receiving a payment to open a currency balance manually. After logging on to your PayPal account, just follow these steps:

1. **Click the <u>Profile</u> link, found under the My Account tab.**

2. **Under the Financial Information column, click the <u>Currency Balances</u> link.**

3. **The Manage Currency Balances page shows the currencies for which you can create balances; it also shows the amount of money you currently have in each balance.**

See Figure 13-6 for an example of the page.

Figure 13-6:
From the
Manage
Currency
Balances
page, you
can open
a new
currency
balance and
check the
funds held in
each of your
existing
balances.

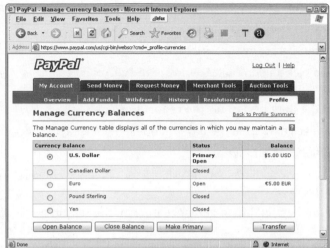

4. **Select a currency that you do not have a balance in and click the Open Balance button.**

5. **A balance opens in the new currency; the balance is zero because you haven't transferred any funds into that balance yet.**

   Later in this chapter, I show you how to transfer funds from one balance to another.

You can select one currency balance to be the primary balance by selecting a balance and clicking the Make Primary button. The primary balance becomes the default for all payments you send and receive.

Closing a currency balance

You can also close a currency balance by selecting the balance on the Manage Currency Balances page and clicking on the Close Balance button. If you have money in the account balance, you will be asked to transfer the money before the account can be closed.

Tracking Currency Conversions

As you accept and send payments in multiple currencies, it helps to be able to track how much money is being transferred and the conversion fees you're paying each time. You can track currency conversion payments from the PayPal Account History page. Here's what you do:

1. **After logging on, click the** <u>History</u> **link under the My Account tab.**

2. **Select Currency Conversions from the Show list.**

3. **Select the currency for which you want to see the records.**

   You can pick all currencies or any of the currency balances you currently maintain in your account.

4. **Select the time period for the report to span.**

   You can see data from the day you opened your PayPal account.

5. **Click the Search function.**

   A list of records that meet the criteria for currency conversions and date range display.

6. **Click the** <u>Details</u> **link to get more information about a specific transaction.**

You can also search by Fee and a specific currency to see how much you are paying in currency conversion fees. See Chapter 11 for more information about how to use the PayPal Account History feature.

The Merchant Sales Report provides weekly summary information broken out by sales channel and by currency. Follow these steps to view the report:

1. **Click the Merchant Tools tab, shown at the top of the page.**

2. **On the Merchant Tools page, click on the** <u>Reporting Tools</u> **link (which can be found under the Receiving and Managing Payments section of the page).**

3. **Click the products link, shown on the left side of the page.**

4. **Click the** <u>Merchant Sales Reports</u> **link. The report will show the sales data for the previous week. (If you haven't had a sale in the past week, the report shows data for the last week in which you made a sale.)**

Handling Currencies Automatically

If you receive payment in a currency (Canadian dollars, for example) and you have a balance in that currency, the funds transfer into the currency account automatically. If you don't maintain balances in different currencies, you can still automate how currency conversions are handled as long as you have a Premier or Business account.

Go to your Account Profile (found under the My Account tab) and click the
Payment Receiving Preferences link. (You find this link under the Selling
Preferences column, on the right side of the page.)

The Payment Receiving Preferences page lets you block all payments in a
currency that you do not hold. If you choose to block payments in other currencies, you can avoid paying currency conversion fees. The buyer needs to
convert the payment to dollars before sending payment, which means the
buyer pays the conversion fee — not you.

You can have the payment converted to U.S. dollars automatically or be asked
what you want to do each time you receive a payment. Figure 13-7 shows the
options you have for managing different currencies on the Payment Receiving
Preferences page.

Figure 13-7:
If you don't
want to be
prompted
every time
you receive
a payment in
a nonlocal
currency,
go to the
Payment
Receiving
Preferences
page to set
up rules for
how PayPal
should han-
dle currency
payments
for you.

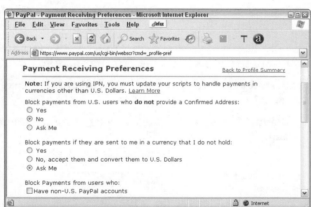

If you want to block currency payments even if you hold a balance in that
currency, select the "Block Payments from users who Have non-U.S. PayPal
accounts" option. This option effectively limits the currency for all your
payments to U.S. dollars.

If a buyer tries to send you payment in pounds sterling, the following message will be displayed: "This recipient does not accept payments denominated in Pounds Sterling. Please select another currency to send your payment."

Transferring Funds Between Currency Balances

You can maintain funds in a specific currency balance to be used the next time you need to make a payment in that currency. But if the funds start adding up in one currency, you may want to transfer them to a different currency (usually your primary currency balance). Follow these steps:

1. **Click the <u>Transfer</u> link, shown on the Account Overview page.**

   You can find the link right above the box that shows how much money you have in each currency balance.

2. **You can also get to the transfer page by going to your Profile, clicking the <u>Currency Balances</u> link, and then clicking the Transfer button.**

3. **On the Transfer Funds page (see Figure 13-8 for an example), type the amount you want to transfer into the Transfer text box.**

4. **Select the currency you want to transfer from and the currency you want to transfer to.**

5. **Click the Calculate button to see the exchange rate for the money you are converting.**

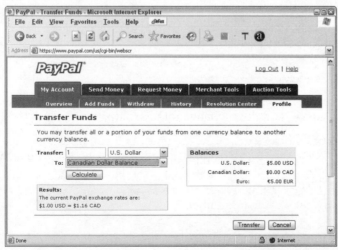

Figure 13-8: Click the Calculate button before transferring the funds to see the current exchange rate PayPal will use.

6. **If you calculated the correct amount to transfer, click the Transfer button.**

   You see a confirmation page that shows the amount to be transferred, the currencies you're transferring from and to, the exchange rate, and the net amount to transfer into the new currency balance.

7. **If the amounts are correct, click the Transfer button.**

   You can go to the Account Overview to check the new amount in each currency balance.

Withdrawing from a Currency Balance

Many people I know transfer their money from their PayPal account to a checking or savings account on a regular basis because they feel more secure when their funds are in a bank.

The process of transferring money held in a currency (non-U.S.) balance is the same as a normal bank transfer, except that you are charged a conversion fee. (Normally, transferring U.S. dollars from a PayPal account to a U.S. bank account is free.)

1. **Click the Withdraw link, found under the My Account section of the site.**

2. **From the list of options, click the Transfer funds to your bank account link.**

3. **On the Withdraw Funds by Electronic Transfer page, you can select the currency balance to use for the transfer from the drop-down list.**

   See Figure 13-9.

4. **After entering the amount to transfer and the bank to transfer to, click the Continue button.**

5. **You see a confirmation page.**

   This page shows the balance the money transfers from, the amount of the transfer, and the exchange rate used. (Although PayPal's fee isn't listed, it comes in the difference between the amount of money you transfer from one currency versus the amount that gets deposited into your bank account in the different currency.) The page also shows the gross (total) amount to be deposited into your bank account, the name of the bank account owner, the name of the bank, and the last four digits of your bank account number.

Figure 13-9:
From the
Withdraw
Funds by
Electronic
Transfer
page, I can
choose to
transfer
funds from
U.S. dollars,
Canadian
dollars, or
euros in my
PayPal
account to
my checking
account.

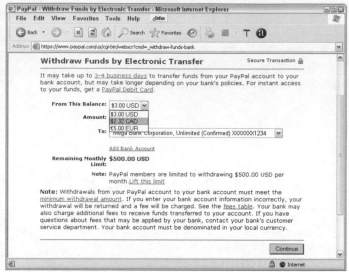

6. **The confirmation page also provides information about resolving problems if the conversion and bank transfer do not go through.**

   • If the money in your bank account is not specifically denominated in U.S. dollars, the currency conversion will fail and the funds will not be transferred to your bank account. (They are still available in your PayPal account, however.)

   • If the information you enter when you linked your bank account to your PayPal account has inaccurate information, the transfer will fail (and the funds will not be deposited, but do remain in your PayPal account).

7. **If the information about the conversion and transfer is correct, click the Submit button.**

   The Your Electronic Funds Transfer Request is in Process page shows. (It takes three to four days before the funds deposit in your bank account.) You can go to the Account Overview page to see the details of this transaction.

Currencies and Web Site Payments

If you use Buy Now, Donations, Subscriptions, or the Shopping Cart on your Web site, you can add support for payment in different currencies. (See Chapters 14 and 16 for more information about integrating PayPal into your Web site to provide e-commerce capability.)

When you use the PayPal button factory to generate Buy Now button code, you can select which currency you want to accept when entering the details of the item you are selling. You can also select the currency for Donations, Subscriptions, or the PayPal Shopping Cart. Depending on how your payment preferences have been set up, payments in different currencies automatically convert to your primary currency when the purchase is made.

Accepting payments in alternate currencies means you can create localized versions of your Web site for many European countries, Great Britain, Canada, and Japan. If you're building a Web site for a specific country, you can choose the country when you're entering the button item detail.

If you tweak the button code (or if you write the code for PayPal buttons yourself), you can modify the code to accept payments in any of the five currencies supported by PayPal.

```
<input type="hidden" name="currency_code" value="EUR">
```

The line shown here describes the currency for the item to be sold. In this example, the currency is euros. The specified currency is used for the cost of the item, shipping, handling, and tax. Table 13-1 shows the values that can be used for the currency_code variable.

Table 13-1	Currency Values for the currency_code Variable
Currency	*Value*
U.S. dollars	USD
Euro	EUR
Pound sterling	GBP
Canadian dollar	CAD
Yen	JPY

Part V

Integrating PayPal into Web Sites and Applications

The 5th Wave   By Rich Tennant

Cleopatra Carpet Cleaners

"So far our Web presence has been pretty good. We've gotten some orders, a few inquiries, and nine guys who want to date our logo."

In this part . . .

Are you ready to get more sophisticated about using PayPal? I show how to create and customize PayPal buttons, and integrate PayPal into an existing Web site. I show you how to add the PayPal shopping cart to your Web site so users can purchase multiple items before beginning the check-out process. PayPal offers wizards that work with many of the applications you may currently use, including Outlook. If you design Web sites with Adobe GoLive, Microsoft FrontPage, or Macromedia Dreamweaver or Flash, there's a PayPal wizard designed to save you many hours of hand-coding, and I show you how to get the most out of these tools.

Chapter 14

Creating PayPal Buttons

· ·

· ·

*B*ack in 1997, I hired a developer to build an e-commerce site for my husband, an antique maps and print dealer who wanted to sell his products online. Back then, many of the automated site generation tools that are available today simply didn't exist. Today, I wouldn't need to hire someone to hand-code the site — I could create the pages myself and use the PayPal button factory to provide the e-commerce functionality.

Like many great tools, the basic services of PayPal are simple to use, but dig a little deeper and you may be surprised at how much PayPal allows you to do. In this chapter, I show you how to turn your current Web site into an e-commerce Web site, quickly and easily.

Although you don't need to be a developer to add PayPal buttons to your Web site, it helps to know a little basic Hypertext Markup Language (HTML), which is the language used to describe Web page layout. If you need a little help brushing up on your HTML tags, two books that can help you are *Web Design For Dummies* by Lisa Lopuck and *HTML For Dummies* by Ed Tittel and Stephen J. James.

Calculating Merchant Fees

Building an online store is a business and before you go into business, you need to know what the costs will be so you can figure out whether selling your items will be profitable. To quote an old, but valid, saying . . . there's no point to losing money on every sale, but hoping to make it up in volume!

There are fees associated with adding PayPal buttons to sell products or services from your Web site and you need to know these in advance before pricing your products. The good news is that the fees are the same as the ones you pay anytime someone sends you a PayPal payment. For each item sold, you pay a $0.30 transaction fee and 2.9 percent of the value of the item or service sold.

If you sell more than $3,000 worth of items/services a month, you can qualify for discounted merchant rates. Table 14-1 shows the discounted merchant rates for which you can qualify, based on your monthly sales volume.

Table 14-1	PayPal's Discounted Merchant Rates	
Sales Volume	*Transaction Fee*	*Percent of Sale Price*
If you sell between $0.00 USD and $3,000.00 USD per month	$0.30 for every transaction	2.9%
If you sell between $3,000.01 USD and $10,000.00 USD per month	$0.30 for every transaction	2.5%
If you sell between $10,000.01 USD and $100,000.00 USD per month	$0.30 for every transaction	2.2%
If you sell more than $100,000.00 USD per month	$0.30 for every transaction	1.9%

To become a PayPal merchant, you need to fill out a special application form (available at `https://www.paypal.com/us/cgi-bin/webscr?cmd=_merchant-app` after you log on to your PayPal account). Additional criteria are that you need to be a PayPal member for at least 90 days, and you must have received more than $3,000 in PayPal payments in the month preceding your application.

During the course of writing this book, I made it a point to ask eBay sellers who don't accept PayPal why they don't. The answer usually has something to do with not wanting to pay merchant fees. If you sell the occasional item on eBay, then this attitude may make sense. But if you want to configure your Web site to accept secure online payments, then you have to resign yourself to paying merchant fees to some company, and PayPal offers a better value than many of the others.

If you accept credit card payments online, you need to work with a credit card processor who verifies the credit card number at the time the purchase is made. You can process cards manually yourself, after the sale is made and before you ship the item, but this becomes impractical for anything other than a few sales a month. Every credit card processor has some type of fee structure, which usually consists of a monthly fee, transaction fee, and percentage of the sale.

On the PayPal Web site (under the Help section) there is a link to a site that lets you compare merchant rates based upon your average monthly sales volume and number of transactions. Go to www.merchantcompare.com, enter your monthly data, and click the Compare Vendor Costs button. Figure 14-1 shows a table comparing PayPal rates with those of other companies.

Because PayPal does not charge fees that many of the other companies do (including a monthly fee, statement fee, gateway fee, daily settlement fee, setup fee, or address verification service fee), it can often be one of the less expensive options to use.

Figure 14-1:
The Digitally Justified. com Web site shows the rates you pay when working with different merchant providers, ordered from the least expensive to the most expensive.

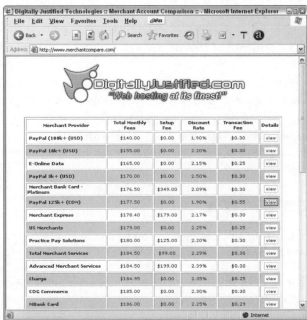

Selecting Which Buttons to Use on Your Site

PayPal offers you four different ways to integrate payment processing into your Web site. You can incorporate Buy Now buttons, Donations buttons, Subscription buttons, or you can add a Shopping Cart. Which button(s) you add depends upon the type of transactions you want to support and the level of complexity with which you're comfortable.

Buy Now buttons

Adding a Buy Now button to a product page on your Web site is the simplest way to support e-commerce payments on your Web site. You generate the code for the Buy Now button by filling out a form on the PayPal Web site (also know as the Button Factory). After filling in the form, PayPal generates the code, which you can paste into the code for your Web page. There are a number of reasons why you would want to add Buy Now buttons to your Web site, including these:

- ✔ **Buttons are easy to add to your Web site.** Because PayPal generates the button code for you, you don't need to know how to write advanced scripts to make the e-commerce functionality work.

- ✔ **There are no additional fees or costs to add PayPal buttons to your Web site.**

- ✔ **Because PayPal saves all transactional data in your Account History, you can download and analyze the sales data whenever you want.**

- ✔ **Taking advantage of the ability to customize the look of the buttons, you can ensure that your Web site looks professional, which makes buyers feel more confident when they decide to purchase an item.**

Donations buttons

The process of creating a Donations button is similar to creating a Buy Now button, but the code for the button is configured to accept payments instead of being linked to the sale of a good or a service. The "Creating Donations Buttons" section, later in this chapter, contains specific information about how to create Donations buttons.

Subscription buttons

Subscription buttons are also similar to Buy Now buttons, but are designed to collect payments on a recurring basis. In Chapter 15, I show you how to create Subscription buttons.

PayPal Shopping Cart

Buy Now buttons are easy to add to your Web site, but they force the user to go through the payment process (giving name, address, and credit card information) each time the customer orders a product from your Web site. If the buyer wants to order more than one type of product, the process becomes tedious and you risk losing that customer's repeat business. If you integrate the PayPal Shopping Cart into your Web site, customers can add the products they want to buy to an online "cart" and decide when to check out. During the checkout process, the buyer only needs to give name, address, and credit card information once. Chapter 16 shows you how to integrate the PayPal Shopping Cart into your Web site.

After you determine which type of button makes sense for your Web site, you can add it by using the PayPal Button Factory.

The Button Factory

The PayPal Button Factory can generate the button code for you, so you can add Buy Now buttons to pages of your Web site. In this example, I want to convert a catalog Web site into a full e-commerce Web site by adding Buy Now buttons to pages that contain the items for sale. To create a button, start by logging on to your PayPal account:

1. **Click the Merchant Tools tab, shown at the top of the page.**

2. **Under the Accepting Website Payments section of the page, click the <u>Buy Now Buttons</u> link.** See Figure 14-2 for an example of the Selling Single Items page — one of the Button Factory pages.

3. **Enter the information about the item you want to sell from your Web site.**

   This information includes the following items:

   • The name of the item or service you're selling.

- An item ID or number. This should be a number you use to track the sales of goods and services (for example, an inventory number or SKU).

- The price of the item or service.

- The currency in which you want to accept payment.

- You can set a default country to feature in the buyer's payment form, if desired.

- You can choose from one of eight default buttons by clicking the <u>Choose a different button</u> link. (See Figure 14-3 for examples.) You can also choose to add a custom image. See the sidebar, "Adding your own button image," which discusses how you can use custom button images on your Web site.

- After choosing the button image, you can opt to encrypt the button code. (See the "Encrypting your buttons" sidebar for more information about encryption.) If you encrypt the buttons, you will not be able to add additional options or manually make changes to the button code.

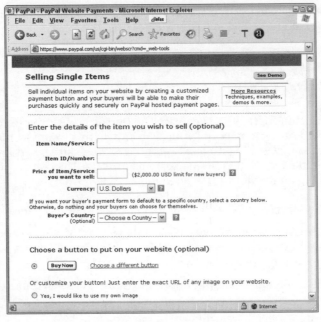

Figure 14-2: After filling in the form on the Selling Single Items page, PayPal generates the button code for you.

Figure 14-3:
When adding a Buy Now button to your Web site, you can choose from one of eight standard PayPal designs, if you don't want to add your own image.

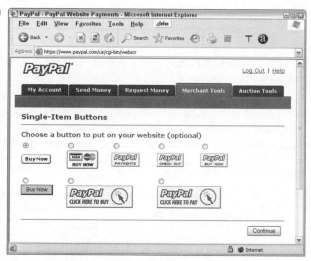

4. **If you want to add additional options to your button code, click the Add More Options button.**

   • **On the second page of the Single Item Purchases, you can choose to add shipping costs to the cost of the item.** See Figure 14-4 for an example of the options you can add to the code for your PayPal button. Shipping costs are calculated as a percentage of the item price or at a flat rate. As the value of the item increases, the shipping costs are increased, too. You can click the Edit button to change the way the shipping costs are calculated. You find more information about shipping costs in Chapter 10.

   • **You can add option fields for the item you are selling.** Option fields let your buyer pick from several options (for example, small, medium, or large) when making a purchase. You find more information about setting options in the next section of this chapter.

   • **You can customize the PayPal payment page that buyers are sent to, to complete the transaction.** These payment pages can be designed to look like the other pages in your Web site. More information about customizing the look of your payment pages can be found later in the section "Customizing the Page Look."

   • **You can elect to send a buyer to a specific page (that is, a "Thank you for your order" page) after a successful transaction.** You can also send them to a specific page after a cancelled transaction. To read more about setting up these pages, see the section "The Customer Experience," later in this chapter.

- **You can decide whether buyers can purchase more than one item of the good or service you're selling.**

- **You can decide whether you want the buyer to provide a shipping address when they are making a purchase.** This is critical if you need to ship an item!

- **You can decide whether buyers can send a note when they send payment for the purchase.** If you have a small number of transactions, getting customer feedback can be valuable to you. If you handle a large volume of transactions, or you automated your fulfillment process, you should turn this option off (because you wouldn't be reading the customer's e-mail).

- **Select the e-mail account to receive the PayPal payment.**

5. **Click the Create Button Now button.**

PayPal generates the button code to add to your Web site. If you're not interested in reading more about product options or customized payment pages, you can jump ahead to the "Adding the Code to Your Web Site" section of this chapter to read how to integrate the PayPal code with the code already featured on your product page.

Figure 14-4:
The second page of the Button Factory lets you add a number of options to your button code, including the ability to add multiple product options, so your buyers can pick from a red, blue, or yellow item.

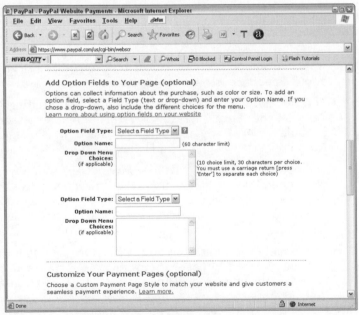

Adding your own button image

You can create your own button image and use it in place of the PayPal button image. If you know the Web address of the location of your logo image (an example is http://www.yourWeb site.com/yourlogo.jpg), you can type it into the box shown on the page. (The first table in Chapter 9 tells you how to find out the Web address of your logo, if you're unsure.)

Image files must be formatted as GIF, JPEG, or PNG files. You can use any size image, but remember that you are fitting it within the context of your Web page, so you probably don't want it to be too big. A good rule of thumb is to keep the size of your button image under the size of PayPal's largest button image, which is 150 pixels wide by 52 pixels long. To make the button look more integrated with the rest of your Web site, use colors already used on your Web pages and use fonts that are similar to the fonts already used on your Web site. If you're not the creative type, many Web sites let you download button images for free. Go to google.com and type **free payment buttons templates** into the text box and click the Search button. Google returns a list of sites that offer free button images. Browse until you find one that works on your Web site.

The code generated by the Button Factory looks like this:

```
<form action="https://www.paypal.com/cgi-bin/webscr"
         method="post">
<input type="hidden" name="cmd" value="_xclick">
<input type="hidden" name="business"
         value="username@e-mail.com">
<input type="hidden" name="undefined_quantity" value="1">
<input type="hidden" name="item_name" value="AMERICAN
         HOMESTEAD - SUMMER">
<input type="hidden" name="item_number" value="33347">
<input type="hidden" name="amount" value="850.00">
<input type="hidden" name="shipping" value="3.85">
<input type="hidden" name="page_style" value="Primary">
<input type="hidden" name="return"
         value="http://yourwebsitehere.com/thankyou.htm">
<input type="hidden" name="no_note" value="1">
<input type="hidden" name="currency_code" value="USD">

<input type="image"
         src="https://www.paypal.com/en_US/i/btn/x-click-
         but23.gif" border="0" name="submit" alt="Make
         payments with PayPal - it's fast, free and
         secure!">
</form>
```

On the next Web page is HTML code that can be copied and pasted into your Web site pages. See Figure 14-5 for an example of what the Add a Button to Your Website page looks like.

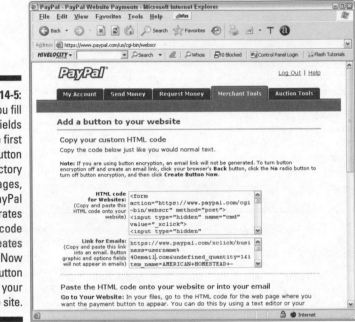

Figure 14-5:
After you fill in the fields on the first two Button Factory pages, PayPal generates the code that creates a Buy Now button on your Web site.

PayPal also generates a link that can be copied into an e-mail that you can send to a buyer. When the buyer clicks this link or copies and pastes the link into a browser, the buyer is sent to a payment page to facilitate payment of the item. (See Figure 14-6.) Sending the link via e-mail, rather than having a button on a Web site page, is useful when you want to sell a service to someone. You can quote the price of the service; if the buyer agrees to your price, you can send the link via e-mail with all payment details already described.

If you want to create multiple buttons quickly, click the Create Another Button button, shown at the bottom of the page. PayPal takes you back to the first page of the Button Factory, but all the values are filled in, based on what you entered for the first button. If the second product is similar to the first, you can edit just a couple of fields and quickly generate the code for the second item button.

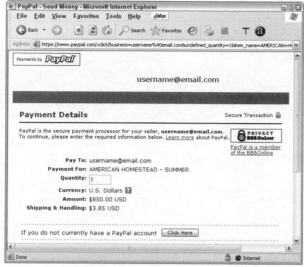

Figure 14-6:
The link, generated by the Button Factory, can be e-mailed to a buyer who is taken to a payment page after clicking the link.

Encrypting your buttons

The PayPal Button Factory makes it easy for you to generate button code and customize the code to meet your needs, but a cost is associated with the simplicity — if it's easy for you to edit the code, it's equally easy for your buyers to alter the code, which means that they may change item prices or decide not to pay for taxes and shipping. Unencrypted code also makes it easier for hackers to get access to user data, which needs to be kept secure.

Without encryption, if you view the source of a Web page with a PayPal button, the button code looks like this:

```
<form action="https://www.paypal.com/cgi-bin/webscr" method="post">
<input type="hidden" name="cmd" value="_xclick">
<input type="hidden" name="business" value="username@e-mail.com">
<input type="hidden" name="item_name" value="Currier &#038; Ives Print">
<input type="hidden" name="item_number" value="100230">
<input type="hidden" name="amount" value="850.00">
<input type="hidden" name="no_note" value="1">
<input type="hidden" name="currency_code" value="USD">
<input type="image" src="https://www.paypal.com/
        en_US/i/btn/x-click-but23.gif" border="0" name="submit" alt="Make payments
        with PayPal - it's fast, free and secure!">
</form>
```

All a user would have to do is change the line that reads:

```
<input type="hidden" name="amount" value="850.00">
```

(continued)

(continued)

and lower the price. If your fulfillment system is automated, and you don't look at each purchase as it is placed, you may never notice the price change.

If you choose to encrypt the button code, the new code looks like this:

```
<form action="https://www.paypal.com/cgi-bin/webscr" method="post">
<input type="hidden" name="cmd" value="_s-xclick">
<input type="image" src="https://www.paypal.com/en_US/i/btn/x-click-but23.gif"
       border="0" name="submit" alt="Make payments with PayPal - it's fast, free and
       secure!">
<input type="hidden" name="encrypted" value="-----BEGIN PKCS7-----MIIHNwYJKoZIhvcNAQcEo
   IIHKDCCByQCAQExggEwMIIBLAIBADCBlDCBjjELMAkGA1UEBhMCVVMxCzAJBgNVBAgTAkNBMRYwFAY
   DVQQHEw1Nb3VudGFpbiBWaWV3MRQwEgYDVQQKEwtQYX1QYWwgSW5jLjETMBEGA1UECxQKbG12ZV9jZ
   XJOczERMA8GA1UEAxQIbG12ZV9hcGkxHDAaBgkqhkiG9w0BCQEWDXJlQHBheXBhbC5jb20CAQAwDQY
   JKoZIhvcNAQEBBQAEgYANWmrAK9phgUq3PvgXRB/dbzWYOMoYoYMYpIJvjx2sgNaSOBw/ryc138DrK
   E/s3MqOM+mxtnj5dYapcSPWXOffaw9iDQ4Gsn4dSSOP88D9oc/loBakGRzKbm/5E+QeXTPdgyQkNsU
   GCr2hSZnntmPansELGVSgUyX1SgPgkF34MzELMAkGBSsOAwIaBQAwgbQGCSqGSIb3DQEHATAUBggqh
   kiG9w0DBwQIRTMdd1ceLwiAgZAqamYPmxncZp0TpDVemChgmJxAv+Ik12uVTjPJ6/d1dPCWfoEJJAt
   bSOtNpgrAvkyJTy4hpSHPqDB299S3jhAdu5YIoOn5RmpuJv1sZieBCgw2UTCgJNbli8FV4nGxg9Dsc
   PNfLZ5wrtEKLRd85rh8VftIZ64VGBGxsA1QYdLM+p405c3tcfxccpg5bODZIiSgggOHMIIDgzCCAuy
   gAwIBAgIBADANBgkqhkiG9w0BAQUFADCBjjELMAkGA1UEBhMCVVMxCzAJBgNVBAgTAkNBMRYwFAYDV
   QQHEw1Nb3VudGFpbiBWaWV3MRQwEgYDVQQKEwtQYX1QYWwgSW5jLjETMBEGA1UECxQKbG12ZV9jZXJ
   OczERMA8GA1UEAxQIbG12ZV9hcGkxHDAaBgkqhkiG9w0BCQEWDXJlQHBheXBhbC5jb20wHhcNMDQwM
   jEzMTAxMzE1WhcNMzUwMjEzMTAxMzE1WjCBjjELMAkGA1UEBhMCVVMxCzAJBgNVBAgTAkNBMRYwFAY
   DVQQHEw1Nb3VudGFpbiBWaWV3MRQwEgYDVQQKEwtQYX1QYWwgSW5jLjETMBEGA1UECxQKbG12ZV9jZ
   XJOczERMA8GA1UEAxQIbG12ZV9hcGkxHDAaBgkqhkiG9w0BCQEWDXJlQHBheXBhbC5jb20wgZ8wDQY
   JKoZIhvcNAQEBBQADgYOAMIGJAoGBAMFHTt38RMxLXJyO2SmS+Nd172T7oKJ4u4uw+6awntALWhO3P
   ewmIJuzbALScsTS4sZoS1fKciBGoh11gIfHzylvkdNe/hJ166/RGqrj5rFb08sAABNTzDTiqqNpJeB
   sYs/c2aiGozptX2R1nBktH+SUNpAajW724Nv2Wvhif6sFAgMBAAGjge4wgeswHQYDVROOBBYEFJaff
   LvGbxe9WT9S1wob7BDWZJRrMIG7BgNVHSMEgbMwgbCAFJaffLvGbxe9WT9S1wob7BDWZJRroYGUpIG
   RMIGOMQswCQYDVQQGEwJVUzELMAkGA1UECBMCQOExFjAUBgNVBAcTDU1vdW50YW1uIFZpZXcxFDASB
   gNVBAoTC1BheVBhbCBJbmMuMRMwEQYDVQQLFApsaXZlX2N1cnRzMREwDwYDVQQDFAhsaXZlX2FwaTE
   cMBoGCSqGSIb3DQEJARYNcmVAcGF5cGFsLmNvbYIBADAMBgNVHRMEBTADAQH/MA0GCSqGSIb3DQEBB
   QUAA4GBAIFfOlaagFr171+jq60KidbWFSE+Q4FqROvdgIONth+8kSK//Y/4ihuE4Ymvzn5ceE3S/iB
   SQQMjyvb+s2TWbQYDwcp1290PIbD9epdr4tJOUNiSojw7BHwYRiPh58S1xGlFgHFXwrEBb3dgNbMUa
   +u4qectsMAXpVHnD9wIyfmHMYIBmjCCAZYCAQEwgZQwgY4xCzAJBgNVBAYTA1VTMQswCQYDVQQIEwJ
   DQTEWMBQGA1UEBxMNTW91bnRhaW4gVm11dzEUMBIGA1UEChMLUGF5UGFsIEluYy4xEzARBgNVBAsUC
   mxpdmVfY2VydHMxETAPBgNVBAMUCGxpdmVfYXBpMRwwGgYJKoZIhvcNAQkBFg1yZUBwYX1wYWwuY29
   tAgEAMAkGBSsOAwIaBQCgXTAYBgkqhkiG9w0BCQMxCwYJKoZIhvcNAQcBMBwGCSqGSIb3DQEJBTEPF
   wOwNDExMDcxOTA0MjZaMCMGCSqGSIb3DQEJBDEWBBRvq9qBCHhSBRz7j/nYxOg8qgqUQTANBgkqhki
   G9w0BAQEFAASBgIDuQp+bDWpTpOchC/aKpY7IDKj2DHSs2R4+Ov5txdEA+za6tX2jT7QAi8mnv4tgf
   mdxu21EwsU2tYtDAwEAin1RNLuwaECkOrhgHn/41mj8KwRAWCAy7z7/ZRUOjn/5D7RpdCql5HGxzNX
   yUhOEzbTPcGl2CqMwbyvozaWEfgqy-----END PKCS7-----
   ">
</form>
```

While encryption is great, there are a couple of drawbacks: You can't add additional option fields to your button, and you can't edit your button options manually, after the encryption has taken place.

PayPal offers a way for developers to encrypt Web site payments; more information is available in Chapter 16, which shows how to integrate the PayPal Shopping Cart into your Web site. If you're not a developer, but you want to tweak the HTML of your button code, a number of products can encrypt the button code for you. LinkLock, from Tunza-Products.com is a software package you can purchase for $38. You can copy and paste your button code into a form, enter a password, and click the Encrypt button. Your button code is encrypted and ready for pasting into a Web page. For more information, you can go to www.tunza-products.com/linklock.

Setting Product Options

Generating a simple button works if the product you sell is always the same, or one-of-a-kind. But what do you do if your product comes in different sizes or colors? Luckily, it's not very difficult to add product options to the PayPal button code. You can use the form on the second page of the PayPal button factory to add two sets of options, or you can add the code yourself to the button code, which is a little more work but gives you more options.

Using the Add Option Fields to Your Page form

On the second Button Factory page, after you set the shipping payment options, you can add up to two sets of option fields.

1. **Start by selecting the type of field from the list.**

   If you choose Drop-Down Menu, the buyer can choose from a list of choices you specify (for example, different colors or sizes). If you choose Text, the user can type into a text box when ordering the item. The text option is good if the user wants to add a personal note or a monogram to the item.

2. **Select an option name.**

   If you chose Drop-Down Menu in the previous step, you might name your option "size" or "color," depending upon the options you want to offer the buyer. If you select Text in the previous step, you type instructions here (for example, **Select up to three initials to be monogrammed on your sweater**). The option name must be 60 characters or less.

3. **If you select Drop-Down Menu in the first step, list the options (for example, small, medium, or large) from which the buyer selects.**

   You can list up to ten options, and each option must be limited to 30 characters. Press the Enter key after each option, so each one is shown on a separate row.

4. **If you want, you can add a second set of options in the same manner you added the first.**

PayPal generates the code to add options to the page where you added the Buy Now button. Figure 14-7 shows what the option fields look like, after you added the button code to your Web page. The list shown in the drop-down menu depends upon the values you enter into the form on the second Button Factory page.

Figure 14-7:
When you use the Button Factory to create product options, drop-down lists and text fields are included for the options you specified.

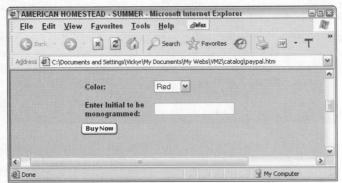

Manually editing the option fields

If you use the PayPal form to generate the code for the options, take a look at the code before pasting it into your Web page. Somewhere within the code is the following text:

```
<input type="hidden" name="on0"
```

The text that follows this string depends on how you configured the options. When I used the Button Factory, I selected colors as my first set of options and let the user enter monogram text for the second option. Within the code for the button generated by PayPal is a table containing my options, which looks like this:

```
<table><tr><td>
<input type="hidden" name="on0" value="Color">Color</td>
<td>
<select name="os0">
<option value="Red">Red
<option value="Blue">Blue
<option value="Green">Green
</select>
</td></tr>
<tr><td>
<input type="hidden" name="on1" value="Enter Initial to be
        monogrammed:">Enter Initial to be monogrammed:
</td>
<td>
<input type="text" name="os1" maxlength="200">
</td></tr></table>
```

The name of the first input type, on0, is how PayPal identifies the first option field name; os0 identifies the field name for the first set of option values. The option values are shown, just as I entered them into the PayPal form.

If you know HTML, you can easily edit the option code to change the options or add additional options. If you edit the code manually, you don't have to be restricted to ten options, and each of the options can be up to 64 characters in length. Text options can be up to 200 characters in length.

Although you can make a lot of changes to the options by editing the HTML, PayPal does not let you incorporate options that change the price of the item. (You can't make the extra-large size cost $2.00 more, for example.) Unless you want to do a lot of custom coding, the easiest way to facilitate options with variable prices is to make each item separate, so that each would get its own Buy Now button.

You can change the layout of the page with respect to where the options are located. You can update the fonts and colors to match the rest of your Web page, or reference a style sheet. Finally, you can substitute different form elements (such as check boxes or radio buttons) for the drop-down list. If I wanted to change the list of options shown in the last example to use radio buttons instead of a drop-down list, I would change the code to

```
<td>
<input type="hidden" name="on0" value="Color">Color
</td>
<td>
<input type="radio" name="os0" value="Red">Red
<input type="radio" name="os0" value="Blue">Blue
<input type="radio" name="os0" value="Green">Green
</td>
```

Figure 14-8 shows the change that the user sees, after I update the button code. The information passed to PayPal via the button code is the same, regardless of the input type.

Figure 14-8:
By changing the input type from a drop-down list to radio buttons in the HTML, I can change the way the interface appears to a potential buyer.

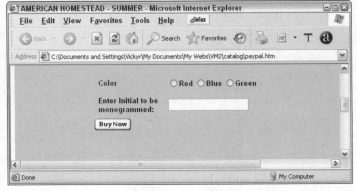

There are 28 HTML variables for the Buy Now buttons, which are used to provide data about the product, how the page displays, and transaction information (for example, currency, tax, shipping data, and so on). Table 14-2 shows the basic item variables. If you want to see the additional variables, which I don't have room to list here, download a copy of the PayPal Integration Guide; Appendix A of the guide lists the variables, gives a description of each, and the character limit (if any). The guide also contains code samples. You can find the guide at `www.paypal.com/en_US/pdf/integration_guide.pdf`.

Table 14-2	PayPal HTML Item Variables	
Variable	*Description*	*Character Limit (If Any)*
Amount	**Optional:** The basic cost of the item (not including shipping, handling, or tax). Although this variable is optional, if you forget to include it, the buyer can change the price of the item when purchasing.	
item_name	**Optional:** The item description. If you don't include it, the customer can enter an item name.	127
item_number	**Optional:** This is where you can enter a SKU or tracking number to identify this item.	127
on0	**Optional:** This variable is for the name of the first option (for example, Color or Size).	64
quantity	**Required:** The number of items being sold. For Shopping Cart transactions, PayPal appends the number of items to the end of the quantity string. (So four items would be quantity4.)	
Undefined_ quantity	**Optional:** If this variable is included in your code and the value is 1, the user can enter the quantity of items.	
on1	**Optional:** This variable is for the name of the first option (for example, Color or Size).	64
os0	**Optional:** This is the first set of values for Option 1 (for example, red, yellow, blue, and so on). You must set on0 before you can specify these values.	Drop-down list or radio buttons: 64 characters; Text box: 200 characters
os1	**Optional:** This is the first set of values for Option 2 (for example, red, yellow, blue, and so on). You must set on1 before you can specify these values.	Drop-down list or radio buttons: 64 characters; Text box: 200 characters

Adding the Code to Your Web Site

After clicking the Create Button Now button, the "Add a button to your Website" page displays. Figure 14-9 shows what the page looks like.

Figure 14-9:
Adding the button code to your Web page is as easy as copying and pasting. If you haven't encrypted the code, you can modify it after pasting it into any application that lets you edit HTML.

To add the button code to a page on your Web site, you need to follow these steps:

1. **Right-click somewhere in the box containing the HTML code for Web sites.**

2. **From the menu, choose the Select All option.**

3. **Right-click again and choose the Copy option.**

   Unless you want to copy the link for e-mails, you can close the PayPal window.

4. **Open the Web page where you want to paste the button code.**

   It doesn't matter if you use DreamWeaver, FrontPage, Notepad, or some other application, as long as you can edit the actual HTML code, not just the page layout.

5. **Making sure you're editing the HTML, paste the button code where you want the button to display.**

    The button code must be pasted in the body of the Web page (somewhere between the <body> and </body> tags).

6. **Open the page in a Web browser and you can test your button code by clicking the link.**

Customizing the Page Look

When you create a Buy Now or Donations button, you have the option of customizing the PayPal page to which buyers are sent to finalize the transaction. Customizing the page by adding your Web site banner and matching the background page color of your Web site makes the payment process seem more integrated. To create a custom payment page, try this:

1. **Log on to your PayPal account and click the Profile tab under the My Account section of the site.**

2. **In the Selling Preferences column on the right side of the page, click the <u>Custom Payment Pages</u> link.**

3. **The Custom Payment Page Styles page shows a list of page styles, if you have created any.**

    You can select one of these existing page styles and edit the style, preview what a page looks like when using the style, or delete the style by clicking the Remove button. You can also choose the Make Primary option, which makes the style you selected the default for all your payment pages, unless you specify otherwise.

4. **Click the Add button to create a new style.**

    You start by naming your style. The style can only be 30 characters long and cannot contain any spaces.

5. **You can use a header image by entering the Web address of the image into the text box.**

    A header image is the big banner-type image that shows at the top of many Web site pages. It usually contains the company logo or some other type of branding. PayPal recommends that the image be 750 pixels wide by 90 pixels long. They also recommend that the image be stored on a secure server.

6. **You can choose a background color for the Header (top portion) of the payment page.**

The color must be specified using HTML hex code (a six character combination of letters and numbers; each unique combination represents a color).

If you click the HTML hex code link, a new window opens, displaying three reference links. Each link takes you to a non-PayPal Web site where you can see the colors and codes that represent them. When entering the hex code into the PayPal form, don't precede the number with a # (pound) symbol.

7. **You can add a border, which surrounds the Header section of the payment page.**

   The border is two pixels in width and you specify the color using hex codes.

8. **You can add a background color to the remainder of the page by using hex codes.**

   PayPal does not accept certain colors (for example, bright red) because it may make PayPal messages too hard to read. Unfortunately, PayPal doesn't give you a list of blocked colors, but recommends trying a color and clicking the Preview button. If you get an error message, you know that you tried using a blocked color.

9. **Click the Preview button to make sure you like the way the page looks.**

   If you're happy with the end result, click the Save button.

Figure 14-10 shows a sample of a customized page. The buyer can see your company's branding when paying for the purchase.

Figure 14-10:
When you create a custom payment page, you set a more professional image and make the payment page feel more like part of an integrated e-commerce Web site.

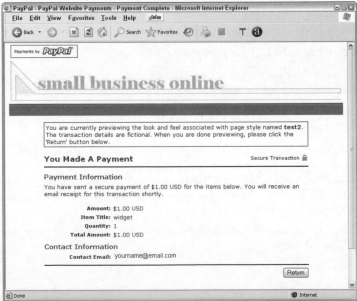

Creating Donations Buttons

The process for creating Subscription buttons is very similar to creating a Buy Now button. After logging on to your PayPal account:

1. **Click the <u>Donations</u> link, which you find under the Accepting Website Payments section of the page.**

   Figure 14-11 shows the Donations screen.

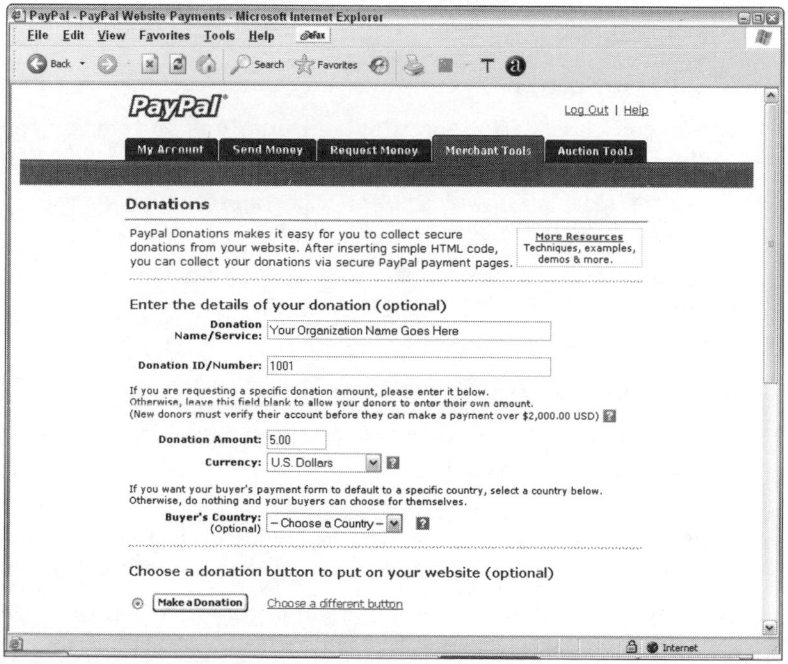

Figure 14-11: The Donations page looks a lot like the Selling Single Items page, except that you enter information about your organi- zation, instead of adding product information.

2. **Although it's optional, entering the name of your organization or char- ity is a good idea.**

   Do this for two reasons: It makes tracking payments easier if you're col- lecting donations through your personal PayPal account; and people are more likely to feel comfortable giving money that they know will go to an organization. You don't want someone wondering whether the donation will go to you or to your charity!

Because we're on the topic of e-mail accounts and donations, it looks more professional and makes it easier to stay organized if you create a separate PayPal account for your organization. While you're at it, you might as well get an e-mail account for your group (if you don't already have one) by going to Yahoo.com and clicking the Mail link.

3. **You can enter a Donation ID or Number.**

   This number is not shown to contributors, but you can use it for tracking purposes because it displays in the transaction item details. You can use it to identify a specific drive or to earmark funds for a specific cause.

4. **You can also enter a donation amount.**

   If you leave this field blank, the contributor can enter any amount.

5. **Select the currency you want; you can also select a country, if desired.**

6. **You can choose from four PayPal Donations buttons, or you can enter the URL of your own image.**

   See the sidebar shown earlier in this chapter if you want to read how to insert your own image.

7. **Select whether you want the button code encrypted.**

   If you plan on making any changes to the button code, be sure to select the No option.

8. **Click the Add More Options button.**

   - This button lets you choose a customized payment page if you already created one.

   - You can also enter a Web address where the Contributor goes after making the donation. (Instead of sending someone back to the home page of your site, send them to a nice thank you page!)

   - There's also a Cancel Payment form where you can enter the URL of a page where the user goes after clicking the Cancel button. This page can provide additional information about why the person may want to donate.

   - You can add a form to the donations page where the contributor can send you a message, if desired.

   - You can select a new e-mail address to receive the donation if you have more than one e-mail address linked to your PayPal account.

   - You can click the Preview button to see what the donations page will look like. If you're happy with the page, click the Return button.

- When you're satisfied with your button settings, click the Create Button Now button where you can copy the code and paste it into a Web page. See the section "Adding the Code to Your Web Site" if you need help with this step.

9. **If you don't need to add more options to your button, click the Create Button Now button, which takes you to a page where you can copy the code that you need to add to the Donations page of your Web site.**

The Customer Experience

When you use PayPal buttons on your Web site, you can control a lot of what your customer sees when purchasing from your Web site. Initially, the buyer is on your Web site and sees a Buy Now button. The button doesn't have a PayPal logo on it (unless you selected one with PayPal branding).

As soon as the customer clicks the Buy Now button, the PayPal Payment Details page displays. The buyer is asked to log on, or has the option to pay with a credit card by clicking the <u>If you have never paid through PayPal, Click Here</u> link. This brings the buyer to a page where a credit card payment can be used; the buyer also has the option of signing up for a PayPal account.

The buyer is taken to the Payment Details page, which looks just like a standard PayPal payment details page, unless you opted to use a customized style. After the buyer fills in the payment details, goes to the payment confirmation page, and clicks the Pay button, you receive the payment. The buyer is redirected back to your Web site to the page that you specified while creating the button.

Chapter 15

Adding Subscriptions and Recurring Payments to Your Web Site

In This Chapter

▶ Creating Subscription buttons

▶ Comprehending the payment flow

▶ Ending subscriptions and recurring payments

▶ Modifying the HTML code for subscriptions

*I*f you sell an ongoing service (such as a newsletter or Web hosting), the PayPal Subscription and Recurring Payments feature can free you from the task of sending an invoice each month. You can offer your buyers a free trial period or special introductory rates before regular billing rates begin. The feature can also be used when you sell an expensive product and want to offer your buyers the option of paying over time.

Another reason to use PayPal is because the fee structure is the same as for any PayPal sale — you pay a $0.30 transaction fee, plus 2.9 percent of the sale price (less if you have high monthly volume and have applied for PayPal's discounted merchant rates). In Chapter 14, I show you how easy it is to add e-commerce functionality to your Web site by creating Buy Now buttons. In this chapter, I show you how to add support for multiple payments, whether they're ongoing or last only for a certain time period.

PayPal does provide some support for generating usernames and passwords, which you use to access subscriber-only content stored in a password-protected Web site folder, but PayPal does not facilitate storing or encrypting your intellectual property (that is, the files you want to sell). If you need a company that can provide these services for you, read about PayLoadz in Chapter 22.

Generating a Subscription Button

Support for subscriptions is a fairly sophisticated feature; many e-commerce site building tools don't provide support for ongoing payments. Setting up subscriptions or recurring payments is easy with PayPal. The first few steps of setting up a subscription are identical to the process of creating a Buy Now button. (See Chapter 14 if you want to discover how to create e-commerce buttons with the Button Factory.) To create a Subscription button, try this:

1. **After logging on to your PayPal account, click the Merchant Tools tab, found at the top of the page.**

2. **Click the <u>Subscriptions and Recurring Payments</u> link, which is under the Accepting Website Payments section of the page.**

3. **Start by entering a name for your subscription, an internal reference number (if you have one), and the currency to use for billing.**

   Like the Button Factory, you can also select the buyer's country.

4. **Check the box if you want to add support for Subscriptions Password Management.**

   Subscription Password Management is an optional feature and requires you to install a PERL script on your Web server (if you run the Apache Web server on Linux). If your Web site is hosted in a different environment (for example, the IIS Web server on Windows 2000), you need to write code to support authentication on your server. Please see Chapter 17 for more information.

In the next section of the Subscriptions and Recurring Payments page, you enter the information to set up a trial period (if desired) and the regular billing cycle.

Setting the trial period

Many magazine subscriptions offer discounts (such as first month free, don't pay for 90 days, and so on) to get you to sign up for their publications. With the Trial Period options, you can offer the same type of deal to entice users to sign up for your product or service.

PayPal lets you offer two different trial periods. You can offer a service free for the first period and discounted for the second period, before the subscriber starts paying the regular periodic amount. Adding a trial period is optional, but it's a great way to get more users to sign up for the product or service you're selling. See Figure 15-1 for an example of the Trial Periods section of the Subscriptions and Recurring Payments page.

Figure 15-1:
You have
the option of
creating two
different
trial periods
before your
subscribers
begin
paying the
full amount
for their
product or
service.

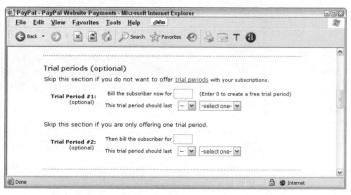

1. **To create a trial period, start by entering the amount that the buyer pays during the first trial period.**

   If you want to sell subscriptions to a newsletter that costs $10 a month, you may decide to offer a 60 percent discount during the first month. In this case, you enter **4.00** as the amount the buyer pays during the first billing cycle. If you don't want to charge the buyer anything during the first trial period, enter **0** in the "Bill the subscriber now for" field.

2. **Enter the length of the trial period by selecting the number and unit of time to use.**

   If you want to make the trial period last one month, you select 1 from the first list and Month(s) from the second list. The units of time include: days, weeks (seven days), months (measured as calendar months), and years.

3. **You can add a second trial period in the same way as you entered the first trial period.**

   If you decided that after the first trial period ends, you want to charge 20 percent of your regular $10 per month newsletter for the second month, you enter **8.00** in the first field, **1** in the second field, and **Month(s)** in the third field.

After entering the trial periods you want to offer, you're ready to set the terms of the regular billing cycle.

Setting the regular billing cycle

If you set any trial periods, the regular billing cycle won't kick in until after the trial periods have ended. Before you start filling in the form (see Figure 15-2 for an example), you need to decide whether you are setting up a subscription or recurring payments. You can also decide whether to cancel a subscription immediately if a payment fails or whether to try twice more to get paid.

Figure 15-2:
When setting the options for the regular billing, you can choose how much to charge, how often to charge, and the length of time for the payments to continue.

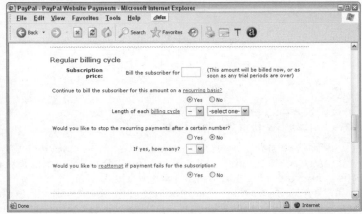

A subscription is forever. (I'm exaggerating a little here.) When you set up a subscription, the subscriber continues to be billed on a regular basis until the subscription is cancelled. The subscriber can decide to cancel, or you can decide to cancel because you're ending the service.

Recurring payments end after a certain number of billing cycles. If you want to offer a buyer the opportunity to pay for an item in installments, you set up recurring payments for a certain period of time. Here's how:

1. **Under the "Regular billing cycle" section of the Subscriptions and Recurring Payments page, enter the amount of the regular subscription rate (the one you plan to charge after the trial period ends).**

   Going back to our magazine example, I enter **10.00** because I intend to bill subscribers $10.00 a month.

2. **Select Yes if you intend to bill the subscriber on a recurring basis. If you select No for this option, the subscriber will be billed just one time, after the end of the trial period.**

   The No option is useful if you want to offer a "No payment for 60 days!" deal. You would set up a 60-day trial period, with 0 as the billing unit. Under the regular billing cycle, enter the payment that is due and select No for billing the subscriber on a recurring basis.

3. **As you did for the trial period, enter the length of the billing cycle by entering a number and the unit of time to be used.**

4. **Decide whether to stop the payments after a certain number.**

   If you select No, you are setting up a subscription. If you select Yes, you are setting up a recurring payment; in the "If yes, how many" list, select the number of payments the user has to make before the billing is ended.

5. **You can decide to reattempt billing if payment fails for the subscription.**

   Failure can occur for many reasons — the subscriber may close the PayPal account, or the credit card linked to the account may be over-drawn. If the payment fails for some reason and you opt to reattempt on failure, payments will reattempt three days after failure, and then again eight days after failure. If the subscriber has still failed to pay, the sub-scription automatically cancels. If you select No for "Would you like to reattempt if payment fails for the subscription," PayPal automatically cancels the subscription.

 Unless you are offering an extremely valuable service, it's always better to reattempt a failed payment. You usually have nothing to lose. If the mistake was an honest one (for example, the buyer's credit card expired), the buyer has two opportunities to make the payment and keep subscribing. If you select the No option, the subscription will be cancelled automatically and you lose the chance to keep a customer.

Choosing a button and setting security options

Adding a Subscription button to feature on your Web site is just like the process of adding a Buy Now button (see Chapter 14). You can use the default button or click the Choose a different button link to see additional options. You can also decide to use a custom image which you host on a Web site. Figure 15-3 shows the Subscription buttons that PayPal offers.

You can't choose a Subscription button without entering at least a subscription period and rate for the regular billing cycle in the Subscriptions and Password Management form.

Figure 15-3:
You can select from PayPal's ten different Subscription buttons or use your own.

In addition to picking a button design to be shown on your Web site, you can choose whether to encrypt the code of your button, so it can't be modified by a user who wants to change the parameters of the subscription. (A user could change the trial period from 1 month to 12 months just by tweaking the code!) Some of the buttons alert subscribers to the trial period(s) or recurring payment schedules you set up (for example, button text that reads "Free Trial" or "Payment Plan").

If you don't plan on modifying the button code, encrypting is a good idea. If you do want to modify the code or add option fields to your buttons, you must select the No option under security settings. Chapters 14 and 17 both offer methods for encrypting button code after making modifications.

Using the Add More Options button

Click the Add More Options button to go to the second Subscriptions and Recurring Payments page, where you can add additional options to the subscription or recurring payment. Some of the options are identical to those available with the Buy Now button:

- **Adding option fields to the subscription page.** To add option fields, you cannot automatically encrypt the buttons by selecting the Yes option on the first page.
- **Choosing (or creating) a Custom Payment page.**

✔ **Sending the buyer to a specific page after successful payment, or to a different page if the buyer cancels before paying.** If you choose to use the Subscription Password Management option, you cannot send subscribers to specific pages after the signup process has ended.

✔ **The Miscellaneous option.** As with the Buy Now buttons, you can choose whether to have buyers provide you with a shipping address. Unlike the Buy Now buttons, the Subscription buttons don't give the option of letting buyers purchase more than one subscription.

There are a number of options available with the Buy Now buttons that are not available when creating a Subscription button. These include adding shipping and sales tax, collecting additional information from your buyers by providing a feedback form, and choosing the e-mail address to receive the payment.

The second page of Subscriptions and Recurring Payments (that is, the More Options page) does offer the option to create a Cancel Subscription button. You have your choice of three PayPal cancellation buttons, or you can enter the URL of your own image if you want a custom cancellation button. Figure 15-4 shows the three button looks available from PayPal. The Cancellation button is then available on your Web site.

Figure 15-4:
In addition
to varied
Subscription
buttons,
PayPal
offers you
a choice
of three
different
cancellation
buttons.

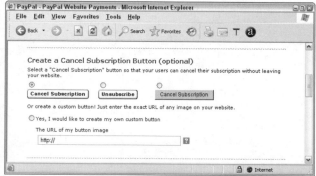

You can click the Preview button to see a sample of the page a user sees after successfully signing up for a subscription. After finalizing your choices, click the Create Button Now button.

Using the button code

After selecting the button options and clicking the Create Button Now button, you go to the "Add a button to your Web site" page. This page provides you with the code to copy and then paste into your Web page code. Code is provided for the Subscription/Recurring Payment button and the Cancellation button. Additionally, code is generated for a link that can be pasted into an e-mail message if you want to let the user sign up after receiving an e-mail from you. Code is also provided to let the user cancel by clicking a link in the e-mail you send.

If you encrypted the button code, you're ready to paste into the HTML of your Web page. Copy the button code, go to your Web page, and paste the button code wherever you want the button to show. Don't forget to include the code for the Cancellation button if you want to include it on the Web page. See Figure 15-5 for a sample Web page with subscription and cancellation buttons.

Figure 15-5:
This sample Web page features subscription and cancellation buttons and gives details of the trial period. If you do not give the trial information on the Web page, the user can see the trial period and terms on the Payment Details page.

You don't have to include the Cancellation button on the Web page when you're trying to get a buyer to sign up. You can choose to include it in the confirmation e-mail you send to the subscriber or at the bottom of a newsletter.

If you choose not to encrypt, you can tweak the HTML if you want. See the last section of this chapter for more information on how to do this.

Sign 'em Up: The Subscription Payment Flow

A user signs up for your subscription-based product by going to your Web site and clicking the subscription or recurring payment button. The user is taken to the PayPal Payment Details page. Users who do not have PayPal accounts are given the opportunity to sign up, as shown in Figure 15-6.

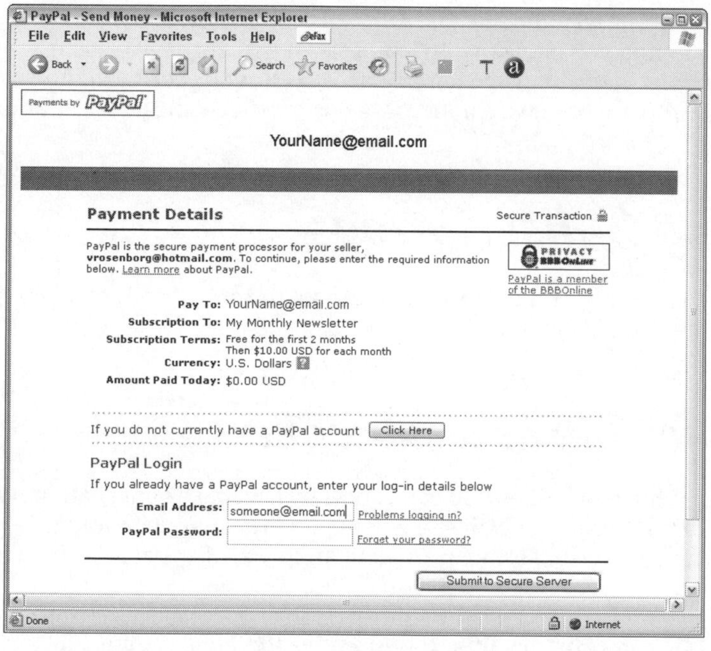

Figure 15-6: The details of the trial period (Free for the first two months; then $10.00 USD for each month) are shown under the Subscription terms on the Payment Details page.

Users who have PayPal accounts but have not linked the account to a credit card need to do so before continuing. On the Confirm Your Payment page, the user is shown the subscription terms again and a Subscription Details message. (This message just warns the user that the subscription will automatically renew at the rates stated unless the user cancels before the end of the billing period.) The user is shown the funding source, typically the credit card that is used to fund the subscription. If the subscription information is correct, the user clicks the Pay button.

The You Made a Payment verification screen appears, which lets the user know that the subscription payment was successful. The user (who is now a subscriber) also gets a verification e-mail noting the following details:

- ✔ **The terms of the subscription or recurring payment.**
- ✔ **A unique subscription ID.**
- ✔ **Instructions on how to configure the PayPal notification settings so an e-mail is sent each time a payment is made.** The subscriber needs to click the <u>Notifications</u> link found on the Profile page and make sure payment notification for making a scheduled subscription payment is selected.
- ✔ **Instructions on how to cancel the subscription.**

You, the seller, also receive a notification e-mail when the subscriber first signs up. If you log on to your PayPal account, you can click the transaction details to see the subscription details. After the trial period ends, you receive another e-mail letting you know that the subscriber's funds have transferred into your account as payment. For each payment cycle, you receive another notification e-mail. You also receive a notice if the user cancels the subscription.

Canceling Subscriptions

Both you and your subscriber can cancel the subscription at any time through the PayPal interface.

Canceling as a subscriber

If you're the subscriber, you can cancel by clicking a cancellation button (if one is available) from the Web site where you first signed up for the subscription. You can also unsubscribe by logging on to your PayPal account. Here's how to do it:

1. **Click the <u>History</u> link, found under the My Account tab.**

2. **Select Subscriptions from the Show drop-down list.**

    If you have multiple subscriptions, you can narrow the list by selecting a specific currency or date range. Click the Search button to see a record for each subscription.

3. **Find the record you want to cancel and click its <u>Details</u> link.**

4. **At the bottom of the page, click the Cancel Subscription button to end your subscription.**

Canceling as a merchant

If you are the merchant who has signed up subscribers, you can unsubscribe an individual subscription by going through the same steps taken by the subscriber. You need to access the subscription record in your account history, click the <u>Details</u> link, and then click the Cancel Subscription button at the bottom of the page.

Under the Hood: Editing the HTML

Like the Buy Now and Donations button code, you can modify the Subscription button code to provide you with more options.

When you copy the code generated by the Button Factory, depending on the options you selected, it looks like this:

```
<form action="https://www.paypal.com/cgi-bin/webscr"
          method="post">
<input type="image"
          src="https://www.paypal.com/en_US/i/btn/x-click-
          but28.gif" border="0" name="submit" alt="Make
          payments with PayPal - it's fast, free and
          secure!">
<input type="hidden" name="cmd" value="_xclick-
          subscriptions">
<input type="hidden" name="business"
          value="yourname@e-mail.com">
<input type="hidden" name="item_name" value="My Monthly
          Newsletter">
<input type="hidden" name="item_number" value="1094">
<input type="hidden" name="page_style" value="PayPal">
<input type="hidden" name="no_shipping" value="1">
<input type="hidden" name="return"
          value="http://www.smallbusinessonline.net">
<input type="hidden" name="no_note" value="1">
<input type="hidden" name="currency_code" value="USD">
<input type="hidden" name="a1" value="0.00">
<input type="hidden" name="p1" value="2">
<input type="hidden" name="t1" value="M">
```

```
<input type="hidden" name="a3" value="10.00">
<input type="hidden" name="p3" value="1">
<input type="hidden" name="t3" value="M">
<input type="hidden" name="src" value="1">
<input type="hidden" name="sra" value="1">
</form>
```

Many of the variables shown previously, including item_name, item_number, currency_code, product options, and so on, are standard button variables. Take a look at Chapter 14 for the basics on how to edit the button code or see Chapter 17 for an in-depth look at how to integrate transactions into the code for your Web site.

Table 15-1 shows a list of variables specific to Subscription buttons.

Table 15-1		PayPal's HTML Item Variables
Variable	*Required?*	*Description*
cmd	Yes	Needs to be set to _xclick-subscriptions.
a1	No	The price for the first trial period; if the value is set to 0 the trial period is free.
p1	No	The length of the first trial period. The value is a number, which gets modified by the time unit (see next).
t1	No	The unit of time to be used, in conjunction with the number value for p1. Possible values are D for days, W for weeks, M for months, or Y for years.
a2	No	The price for the second trial period; if the value is set to 0 the trial period is free.
p2	No	The length of the second trial period. The value is a number, which gets modified by the time unit (see next).
t2	No	The unit of time to use in conjunction with the number value for p2. Possible values are D for days, W for weeks, M for months, or Y for years.
a3	Yes	A number value for the regular ongoing rate of the subscription.
p3	Yes	The length of the regular billing cycle. The value is a number, which gets modified by the time unit (see next).

Variable	Required?	Description
t3	Yes	The unit of time to use in conjunction with the number value for p3. Possible values are D for days, W for weeks, M for months, or Y for years.
src	Yes	The value for recurring payments. If the value is set to 1, payments will recur. If this variable is not included, payments will end when the billing cycle ends.
sra	Yes	The value for reattempting if payment fails. If the value is set to 1, payment will be reattempted. If the variable is not included, the subscription will be canceled on failure of payment.
srt	Yes	The value for this variable is a number that determines the number of payments (after the trial period has ended). If the variable is not included, payments will be ongoing, unless the subscription is canceled.
no_note	Yes	Subscription code does not allow the subscriber to send a note to the merchant. This variable must be included and set to 1.
usr_manage	Yes	If the variable is included, and set to a value of 1, PayPal will generate usernames and passwords.
modify	Yes	If this variable is included, and set to a value of 1, subscribers can modify existing subscriptions according to parameters specified by the subscriptions button. If the value is set to 2, subscribers can modify existing subscriptions or sign up for new subscriptions. If value is set to 0 or the variable is not included, no modifications will be permitted; buyers can only sign up for new subscriptions.

You can find a comprehensive guide to the subscription code variables and sample code in the PayPal Subscriptions and Recurring Payments Manual, available at https://www.paypal.com/en_US/pdf/subscriptions.pdf.

The variables used in the button code can also be used to modify the link generated by the Button Factory. See the link code shown next (which creates a button with the same variables as the HTML script shown earlier in the chapter).

```
https://www.paypal.com/subscriptions/business=yourname%40e-ma
          il.com&item_name=My+Monthly+Newsletter&item_number
          =1094&page_style=PayPal&no_shipping=1&return=http%
          3A//www.smallbusinessonline.net&no_note=1&currency
          _code=USD&a1=0.00&p1=2&t1=M&a3=10.00&p3=1&t3=M&src
          =1&sra=1
```

Changing subscriptions

The last variable shown in Table 15-1 lets you create a button that can modify an active subscription. If you want to change the terms of the subscription (lower the price or change the length of the billing cycle), you can create a Modify Subscription button. You can add this button to a page on your Web site, or you can create an e-mail link to send to your current subscribers.

You can make changes to the following when you modify a subscription:

✔ Subscription name

✔ Number

✔ Ongoing price of the subscription

✔ Length of the billing cycle

✔ The time unit of the billing cycle

✔ Currency of an existing subscription

If you omit the lines for any of these variables, the subscriber can decide what values to enter (that is, if you don't enter a value for the price variable, subscribers can choose their own price).

To create a Modify button, use the Button Factory to create a Subscription button but don't encrypt the code. Copy the resulting HTML code into Notepad (or any HTML editing tool that you like to use) and add the following line within the form (between the `<form>` and `</form>` tags).

```
<input type="hidden" name="modify" value="1">
```

If you use a value of 1 for the modify variable, the button that displays takes the subscriber to a Payment Details page that shows the terms of the old subscription and the terms of the revised subscription. If the user clicks on the Modify Subscription button, the revised terms for the subscription will be implemented. The user can choose to keep the current subscription but also sign up for a new subscription (with the new terms) by clicking the Keep your current subscriptions and sign up for a new one link.

If you use a value of 2 for the `modify` variable:

```
<input type="hidden" name="modify" value="2">
```

The user can change from the old subscription terms to the modified terms, but won't have the option of signing up for a new subscription (while keeping the terms of the old one).

If you want to add the `modify` variable to the link for the Subscription button code, you just need to append the following to the URL string:

```
&modify=1
```

After appending the variable, the new URL string looks like this:

```
https://www.paypal.com/subscriptions/business=yourname%40e-ma
           il.com&item_name=My+Monthly+Newsletter&item_number
           =1094&page_style=PayPal&no_shipping=1&return=http%
           3A//www.smallbusinessonline.net&no_note=1&currency
           _code=GBP&a1=0.00&p1=2&t1=M&a3=10.00&p3=1&t3=M&src
           =1&sra=1&modify=1
```

As with the HTML code, the value of the variable shown previously can be 0, 1, or 2. If 0, the subscription cannot be modified. If 1, the subscription can be modified, or the subscriber can keep the existing subscription and sign up for a second subscription with the new terms. If the value is 2, the user can only sign up for the new subscription.

Chapter 16

The PayPal Shopping Cart

*B*uy Now buttons are a great way to dip your toe into the waters of e-commerce, but before long, you'll probably want a Shopping Cart. With a Shopping Cart, buyers can put multiple items into a basket before going to the PayPal Payment Details page to check out. Shopping Carts are good for you and your customers. Having a shopping cart encourages the purchase of multiple products from your site (more profit for you) and keeps the buyer from having to enter payment information for each product they want to buy (less aggravation for them).

Creating a Shopping Cart is almost as easy as creating Shopping Cart buttons. The beginning of this chapter shows you how. If you're the type that likes writing your own code (or tinkering with other people's code), keep reading. The latter part of the chapter shows you how to integrate the Shopping Cart with your existing Web site, even if you already sell products online.

Generating Shopping Cart Buttons

Creating a Shopping Cart button starts off the same way as creating a Buy Now button. (See Chapters 14 and 15 if you want to read how to create PayPal buttons.) Start by logging on to your PayPal account and clicking the Merchant Tools tab.

1. **On the PayPal Shopping Cart page under Accepting Website Payments, enter the name of the item or service you want to sell; the item ID.**

   This can be a SKU or tracking number you use, the price of the item, and the currency and country, if desired.

2. **Under the Select an Add to Cart button section of the page, choose which Add to Cart button you want to feature in your Web site.**

   You can also decide to use your own button image. (See Chapter 14 if you need help.) Figure 16-1 shows the button styles from which you can pick.

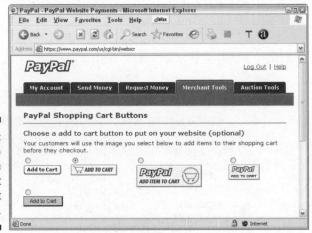

Figure 16-1: You get to choose from five different Add to Cart buttons.

3. **Click the Add More Options button if you want to specify tax, shipping, and other options, including:**

   • **Setting product options (for example, small, medium, or large).** See Chapter 14 for more information on how to set or change your product options.

   • **Selecting a View Cart button.** The View Cart buttons are styled to match the look of the Add to Cart buttons. Make sure you pick the button that matches your Add to Cart choice. You also have the option of entering the Web address of your own image to use for the View Cart button. See Figure 16-2, which shows the View Cart button styles.

   • **You can customize the Payment Details page, which the user is sent to at the time of payment.** You can create page styles featuring custom headers and background page colors. See Chapter 14 for information on how you can customize the Payment Details page.

Figure 16-2:
The View Cart button styles match the look of the Add to Cart buttons; when you coordinate the two, it makes your site look more professional.

- **You can further customize the customer experience by entering a Web address the buyer returns to after payment is completed (that is, a "thank you" page).** You can also enter the Web address where the buyer returns if the payment is cancelled before the transaction has completed.

- **Another way to customize the payment process is to turn on the Payment Data Transfer (PDT) feature by clicking the Edit button.** PDT passes transaction data back to your Web site after a payment completes. The payment data displays in a confirmation page, hosted on your site or written to a database. (Chapter 18 has more information about PDT.) Before you can implement PDT, you must turn on the PayPal Auto-Return option to ensure the buyer returns to your site (along with the transaction data!).

- **You can choose whether the buyer should supply a shipping address at the time of purchase, and whether you want to collect additional information (by providing a form where buyers can send you feedback).**

- **The last of the additional options lets you select which e-mail address should receive the notification after a sale is made.**

- **On the second page of the Shopping Cart setup (the More Options page), you can click the Preview button to preview what the Payment Details page looks like.**

4. **Click the Create Button Now button if you are ready to generate the button code.**

Adding the code to your Web site

The code for the Add to Cart button is shown here:

```
<form target="paypal" action="https://www.paypal.com/cgi-
        bin/webscr" method="post">
<table><tr><td><input type="hidden" name="on0"
        value="Size:">Size:</td><td><select
        name="os0"><option value="Small">Small<option
        value="Medium">Medium<option
        value="Large">Large</select>
</td></tr></table><input type="image"
        src="https://www.paypal.com/en_US/i/btn/sc-but-
        03.gif" border="0" name="submit" alt="Make
        payments with PayPal - it's fast, free and
        secure!">
<input type="hidden" name="add" value="1">
<input type="hidden" name="cmd" value="_cart">
<input type="hidden" name="business"
        value="username@email.com">
<input type="hidden" name="item_name" value="Widget One">
<input type="hidden" name="item_number" value="1001">
<input type="hidden" name="amount" value="65.00">
<input type="hidden" name="shipping" value="3.85">
<input type="hidden" name="return"
        value="http://www.smallbusinessonline.net">
<input type="hidden" name="no_note" value="1">
<input type="hidden" name="currency_code" value="USD">
</form>
```

The code for the View Cart button is also shown here:

```
<form target="paypal" action="https://www.paypal.com/cgi-
        bin/webscr" method="post">
<input type="hidden" name="cmd" value="_cart">
<input type="hidden" name="business"
        value="username@email.com">
<input type="image"
        src="https://www.paypal.com/en_US/i/btn/view_cart.
        gif" border="0" name="submit" alt="Make payments
        with PayPal - it's fast, free and secure!">
<input type="hidden" name="display" value="1">
</form>
```

After the code is generated, copy and paste it into the HTML of your product information Web page. When figuring out where to add the code for each button, the Add to Cart code should be located somewhere close to the item price. The Add to Cart button should be located near the top of page. After you paste the code into your Web page, the page looks like the one shown in Figure 16-3.

Figure 16-3:
After generating both sets of button code, I pasted it into this sample Web page. In addition to the Add to Cart and View Cart buttons, the list of "Size" product options is added (above the Add to Cart button).

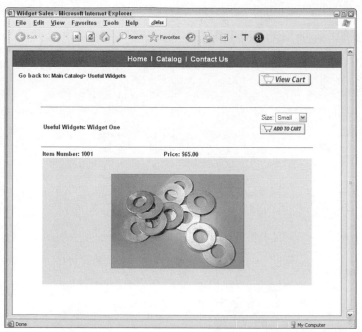

After the code is generated, you can click the Create Another Button button, which creates a second button with the values already filled in based upon the selections you made for the first button. You can quickly create a second button by modifying the values and then generating the code. Create buttons for every product page in your Web site. Paste the Add to Cart buttons on each page, and remember to add the View Cart button code to each page.

The customer experience

Unlike the Buy Now buttons, which take the buyer directly to the Payment Details page, the PayPal Shopping Cart appears in a new window when the buyer clicks the Add to Cart button. The Shopping Cart shows the quantity, the name of the item (and item number, if available), the options selected, and the price.

The user can type in a new number to change the quantity although the quantity won't be changed until after the Update Cart button is clicked. The user can remove an item from the cart by checking the Remove box and clicking the Update Cart button.

After viewing the items in the cart, the user can click the Continue Shopping button or click the Checkout button. If the user clicks the Continue Shopping button, the product page shows, and the Add to Cart window remains in the background until another item is added to the cart or the View Cart button is clicked. The user can add additional items to the cart. (See Figure 16-4, which shows multiple items in the Shopping Cart.)

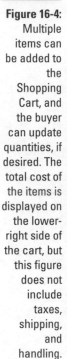

Figure 16-4: Multiple items can be added to the Shopping Cart, and the buyer can update quantities, if desired. The total cost of the items is displayed on the lower-right side of the cart, but this figure does not include taxes, shipping, and handling.

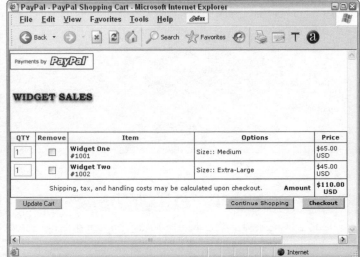

When the user has finished shopping and clicked the Checkout button on the Shopping Cart, the Payment Details page appears (see Figure 16-5). The items are totaled together. Taxes, shipping, and handling charges are added to the total. The buyer can see individual product information by clicking the View Contents link. This opens the Shopping Cart again. To complete the transaction, the buyer needs to click the Checkout button again.

After payment is completed for a item, an e-mail receipt is sent to the buyer, and you receive an e-mail notification letting you know the funds transferred into your PayPal account.

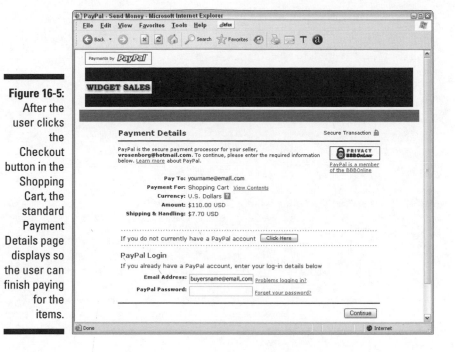

Figure 16-5:
After the
user clicks
the
Checkout
button in the
Shopping
Cart, the
standard
Payment
Details page
displays so
the user can
finish paying
for the
items.

Converting Buy Now Buttons to Shopping Cart Buttons

What if you spent a lot of time creating Buy Now buttons, and you want to convert these to Add to Cart buttons so you can integrate the Shopping Cart into your Web site? Luckily, the process is very straightforward, and should be easy for you if you're comfortable editing HTML code.

Converting the Buy Now buttons

First, copy the Buy Now button code into Notepad, or whichever application you use to modify Web pages. The Buy Now button code has many of the same variables as those used for the Add to Cart buttons:

```
<form action="https://www.paypal.com/cgi-bin/webscr"
          method="post">
<input type="hidden" name="cmd" value="_xclick">
<input type="hidden" name="business"
          value="username@email.com">
<input type="hidden" name="undefined_quantity" value="1">
<input type="hidden" name="item_name" value="AMERICAN
          HOMESTEAD - SUMMER">
<input type="hidden" name="item_number" value="33347">
<input type="hidden" name="amount" value="850.00">
<input type="hidden" name="shipping" value="3.85">
<input type="hidden" name="page_style" value="Primary">
<input type="hidden" name="return"
          value="http://yourwebsitehere.com/thankyou.htm">
<input type="hidden" name="no_note" value="1">
<input type="hidden" name="currency_code" value="USD">
<input type="image"
          src="https://www.paypal.com/en_US/i/btn/x-click-
          but23.gif" border="0" name="submit" alt="Make
          payments with PayPal - it's fast, free and
          secure!">
</form>
```

To convert your Buy Now button, you need to add new variables and change the values for others. Here's how:

1. **Include** `target="paypal"` **within the form tag.**

    The revised form tag looks like this:

    ```
    <form target="paypal" action="https://www.paypal.com/cgi-
              bin/webscr" method="post">
    ```

2. **Replace** `_xclick` **with** `_cart` **in the line that reads** `<input type="hidden" name="cmd" value="_xclick">`.

    The revised line looks like this:

    ```
    <input type="hidden" name="cmd" value="_cart">
    ```

3. **Insert the following line somewhere between the** `<form>` **and** `</form>` **tags:**

    ```
    <input type="hidden" name="add" value="1">
    ```

4. **Find the line that contains the link to the Buy Now button image (a standard PayPal button image or your own image):**

    ```
    <input type="image"
              src="https://www.paypal.com/en_US/i/btn/x-click-
              but23.gif" border="0" name="submit" alt="Make
              payments with PayPal - it's fast, free and
              secure!">
    ```

5. **Replace the Buy Now button image with an Add to Cart button image (or use your own image):**

```
<input type="image"
       src="http://images.paypal.com/en_US/i/btn/x-
       click-but22.gif" border="0" name="submit"
       width="87" height="23" alt="Make payments with
       PayPal - it's fast, free and secure!">
```

The revised code looks like this (changes are in bold):

```
<form target="paypal" action="https://www.paypal.com/cgi-
       bin/webscr" method="post">
<input type="hidden" name="cmd" value="_cart">
<input type="hidden" name="add" value="1">
<input type="hidden" name="business"
       value="username@email.com">
<input type="hidden" name="undefined_quantity" value="1">
<input type="hidden" name="item_name" value="AMERICAN
       HOMESTEAD - SUMMER">
<input type="hidden" name="item_number" value="33347">
<input type="hidden" name="amount" value="850.00">
<input type="hidden" name="shipping" value="3.85">
<input type="hidden" name="page_style" value="Primary">
<input type="hidden" name="return"
       value="http://yourwebsitehere.com/thankyou.htm">
<input type="hidden" name="no_note" value="1">
<input type="hidden" name="currency_code" value="USD">
<input type="image"
       src="https://www.paypal.com/en_US/i/btn/sc-but-
       03.gif" border="0" name="submit" alt="Make
       payments with PayPal - it's fast, free and
       secure!">
</form>
```

Apply the same changes to each instance of the Buy Now code leaving the product variables unchanged.

Creating View Cart buttons

After you replace all the Buy Now buttons, you need to add the View Cart code to the product pages.

```
<form target="paypal" action="https://www.paypal.com/cgi-
       bin/webscr" method="post">
<input type="hidden" name="cmd" value="_cart">
<input type="hidden" name="business"
       value="username@email.com">
```

```
<input type="image"
         src="https://www.paypal.com/en_US/i/btn/view_cart.
         gif" border="0" name="submit" alt="Make payments
         with PayPal - it's fast, free and secure!">
<input type="hidden" name="display" value="1">
</form>
```

Both the Buy Now buttons and the Shopping Cart buttons let you choose which e-mail account to use when generating the button code. If you are editing the HTML manually, make sure that you consistently use the same e-mail address for each of the Add to Cart buttons and the View Cart code included on every page. If you start mixing your e-mail accounts, you won't be able to add all items to a single Shopping Cart.

If you do want to create several different storefronts, tie each group of products plus the View Cart code to one e-mail account, and the second group of products plus the second View Cart code to a different e-mail account.

Customizing the HTML of the PayPal Shopping Cart

PayPal button code (whether Buy Now, Donations, Subscription, or Add to Cart) is easy to modify, as long as you know the variables that you can use and the valid values for each.

PayPal HTML variables

Table 16-1 shows a list of display variables created to use with Buy Now buttons. These variables can be used with the Add to Cart buttons, as well.

Table 16-1	PayPal HTML Display Variables	
Variable	*Description*	*Character Limit (If Any)*
cn	**Optional:** This contains the label shown above the note field, if included. The variable is not saved and does not show in notifications.	40 characters
Cs	**Optional:** This sets the background color of the payment pages. If the value is 1, the background color will be black; if 0 or not included, the color will be white.	

Variable	Description	Character Limit (If Any)
image_url	**Optional:** The Web address of your 150 pixel x 150 pixel logo image. If you do not include this variable, your e-mail address or business name will display.	
no_note	**Optional:** If the value is set to 1, the buyer will not be prompted to enter a note when paying; if omitted or set to 0, the buyer will be prompted.	
no_shipping	**Optional:** If the value is set to 1, the buyer will not be prompted to enter a shipping address when paying; if omitted or set to 0, the buyer will be prompted.	
cancel_return	**Optional:** The URL where the buyer is sent if the payment is cancelled before the sale completes. If omitted, the user is redirected to the PayPal Web site.	
return	**Optional:** The URL where the buyer is sent if the payment is successfully completed. If omitted, the user is redirected to the PayPal Web site.	
rm	**Optional:** This variable controls whether transaction information is passed back to the seller's Web site after the sale is complete. The return variable (see previous information) needs to be set. If rm is set to 1, the buyer is returned to the seller's Web site using a GET method and no transaction variables are returned. If the rm value is 2, the buyer is returned to the seller's Web site using a POST method and all available transaction variables are posted. If rm is set to 0 or omitted, the GET method is used and no variables are returned unless IPN is enabled (in which case, the POST method is used for any additional variables).	

(continued)

Table 16-1 *(continued)*

Variable	Description	Character Limit (If Any)
page_style	**Optional:** If included, it should be set to the name of the custom payment page style you created at the PayPal Web site. You can also use `primary` as a value to set the page style to the style designated as the Primary style on the PayPal Web site.	30 characters (Must be alpha-numeric ASCII lower-bit characters. An under-score can be included, but no spaces.)
address_ override	**Optional:** If you want to collect address information from the user at your Web site, set the `address_override` value to `1` to pass the address data to PayPal. The buyer can see, but not edit, the address passed in. If any of the address data is invalid or missing, the address will not be shown.	
cbt	**Optional:** The `cbt` variable lets you define the text that is used in the Continue button at the payment confirmation page. (This variable requires that the return variable be set.) After clicking the button, the user is redirected to the seller's Web site.	

In addition to display variables, you can also change the transaction variables in the Buy Now and Add to Cart button code; Table 16-2 shows the transaction variables that you can use.

Table 16-2   **PayPal HTML Transaction Variables**

Variable	Description	Character Limit (If Any)
currency_ code	**Optional:** Sets the currency to be used in all money-related variables (amount, shipping, shipping2, handling, and tax). Values are `USD`, `EUR`, `GBP`, `CAD`, and `JPY`. If variable is omitted, `USD` (U.S. dollars) is used as the default.	

Variable	Description	Character Limit (If Any)
custom	**Optional:** It shouldn't come as a surprise that this variable lets you define a "custom" variable. The value never displays to a buyer; if omitted, no variable is passed back to you.	256
handling	**Optional:** The cost of handling charged to your buyer. Please note that handling is charged for each item purchased; if omitted, no handling charges add to the final cost.	
invoice	**Optional:** This is a pass-through variable that you can use to identify an invoice number for the purchase. If omitted, no variable is passed back to you.	
shipping	**Optional:** If you have enable item-specific shipping costs on the PayPal Web site, this variable is used to define the shipping cost. (The "override the profile shipping settings" checkbox must be checked in Shipping Calculations in the Account Profile.) If the shipping variable is defined (but not shipping2), a flat amount will be charged for the shipping of each item. If this variable is omitted, the customer will be charged the amounts you defined for Shipping Calculation in your Account Profile.	
shipping2	**Optional:** The cost of shipping every item after the first, as opposed to charging the same amount for each item. If omitted, the values set in your Shipping Calculation, in the Account Profile, will be used.	
tax	**Optional:** The value for this variable overrides any settings that may be set in your Account Profile. Warning: If you use this variable, the same tax will be added to every purchase, no matter where the buyer is located. If this variable is omitted, the values set up in your Account Profile will be used.	

(continued)

Table 16-2	**PayPal HTML Transaction Variables**	
Variable	*Description*	*Character Limit (If Any)*
tax_x	**Optional:** The tax charged for a specific item (the _x describes the item number; the variable defining the tax for item 2 would be tax_2).	

There's one additional Shopping Cart variable you should know about. The handling_cart variable is optional and lets you assign a single handling charge to all the items in your cart. If there are multiple items in a Shopping Cart, the handling_cart value of the first item is used and the rest ignored.

Tinkering with PayPal's button code

You can modify the value for any button variable with the exception of the following line (which cannot be changed or the Shopping Cart breaks):

```
<form target="paypal" action="https://www.paypal.com/cgi-
        bin/webscr" method="post">
```

After you generate the code for one Add to Cart button, modifying the code to create a different button for every item you sell is easy. The code for a very simple Add to Cart button is shown here:

```
<form target="paypal" action="https://www.paypal.com/cgi-
        bin/webscr" method="post">
<input type="image"
        src="https://www.paypal.com/en_US/i/btn/sc-but-
        03.gif" border="0" name="submit">
<input type="hidden" name="add" value="1">
<input type="hidden" name="cmd" value="_cart">
<input type="hidden" name="business"
        value="yourname@email.com">
<input type="hidden" name="item_name" value="Widget One">
<input type="hidden" name="item_number" value="1001">
<input type="hidden" name="amount" value="65.00">
</form>
```

In order to create a second button for a different product, I can just change the values for the item_name, item_number, and amount variables (shown in bold text in the previous code):

```
<form target="paypal" action="https://www.paypal.com/cgi-
        bin/webscr" method="post">
<input type="image"
        src="https://www.paypal.com/en_US/i/btn/sc-but-
        03.gif" border="0" name="submit">
<input type="hidden" name="add" value="1">
<input type="hidden" name="cmd" value="_cart">
<input type="hidden" name="business"
        value="yourname@email.com">
<input type="hidden" name="item_name" value="Widget Two">
<input type="hidden" name="item_number" value="1002">
<input type="hidden" name="amount" value="70.00">
</form>
```

Creating multiple buttons in this fashion works if you have a small number of items to sell, but what if you have hundreds of items? Or you want to show all products within a certain category on a single page (each with its own Add to Cart button)? To bring your PayPal Shopping Cart to the next level, you need to dynamically generate your Add to Cart buttons. (I show you how to do this later in the chapter.)

After you have the button code for a new item, it should be a simple matter to paste the code into the HTML of your Web page. But what if the buttons aren't placed exactly where you need them to be (or even more frustrating, what if the buttons aren't lining up properly)? Here are a couple of tips to help you with a product Web page layout.

Making Your Page(s) Look Good

When designing an online store, the product pages need to look good, if you want to have people order from you. (I'm always amazed at how many companies with quality products have Web sites that look as if a high school student put the site together.) The following are a few pointers to help you with page layout when you incorporate PayPal's button code into your Web site.

Lining up the buttons with the other page elements

If you tried pasting the Add to Cart button code into the HTML of your product page, you may have had some problems in getting the button to line up with the other elements on your page. The problem is especially noticeable when you add product options to the button code.

If I paste the button code into my Web page without any modifications, the result looks like Figure 16-6. Notice how the Size drop-down list doesn't line up with the Add to Cart button.

Figure 16-6:
If you paste
the button
code into
the HTML of
your Web
page
without
making any
modifica-
tions to the
layout, the
layout may
be a little
off.

The fastest way to get control over the layout is to add a table within the PayPal form (between the <form> and the </form> tags) and place the button elements (in this case, the product options and the button) in sepa-rate cells. In this way, you can choose to stack the elements in a column or display them in a single row. If I add a table to the button code, the resulting HTML looks like this:

```
<form target="paypal" action="https://www.paypal.com/cgi-
          bin/webscr" method="post">
<table>
<tr>
<td>
<input type="hidden" name="add" value="1">
<input type="hidden" name="cmd" value="_cart">
<input type="hidden" name="business"
          value="username@email.com">
<input type="hidden" name="on0" value="Color"></font>
<font face="ARIAL, HELVETICA" size="2">
Size:</font><font face="ARIAL, HELVETICA" size="2"
          color="#365680">
<select name="os0">
<option value="Small">Small
<option value="Medium">Medium
```

```
<option value="Large">Large
</td>
<input type="hidden" name="undefined_quantity" value="1">
<input type="hidden" name="item_name" value="Big Widget">
<input type="hidden" name="item_number" value="1006">
<input type="hidden" name="amount" value="60.00">
<input type="hidden" name="shipping" value="3.85">
<input type="hidden" name="page_style" value="Primary">
<input type="hidden" name="return"
          value="http://yourwebsitehere.com/thankyou.htm">
<input type="hidden" name="no_note" value="1">
<input type="hidden" name="currency_code" value="USD">
<td>
<input type="image"
          src="https://www.paypal.com/en_US/i/btn/sc-but-
          03.gif" border="0" name="submit">
</td>
</tr>
</table>
</form>
```

The table, row, and cell tags are shown in bold in the previously listed code. Notice how only the elements that actually show on the page (the drop-down list and button) need to be within the cell tags. Figure 16-7 shows the revised page.

Replacing buttons with links

If you don't like the look of the PayPal buttons, you can replace the button image (and code) with a link, which serves the same function. When you use PayPal to create Buy Now buttons, the code for a link is generated, too. Unfortunately, when you create an Add to Cart button, no link code is generated. You can, however, easily create your own. Try this:

✔ **Get rid of the** `<form>` **and** `</form>` **tags.**

✔ **The beginning of the link starts with** `<a target="_blank"` `href=https://www.paypal.com/cgi-bin/webscr` **followed by a question mark.**

✔ **If you want to have a** <u>Continue Shopping</u> **link displayed in the View Cart window, you need to open the cart in a new instance of the browser, so make sure you don't forget to add** `target="_blank"` **within the tag.**

✔ **Each of the variables is listed, followed by an equal sign and the value to be used for that variable.**

✔ Each variable is separated by an ampersand.

✔ If you have any spaces in your item name, substitute a plus sign for the space.

✔ Don't forget to add `&target=paypal` to the end of the string if it isn't already included.

✔ End with a right angle bracket > and add your link text, ending with `</a>`.

Figure 16-7:
By putting a table inside the form tags and putting the different page elements in separate cells, I have much more control over the layout presented by the button code. The only other item I need to add is the View Cart button.

Using this formula, the following button code:

```
<form target="paypal" action="https://www.paypal.com/cgi-
          bin/webscr" method="post">
<input type="hidden" name="cmd" value="_cart">
<input type="hidden" name="add" value="1">
<input type="hidden" name="business"
          value="yourname@email.com">
<input type="hidden" name="quantity" value="1">
<input type="hidden" name="item_name" value="Bigger Widget">
```

```
<input type="hidden" name="item_number" value="1007">
<input type="hidden" name="amount" value="90.00">
<input type="image"
        src="https://www.paypal.com/en_US/i/btn/sc-but-
        03.gif" border="0" name="submit">
</form>
```

becomes the following link:

```
<a target="_blank" href=https://www.paypal.com/cgi-
        bin/webscr?&cmd=_cart&add=1&business=yourname%40em
        ail.com&quantity=1&item_name=Bigger+Widget&item_nu
        mber=1007&amount=90.00&target=paypal>link text
        goes here</a>
```

If you are handy with Notepad, or any text editor, using the Replace All function helps speed up the process of turning button code into links:

1. **Search for the following string: <input type="hidden" name="**

2. **And replace with an ampersand: &**

3. **Search for the following string: "value="**

4. **And replace with an equal sign: =**

5. **Search for the following string: ">**

6. **And replace with nothing.**

7. **You still need to massage the code a little and remove the blank spaces, but searching and replacing lessens the amount of time you need to spend, especially for buttons with a lot of options.**

Converting the View Cart button code to a link is even easier:

```
<a target="_blank" href=https://www.paypal.com/cgi-
        bin/webscr?cmd=_cart&business=username@email.com&d
        isplay=1>View Cart</a>
```

After you create a link in place of a button, you can match the look of other links in your navigation bar, or you can create a rollover button with just a little JavaScript.

Building a better button

Sure, you can create your own button image, and link to it from the button code, but the button image will be static. (Yawn.) With just a little JavaScript, and a couple of images, you can create rollover buttons, where the image changes as you pass the mouse over it.

There are many different ways to create a rollover effect, but one of the easiest is to use the JavaScript event handlers `onMouseOver` and `onMouseOut`. Don't worry if you don't write much JavaScript . . . the code is so simple, you can adapt it for your needs.

You need two images that you want to use as a button; one shows when the mouse passes over the image; the other shows the rest of the time. Insert this code into your HTML at the point where you want the button to show.

```
<img src="yourimage.jpg"
name="displaypic"
onmouseover="document.displaypic.src = 'otherimage.jpg';"
onfocus="document.displaypic.src = 'otherimage.jpg';"
onmouseout="document.displaypic.src = 'yourimage.jpg';"
onblur="document.displaypic.src = 'yourimage.jpg';"
/>
```

In the code shown previously, the image that shows as the default is `your image.jpg`; the image that shows when the user mouses over is `other image.jpg`. You can add the link that you created in the last section of this chapter, so when the user clicks the link, the product item gets added to the PayPal Shopping Cart:

```
<a target="_blank" href=https://www.paypal.com/cgi-
          bin/webscr?&cmd=_cart&add=1&business=yourname%40em
          ail.com&quantity=1&item_name=Bigger+Widget&item_nu
          mber=1007&amount=90.00&target=paypal>
<img src="yourimage.jpg"
name="displaypic"
onmouseover="document.displaypic.src = 'otherimage.jpg';"
onfocus="document.displaypic.src = 'otherimage.jpg';"
onmouseout="document.displaypic.src = 'yourimage.jpg';"
onblur="document.displaypic.src = 'yourimage.jpg';"
/>
</a>
```

You can use the same JavaScript (with two different images) to create a rollover button that lets the user view the Shopping Cart:

```
<a target="_blank" href=https://www.paypal.com/cgi-
          bin/webscr?cmd=_cart&business=username@email.com&d
          isplay=1>
```

```
<img src="viewcart1.jpg"
name="displaypic"
onmouseover="document.displaypic.src = 'viewcart2.jpg';"
onfocus="document.displaypic.src = 'viewcart2.jpg';"
onmouseout="document.displaypic.src = 'viewcart1.jpg';"
onblur="document.displaypic.src = 'viewcart1.jpg';"
/>
</a>
```

These tips can improve the design of your product page, but what if you're more concerned with button quantity, rather than quality? The next section of this chapter shows you how to create buttons if you have hundreds of products.

Dynamically Generating Add to Cart Buttons

If you're comfortable with scripting and doing database queries, you can write code to dynamically generate your Add to Cart buttons from a database. The product information is stored in a database; the product name, price, and other fields are pulled from the database to populate the button code.

I spent six years at Microsoft, so it shouldn't come as a shock when I tell you that I use VBSCRIPT and ASP for writing scripts and Microsoft SQL for my databases. You may be a PERL and MySQL kind of person. It doesn't really matter. I explain the theory behind the code in the examples I show you. You should be able to figure out how to adapt my examples to your preferences.

If you need help figuring out how to adapt the code shown here, or if you're 90 percent of the way there, but you can't solve a bug, don't despair! You can go to `https://www.paypal.com/us/cgi-bin/webscr?cmd=p/pdn/software_dev_kit`. At the bottom of the page are links to free software development kits, which provide documentation and sample code. Unfortunately, only PHP and ASP.NET are available now, but SDKs for PERL and ColdFusion are coming soon. If you need additional help, go to `www.paypaldev.org`; click the <u>Search</u> link at the top-right corner of the page and search on the phrase "dynamically generate buttons". Scroll through the forum threads and you'll probably find information to help you. (Or you can post a message requesting help and someone can steer you in the right direction.)

In the beginning was the database

Before you can generate anything, you need to get your product data into a database table. When deciding which columns to include in your table, remember that some of the PayPal button code variables can be hard-coded (because your e-mail address, currency code, and so forth, stays the same, no matter which product you're selling).

If I were creating a complex database, I would design multiple tables and attempt to normalize the database. (This is a single-table example, so I hope you purists out there forgive me!) For each button, I want to include the following information:

Record_no (I give each record a unique ID for tracking purposes)

item_name

item_number

short_desc (short description)

amount

shipping

on0 (I plan to offer options for each item I'm selling, but the options don't have to be the same for each item)

os01 (option 1)

os02 (option 2)

os03 (option 3)

Figure 16-8 shows what my database table (candy) looks like in SQL Server Enterprise Manager. After I create my table, I need to write the code that will generate my PayPal buttons.

Figure 16-8:
I created a table with a record for each of my seven products. In addition to basic product information (item name, price, and so forth), I chose to include product options.

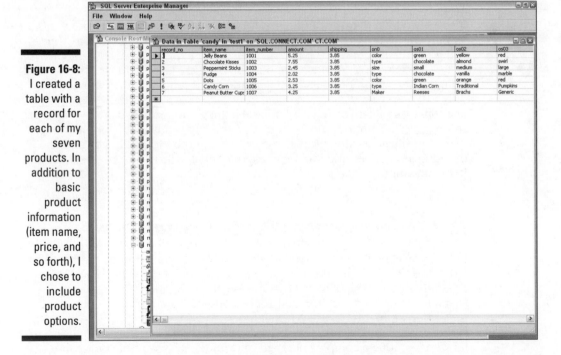

Writing the script to generate the buttons

I'm now ready to add script to my Web page that will pull the product data from each record to create my buttons. First, using VBScript, I need to attach to my database. (Please note: Your script will be different, depending on the type of database you use and the language you script in.)

```
<%
Dim conn
Set conn = Server.CreateObject("ADODB.Connection")
conn.Open "Provider=SQLOLEDB; Data Source = sql.connect.com;
          Initial Catalog = test1; User Id = myname;
          Password = mypassword"
```

After connecting to the database, I need to write a simple SQL query to grab the data for the records and write them to a recordset (RS):

```
SQL_query = "SELECT * FROM candy"
  Set RS = conn.Execute(SQL_query)
```

For each record until the last record, or end of file (EOF), I want to display a row with the product name, short description, and price shown in separate table cells. After displaying each record, I want to close my connection to the database:

```
WHILE NOT RS.EOF
%>
    <tr><td><%=RS("item_name")%></td>
    <td><%=RS("short_desc")%></td>
    <td><%=RS("amount")%></td></tr>
<%
 RS.MoveNext
 WEND
 RS.Close
conn.Close
%>
```

All I've done until now is display a table on a Web page, showing the rows contained in my database table. Now, I want to put an Add to Cart button on each row. To do this, I'm going to substitute the value shown in each button code variable with the string <%=RS("xxx")%>. (In this string, the xxx is replaced with the column name in the SQL table I created.)

For a button without options, the dynamic button code looks like this:

```
<form target="paypal" action="https://www.paypal.com/cgi-
          bin/webscr" method="post">
<input type="hidden" name="cmd" value="_cart">
<input type="hidden" name="add" value="1">
```

```
<input type="hidden" name="business"
          value="yourname@email.com">
<input type="hidden" name="quantity" value="1">
<input type="hidden" name="item_name"
          value="<%=RS("item_name")%>">
<input type="hidden" name="item_number"
          value="<%=RS("item_number")%>">
<input type="hidden" name="amount" value="<%=RS("amount")%>">
<input type="image"
          src="https://www.paypal.com/en_US/i/btn/sc-but-
          03.gif" border="0" name="submit">
</form>
```

Notice that I left some of the values (the business variable that displays the e-mail address, the button image, and so on) hard coded because the values are the same for each button. This puts an Add to Cart button on each row; when a buyer clicks the button, the item is added to the Shopping Cart. See Figure 16-9.

Figure 16-9:
By substituting a little VBScript in place of the value for PayPal button variables, I can dynamically generate buttons for a page that displays a list of products.

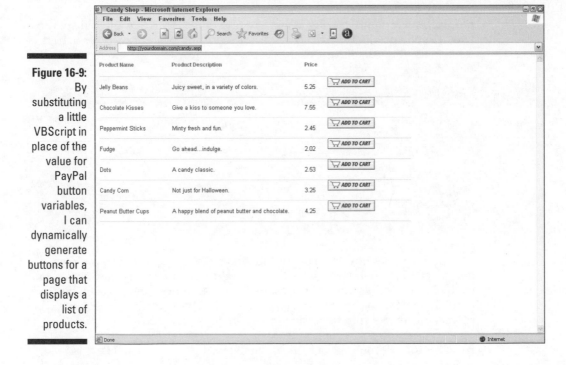

Adding product options

The process of dynamically generating the product options is exactly the same; all you have to do is substitute some script for the button option values and add the options in a cell to the left of the Buy button. See the code shown here, which should be included somewhere between the form tags:

```
<input type="hidden" name="on0" value="<%=RS("on0")%>">
<%=RS("on0")%>:
<select name="os0">
<option value="<%=RS("os01")%>"><%=RS("os01")%>
<option value="<%=RS("os02")%>"><%=RS("os02")%>
<option value="<%=RS("os03")%>"><%=RS("os03")%>
```

Remember to put a table within the `<form></form>` tags and to use a `valign="bottom"` tag in each cell to help with the formatting when you're trying to position the option next to the Add to Cart button.

In the example shown previously, I cheated by using the same number of options, even though I didn't use identical options for each product. With a little more script, you could have a different number of options for each product.

Putting it all together

Taking all the code snippets already mentioned (plus throwing in a little old fashioned HTML formatting), the code for my Web page displaying the products and dynamic buttons looks like this:

```
<html>
<head>
<title>Candy Shop</title>
<style>
.bodytext {font-family: Arial, Helvetica, sans-serif; font-
          size: 13px; color: #000000}
h1 {font-family: Arial; font-size: 12px; font-weight: 700;
          color: #1874A3;}
</style>
</head>
<body>
<table border="0" width="72%" id="table1" cellspacing="0"
          cellpadding="0">
  <tr>
    <td width="165" style="border-bottom-style: solid;
          border-bottom-width: 1px">
    <h1><b>Product Name</b></h3>
    </td>
```

```
    <td width="302" style="border-bottom-style: solid;
          border-bottom-width: 1px">
    <h1><b>Product Description</b></h3>
    </td>
    <td style="border-bottom-style: solid; border-bottom-
          width: 1px">
    <h1><b>Price</b></h3></td>
  </tr>
<%
Dim conn
Set conn = Server.CreateObject("ADODB.Connection")
conn.Open "Provider=SQLOLEDB; Data Source =
          sql2k3.smallbusinessconnect.com; Initial Catalog =
          rosenbo_test1; User Id = rosenbo_vicky1; Password
          = snicky"
SQL_query = "SELECT * FROM candy"
 Set RS = conn.Execute(SQL_query)
 WHILE NOT RS.EOF
%>
    <tr><td width="165" style="border-bottom-style: solid;
          border-bottom-width: 1px"
          class="bodytext"><%=RS("item_name")%></td>
    <td width="302" style="border-bottom-style: solid;
          border-bottom-width: 1px"
          class="bodytext"><%=RS("short_desc")%></td>
    <td style="border-bottom-style: solid; border-bottom-
          width: 1px"
          class="bodytext"><%=RS("amount")%></td>
    <td width="20"></td>
    <td style="border-bottom-style: solid; border-bottom-
          width: 1px" class="bodytext">
<form target="paypal" action="https://www.paypal.com/cgi-
          bin/webscr" method="post">
<table><tr>
 <td style="border-bottom-style: solid; border-bottom-width:
          1px" class="bodytext" valign="bottom">
<input type="hidden" name="cmd" value="_cart">
<input type="hidden" name="add" value="1">
<input type="hidden" name="business"
          value="yourname@email.com">
<input type="hidden" name="quantity" value="1">
<input type="hidden" name="on0" value="<%=RS("on0")%>">
<%=RS("on0")%>:
<select name="os0">
<option value="<%=RS("os01")%>"><%=RS("os01")%>
<option value="<%=RS("os02")%>"><%=RS("os02")%>
<option value="<%=RS("os03")%>"><%=RS("os03")%></td>
<td valign="bottom">
<input type="hidden" name="item_name"
          value="<%=RS("item_name")%>">
<input type="hidden" name="item_number"
          value="<%=RS("item_number")%>">
```

```
<input type="hidden" name="amount" value="<%=RS("amount")%>">
<input type="image"
            src="https://www.paypal.com/en_US/i/btn/sc-but-
            03.gif" border="0" name="submit">
</td></tr></table>
</form>
</td></tr>
<%
 RS.MoveNext
 WEND
 RS.Close
conn.Close
%>
</table>
</body>
</html>
```

Figure 16-10 shows the final result with product options and Add to Cart buttons.

Figure 16-10:
By replacing the values for the product option variables, I can let a buyer select Yellow Jelly Beans before clicking the Add to Cart button. After the product is added to the basket, the View Cart page displays with the product payment details that are submitted to PayPal.

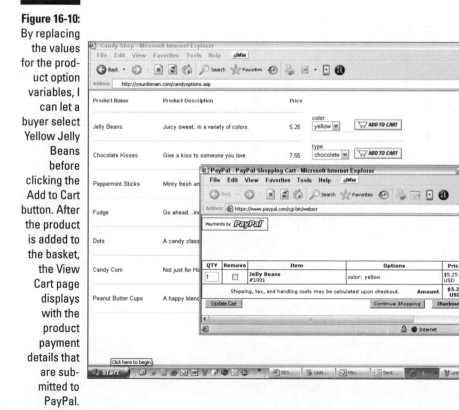

Generating dynamic Add to Cart links

If you want to, you can also dynamically generate Add to Cart links, instead of buttons. The following shows the code for a simple link (that is, no product options are included):

```
<a target="_blank" href=https://www.paypal.com/cgi-
       bin/webscr?&cmd=_cart&add=1&business=yourname%40em
       ail.com&quantity=1&item_name=<%=RS("item_name")%>&
       item_number=<%=RS("item_number")%>&amount=<%=RS("a
       mount")%>&target=paypal>ADD TO CART</a>
```

Chapter 17

PayPal Integration

*I*f you build Web sites using software such as Dreamweaver or FrontPage, there are some cool third-party tools that will add PayPal functionality to the pages you build. PayPal also offers a wizard for merchants who send e-mail with Outlook or Outlook Express and want a quick way to include PayPal buttons. In this chapter, I show you tools that are available for Outlook/Outlook Express, FrontPage, Dreamweaver, Flash, and Adobe GoLive.

If you haven't done so already, try using the PayPal Button Factory at least once to familiarize yourself with the information that needs to be provided with each button. You can get more information on creating buttons through the PayPal Web site in Chapter 14.

The Payment Request Wizard for Microsoft Outlook

When you use PayPal to send a Money Request, PayPal sends an e-mail containing the details of the Money Request and a Pay Now button to the person or company you requested money from. By clicking the Pay Now button, the recipient is taken to the PayPal Payment Details page to complete the transaction.

You can create your own version of an e-mail Money Request. This has the advantage of letting you customize the message sent to the recipient and add branding for your company or organization (instead of having PayPal's branding featured prominently in the e-mail). Before the Payment Request Wizard, you had to create a Buy Now button. (See Chapter 14 for details on how to do this.) Along with the HTML code for the button, PayPal generates a link that can be included in an e-mail. The process is somewhat cumbersome, and the end result (a link in your e-mail message) is not nearly as eye-catching as a PayPal button.

Thanks to the PayPal Payment Request Wizard, you can now create buttons without ever leaving your e-mail program. To take advantage of the wizard, you need to be using Windows 98, 2000, or XP. The wizard works with Outlook 2000, Outlook 2002/XP, and Outlook 2003.

Installing the wizard

To install the wizard for either Outlook or Outlook Express, go to `https://www.paypal.com/outlook`. In the example given next, I download and install the wizard for Outlook. (But the process is the same for Outlook Express.) Here's how:

1. **Click the <u>for Microsoft Outlook</u> link, located on the left side of the page.**

   If you use Outlook Express, click the <u>for Outlook Express</u> link. The File Download window appears.

2. **Click the Save button and save the file to your desktop.**

3. **After the file has finished downloading, make sure the Outlook (or Outlook Express) application is not running and double-click the file icon.**

   The installation program takes you through several steps to install the wizard; just follow the instructions to complete the installation. (See Figure 17-1, which shows the installation wizard.)

   • **During the installation, you need to provide a username (use the e-mail address associated with your PayPal account).**

   • **You also are prompted for a Company Name; if you don't use your PayPal account for a business, just enter your first and last name instead.**

4. **After the wizard has finished installing, open Outlook.**

   The newly installed Payment Request toolbar appears below your other Outlook toolbars. (If you don't see it, select the Toolbars option from the View menu; make sure that the PayPal toolbar is checked.)

After you install the wizard, you can start using the toolbar to generate payment request buttons.

Figure 17-1:
Just follow
the
instructions
shown on
the screen
to complete
the
installation
of the
Payment
Request
Wizard.

Using the wizard

After the wizard is installed, and you open Outlook or Outlook Express, you can use it to send payment requests. Just follow these easy steps:

1. **Click the Payment Request Wizard button on the new PayPal toolbar.**

   The Payment Request Wizard window opens, as shown in Figure 17-2.

2. **Click the Next button.**

3. **Select the type of payment you want to request:**

   - **Basic Payment.** This is the equivalent of requesting money or a Quasi-cash request. In the next step, you are asked to enter your e-mail address, the amount, the currency you want to receive payment in, and what the payment is for.

   - **Request payment for a product.** You are asked to enter your e-mail address; the buyer's e-mail address; the subject header of the e-mail; the buyer's first and last name; whether the buyer should send address information with the payment; the name, ID, and quantity of the product; the product price; shipping and handling costs; the currency; and the total amount to be paid.

- **Request payment for a service.** You are asked to enter your e-mail address; the customer's e-mail address; the subject header of the e-mail; the buyer's first and last name; a description of the service; the amount of payment requested; and the payment currency.

- **Request payment for an auction.** You are asked for your e-mail address; the e-mail address of the winning bidder; the eBay item number; and an optional note. (Unfortunately, eBay is the only type of auction supported by the wizard.)

Figure 17-2:
After installing the wizard, click the Payment Request Wizard button (shown on the left side of the Outlook window, under the standard toolbars). This launches the wizard, which takes you through the steps of inserting a payment button.

- **Request a donation.** You are asked to enter your e-mail address; the donor's e-mail address; the subject header of the e-mail; the donor's first and last name; and for what you are requesting a contribution.

4. **After selecting the type of payment and clicking the Next button, you are asked to enter specific payment details.**

The details depend upon the type of button you're creating (see the previous list for the information you need to provide). If you have default shipping details set up in your PayPal profile, these will be used if you don't enter a shipping and handling amount through the wizard's form.

5. **Select the button you want included in the e-mail.**

   You can select one of the PayPal default Pay Now or Buy Now buttons, enter the URL of an image file you want to use as a button, or enter a line of text that is formatted as a link (instead of using a button within your e-mail).

6. **Always select the Link text option if you send e-mail formatted as plain text.**

   You should also select the Link text option if you're not sure whether the e-mail's recipient can view HTML-formatted e-mail.

7. **After selecting the button or link, click the Next button.**

8. **The payment details display.** You can select the Save Setting option if you want to save the payment details to use as a default for future e-mails. You can click one of the following buttons:

   • **Click the Back button to change the payment details.**

   • **Click the Test button to see the Payment Details page that display when the e-mail recipient clicks the payment button or link incorporated into the e-mail you send.**

   • **Click Cancel to end the wizard without creating a button.**

   • **You can click the Insert button.** A new e-mail opens; the Subject header is filled out and the button or link is inserted into the page (along with a PayPal promotional message, which you can delete if you want). Figure 17-3 shows what the button looks like after being inserted in the e-mail. You can add your e-mail message and address it to the recipient(s).

Removing the wizard

If, after trying the wizard, you run into problems or you find you no longer want to use it, it's pretty easy to uninstall the wizard by going to your Control Panel and clicking the Add/Remove Program icon. Select the PayPal Payment Request Wizard from the list of programs. Click the Remove button and follow the instructions to uninstall the wizard.

Figure 17-3:
After the
PayPal
wizard
inserts the
button or
link into
your e-mail
message,
you can use
your own
text and
format the
e-mail.
When the
button was
first
generated,
the button
was
centered,
but I
changed it
to be left
justified.

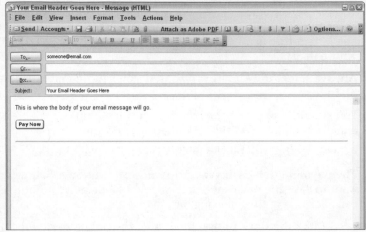

Auction Messenger for FrontPage

Auction Messenger is a software development company that develops
Windows-based applications for eBay auction management. Although most of
their applications are for sale, they do offer a free utility called 1-2-3 PayPal
Website Payments for Microsoft FrontPage. You can download a copy from
the Auction Messenger Web site at www.auctionmessenger.net/paypal/
index.asp.

Installing the 1-2-3 add-in

With the 1-2-3 PayPal tool, you can create PayPal buttons within FrontPage
(as opposed to having to create the buttons on the PayPal Web site and paste
the code into your FrontPage pages). The tool works with FrontPage 2000, XP
(2002), and 2003. To install the utility:

1. **Go to the Auction Messenger site (use the URL shown previously) and click the <u>Free - Download the FrontPage PayPal Website Payments Wizard Now!</u> link.**

   Auction Messenger asks you to make a donation if you use the tool; you can do so by clicking the PayPal Donate button shown at the bottom of the page.

2. **You need to fill out a form, giving your e-mail address, name, title, company, Web site URL, and telephone number.**

   You also need to provide information about whether you, or someone else, is developing your e-commerce Web site. Finally, you need to say whether you're a member of the PayPal Developer Network or have registered for PayPal Shops. (Auction Messenger shares this data with the PayPal Developer Network.)

3. **After filling out the form, click the Download button; then click the <u>Click here to download the FrontPage Payment Button Wizard Now (Windows 2000, 2002 (XP) or 2003)!</u> link, which appears on the next page.**

4. **When the File Download window appears, click the Save button and save the file to your desktop.**

5. **After the file has finished downloading, double-click the fppaypal.exe icon to start the installation process.**

   See Figure 17-4, which shows the installation program. You need to shut down all windows applications — don't forget any virus protection software — before continuing with the installation.

6. **Read the add-in information and then click the Next button.**

   Install the add-in to the location given as the default or click the browse button to save to a new location.

7. **Click the Next button.**

8. **Select the folder for the add-in, click the Next button, and then click the Install button shown on the next screen.**

9. **Click the Finish button and open FrontPage.**

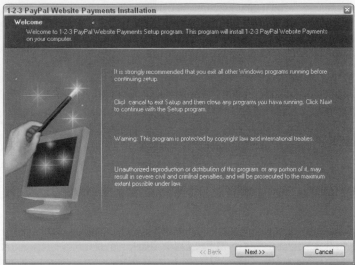

Figure 17-4:
Follow the
instructions
given in the
1-2-3 tool
installation
program to
ensure the
tool is
available
when you
start
FrontPage.

Using the add-in

After the add-in installs, you can open a page in an existing Web site and add a payment button.

1. **After opening the page, click in the place where you want the button or link to insert.**

   Select the PayPal Purchase Button Wizard option from the Insert menu. The 1-2-3 PayPal Website Payments Wizard opens in a new window. (See Figure 17-5 for an example.)

2. **If you already have a PayPal account, click the Start Building Buttons button.**

3. **Enter the e-mail address for your PayPal account and then click one of the tabs shown under the big buttons.**

   These tabs let you create Add to Cart, View Cart, Buy Now, Donations, and Subscriptions buttons.

4. **Select the button image you want to add to your Web page or enter the URL for your own image.**

   Click the Next button. The fields you need to fill out vary according to the type of button you're creating:

   • **Add to Cart:** Enter the name of the item or service; item ID number (if you have one); price of the item and currency; and whether you want to create a text box so the buyer can send you a note, along with payment.

Figure 17-5:
The first screen of the wizard provides you with links to let you sign up for a PayPal account, go to the PayPal Developer Network, and go to pages where you can learn more about Web site payments and auction payments.

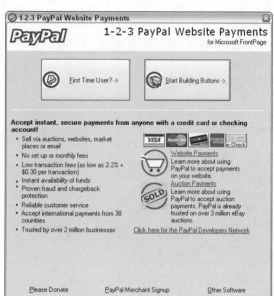

- **View Cart:** After selecting the button, you can use the previous button to make changes, or click the Insert HTML button to add the View Cart button to your Web page.

- **Buy Now:** Enter the name of the item or service; item ID number (if you have one); price of the item and currency; and whether you want to create a text box so the buyer can send you a note, along with payment. Click the Next button. On the next screen, enter the base-shipping price, the price for each additional shipped item, and the handling charge. Click the Next button.

- **Donations:** Enter the name of the donation or service; donation ID number (if you have one); a specific donation amount and currency; and whether you want to create a text box so the buyer can send you a note along with payment. Click the Next button.

- **Subscription:** Enter the name of the subscription, a reference number (if you have one), and the currency. Click the Next button. Enter the amount you charge subscribers and the billing cycle. You select whether to keep charging or to end charges after a certain number of billing cycles. You can also enter a price and duration for a trial billing period. (See Figure 17-6, which shows the fields that need to be filled out in order to create a Subscription button.) Click the Next button.

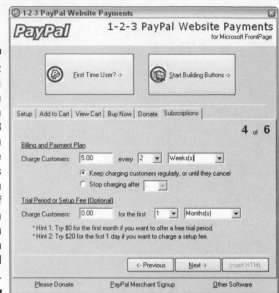

Figure 17-6:
To create a
Subscription
button with
the 1-2-3
add-in, you
enter the
same details
that you
enter if
creating a
subscription
button on
the PayPal
Web site.

5. **After filling out the required fields for specific buttons, enter the URL of the image to display on your custom payment page.**

   You can also enter URLs where the buyer is sent after successful or cancelled payments. Click the next button.

6. **On the final screen, you can click the Previous button to make changes, or click the Insert HTML button to insert the button into your Web page.**

After the button or link inserts into your Web page, you can edit the HTML code as if the button is generated through the PayPal interface. See Chapter 16 for more information on how to do this.

Using Web Assist for Dreamweaver

Web Assist, a company that makes extensions (add-in tools) for Macromedia products, offers a free e-commerce toolkit to enable you to easily add PayPal product support to the Web sites you create with Dreamweaver. Not only can you download the extension for free, but the Web Assist Web site also offers a lot of technical support and code samples to help get you started.

Installing the Web Assist Dreamweaver Extension

It may seem counter-intuitive to go through a checkout process to buy a free tool, but that's what you'll have to do to download the Dreamweaver Extension from the Web Assist Web site. Just follow these steps:

1. **Go to** www.webassist.com/Products/ProductFeatures.asp?PID=18 **and click the Get Now button, found at the upper-right corner of the page.**

2. **Click the Checkout button.**

   On the next page, select the Check Box To Accept Software License option, enter your name and e-mail address, and click the Get Software Now button.

3. **On the Order Receipt page (which is displayed, even though you haven't paid for anything), click the small button (located to the left of the** WA PayPal eCommerce Toolkit **link).**

4. **When the File Download window appears, click the Save button and save the file to your desktop.**

5. **After the file has finished downloading, double-click the fPayPal401.mxp icon to start the installation process.**

6. **The Macromedia Extension Manager window opens; click the Accept button and then click the OK button to install the extension.**

   Before closing the Macromedia Extension Manager window, you can read about the extension before using it.

Using the eCommerce Toolkit with Dreamweaver

Start Dreamweaver and open a Web page to which you want to add the e-commerce button.

1. **Start by clicking in the cell where you want to insert the PayPal button.**

   You can add a button two ways: by using the Insert menu or by clicking the PayPal tab in the insert bar (which is the way I do it in the example shown here).

2. **Select a Buy Now, Add to Cart, View Cart, Subscription, or Donation button by clicking one of the small insert buttons.**

3. **Enter your PayPal e-mail account and click the Next button.**

4. **Choose the button image you want to add to your page (or enter the URL of a custom image) and click the Next button.** (See Figure 17-7, which shows how the Web Assist eCommerce extension integrates with Dreamweaver.)

Figure 17-7: The Web Assist toolkit lets you pick from the PayPal standard Buy Now buttons (or you can use a custom image by entering its location in the form of a URL).

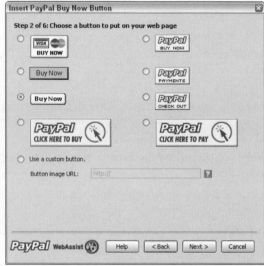

As with the add-in tools for Outlook or FrontPage, the fields you need to fill in depend upon the button you select:

- **Buy Now Button:** You need to provide the following information: item name or service; item ID number; price; currency; an option to let buyers purchase more than one of the item; the base shipping price; the shipping price for each additional item ordered; the handling charges; whether buyers should provide a shipping address; whether buyers can include a note with the payment information; the Web address of your logo image (which is included on a customized payment details page); and the URLs where the user is redirected for successful or cancelled payment.

- **Add to Cart Button:** You need to provide the following information: item name or service; item ID number; price; currency; whether buyers should provide a shipping address; whether buyers can include a note with the payment information; the Web address of your logo image (which is included on a customized payment details page); and the URLs where the user is redirected for successful or cancelled payment.

- **View Cart Button:** After picking the image for the View Cart button, you don't need to provide any additional detail.

- **Subscription Button:** You need to provide the following information: subscription name, a reference ID; the currency; the price to be charged and the length of the billing cycle; whether to charge for a certain number of cycles; the price of the trial period and the length of the trial period; whether to reattempt billing if a payment fails; whether customers should provide a shipping address when making a payment; the URL of your logo image (to be shown on a customized payment details page); and the URLs where the buyer is redirected in the event of a successful payment or a cancelled transaction.

- **Donation Button:** You need to provide the following information: name of the donation or service; an ID number; the currency; whether donors should provide a shipping address when sending in a donation; whether donors can include a note with the donation; the URL of your logo image (to be shown on a customized payment details page); and the URLs where the buyer will be redirected in the event of a successful payment or a cancelled transaction.

5. **After entering all of the button information, review your selections.**

   If you want to make changes, click the Back button. To insert the button into your Web page, click the Finish button.

 For more information about using the Web Assist eCommerce extension, you can download the Web Assist eCommerce Toolkit Recipes. After downloading and installing this extension, you have access to documentation (available from the Web Assist option under the Dreamweaver Help menu). The Recipes toolkit also provides code snippets, which you can add to the e-commerce pages you're building.

To get a copy of the free Recipes toolkit, go to `www.webassist.com/Products/ProductDetails.asp?PID=29` and click the Get Now button (shown in the upper-right corner of the page). Go through the checkout process and install in the same way you installed the Web Assist eCommerce Toolkit.

Using Web Assist for Flash

In addition to the Web Assist eCommerce Toolkit for Dreamweaver, Web Assist also makes an eCommerce snap-in that integrates with Macromedia Flash. The snap-in provides much of the same functionality as the Dreamweaver extension, but you can create a much more dynamic-looking e-commerce site.

Installing the Web Assist Flash snap-in

As with the Dreamweaver Extension from Web Assist, you will need to buy the free Flash snap-in and add to your shopping cart before you can download the file. Here's how:

1. **Go to** www.webassist.com/Products/ProductDetails.asp?PID=24 **and click the Get Now button, found at the upper-right corner of the page.**

2. **Click the Checkout button.**

3. **On the next page, select the Check Box To Accept Software License option and type in your name and e-mail address.**

   After you finish, click the Get Software Now button. The Order Receipt page appears.

4. **Click the small button (located to the left of the <u>WA PayPal eCommerce Snap-ins for Flash MX</u> link).**

   The File Download window appears.

5. **Click the Save button and save the file to your desktop.**

6. **After the file finishes downloading, double-click the PayPalFlash102.mxp icon to start the installation process.**

   The Macromedia Extension Manager window opens.

7. **Click the Accept button and then click OK after the extension installs.**

Using the eCommerce snap-in for Flash

After installing the snap-in, open a product page from your soon-to-be e-commerce Web site. The eCommerce snap-in makes it easy to add PayPal buttons to your product pages:

1. **Open a product page (or any page that you want to add a PayPal button).**

2. **Import an image to use as your Buy Now button and convert it to a movie or symbol.**

   The snap-in offers some standard PayPal buttons you can use if you like. Go to the Common Libraries option and select PayPal buttons to open the PayPal Buttons panel. To add a Buy Now button, drag the button onto the stage in the position where you want the button to be placed.

3. **From the Window menu, select the Components option.** From the Components list, select WA PayPal eCommerce.

4. **If you're adding a Buy Now button to the page, drag the Buy Now object and place it over your Buy Now button.**

   The snap-in object displayed in the upper-left corner of the stage won't show after you publish your movie.

5. **Click the eCommerce snap-in to select it and click the Launch Component Parameters Panel button, which you find in the Property inspector.**

6. **In the Component Parameters window (see Figure 17-8), fill out the information required in each of the tabs:**

   • **General Tab:** Enter your PayPal e-mail account, the URL of your logo (which is featured on the customized Payment Details page), the URL where the user is redirected after paying for the item, and the URL where the user is sent if he or she cancels the transaction before payment completes.

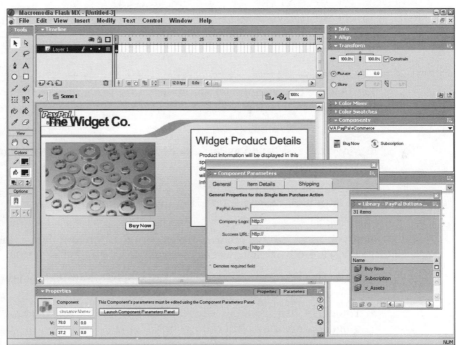

Figure 17-8: By filling out the Flash Component Parameters, you are providing values for the button variables that need to be passed to PayPal.

- **Item Details Tab:** Enter the name of the item, item ID, price of the item, currency, and whether you let a buyer buy more than one of the item.

- **Shipping Tab:** Enter the base shipping price, the extra price for shipping each additional item, the handling charge, whether you want the buyer to provide you with shipping information, and whether buyers can send you a note at the time of purchase.

7. **After entering the PayPal button information, you can publish the movie.**

When a buyer clicks the Buy Now button in your Flash movie, the PayPal Payment Details page opens in the browser window.

PayPal for Adobe GoLive (Transmit Media)

Transmit Media, a Web design and development company, offers a free PayPal eCommerce extension for people who prefer to use Adobe GoLive for designing Web pages. You can download the extension from www.transmitmedia.com/golive/paypal.

1. **Click the Download PayPal Extension button and save the paypal.zip file to your desktop.**

2. **Double-click to unzip the file.**

3. **Move the resulting PayPal folder to the Adobe GoLive\Modules\Extend Scripts folder.**

   The folder on my computer is C:\Program Files\Adobe\Adobe GoLive CS\Modules\Extend Scripts, but may be somewhat different for your installation.

4. **If you have GoLive open, close the application and then relaunch it.** Open a product page, where you want to add a PayPal button.

5. **From the Windows menu, select the Objects palette.** From the Palette Options list, select PayPal E-Commerce.

6. **You can select from the Buy Now, Add to Cart, View Cart, or Subscribe objects.** Drag the object onto your Web page.

   This launches the Insert PayPal Add to Cart Button Wizard, where you can enter specific details about the product or service you're selling. The details you need to enter depend upon the type of button you're adding to the page. See Figure 17-9 for an example.

Figure 17-9:
The eCommerce extension for Adobe GoLive works much like the wizards and snap-ins for FrontPage, Dreamweaver, and Flash. After dragging a button object to your Web page, you need to provide values for the PayPal button variables.

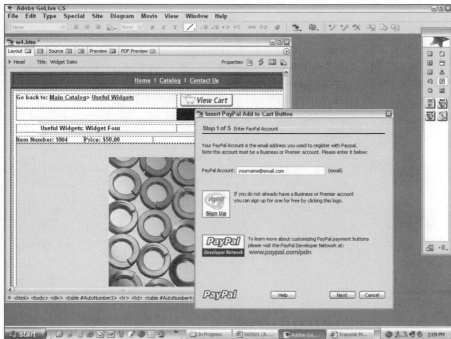

- **Add to Cart:** You need to enter your PayPal account; the button image you want to use; the name of the item or service; the item's ID number; the price of the item and currency to be used; whether a buyer can purchase more than one item; whether the buyer needs to enter a shipping address at the time of purchase; and whether the buyer can leave a note when making payment. You can also enter URLs for your logo image and where the buyer goes either after completing the purchase or canceling the purchase before payment is made.

- **View Cart:** You need to enter your PayPal account and the button image you want to use.

- **Buy Now:** You need to enter your PayPal account; the button image you want to use; the name of the item or service; the item's ID number; the price of the item and currency to be used; and whether a buyer can purchase more than one item. You can also enter the URLs of your logo image and where the buyer can go either after completing the purchase or canceling the purchase before payment is made.

- **Subscribe:** You need to enter your PayPal account; the button image to be used; a subscription name and reference ID; the amount to be charged and the billing cycle; the amount to be charged and the length of the trial period (if you plan on offering one); whether you want to reattempt billing if payment fails for some reason; and whether the buyer needs to provide a shipping address. You can also enter the URLs for your logo image where the buyer will go either after completing the purchase or canceling the purchase before payment is made.

7. **After entering all of the button parameters, click the wizard's Finish button.**

   The button is added to your Web page. After adding a button to one page, the button objects retain data you entered the first time. This makes adding a second (and subsequent) button a very quick process.

8. **Save your Web pages.**

   When the buyer clicks the Add to Cart button, the Cart window opens, just as if you generated the button from the PayPal Web site.

Part VI
PayPal Web Services

The 5th Wave   By Rich Tennant

@RICHTENNANT

"If they solve that, maybe they can help me understand
PayPal's terms of service."

In this part . . .

For developers, this section contains information about PayPal's newly published APIs. I show you how to get an account on the PayPal Developer Central Web site, as well as how to set up your testing environment. Finally, I give you an overview of the APIs you'll be working with.

Chapter 18

The PayPal Sandbox

*U*nless you have access to unlimited funds, you want a way to test the functionality of your applications as you begin developing with PayPal Web Services. Luckily, PayPal Developer Central provides a safe, self-contained testing environment, called the Sandbox, which is similar to the real PayPal world (except for the fact that you won't be paying with real money!).

You can use the Sandbox to test your applications and to learn more about how to work with PayPal APIs. Specifically, the Sandbox can test the following:

✔ Website payments

✔ Shopping Cart purchases

✔ Subscriptions

✔ Refunds

✔ IPNs (Instant Payment Notifications)

Setting Up Testing Accounts

Before you can get access to the PayPal API Sandbox, you need to sign up for a PayPal Developer Central account. This gives you access to

✔ Code samples and reference guides for PayPal APIs

✔ Access to PayPal Developer Forums

✔ Access to the Sandbox test environment, which I cover in this chapter

✔ Information on how to test your PayPal applications

✔ Testing for Instant Payment Notification (IPN)

To sign up for a Developer Central account, go to PayPal Developer Central (`https://developer.paypal.com`) and click the <u>Sign Up Now</u> link. The Sign Up page shown in Figure 18-1 appears. You're asked to provide information about your company and to agree to the PayPal terms of use. The information you need to provide includes

✔ Your e-mail address and password. For security reasons, PayPal recommends that you do not use your regular PayPal user ID and password.

✔ Optional information about your company.

After entering all of the information, click the Sign Up button. PayPal sends you a confirmation e-mail. After you receive the e-mail, click the link to activate your Developer Central account and log on.

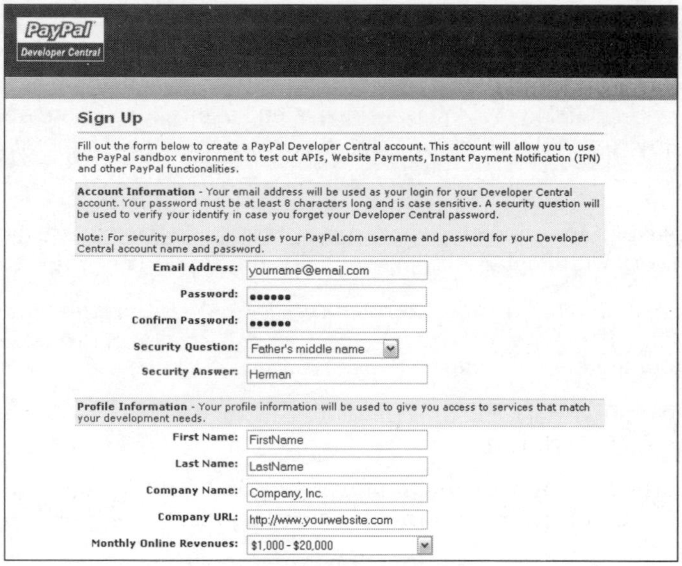

Figure 18-1:
You need to provide information about your company and the reason why you're interested in getting access to PayPal Developer Central when you sign up.

Playing in the Sandbox

Although the Sandbox environment seems a lot like the actual PayPal Web site, there are some important differences between the two, which you need to be aware of:

✔ **Nothing is real.** (I know, I'm being melodramatic, but you need to keep this in mind.) The Sandbox environment contains only fictional PayPal user accounts, bank accounts, credit cards, and transactions. As you move "money" from a test user's bank account to a PayPal account, or transfer money through various transactions, it may seem real but Sandbox cash cannot be used to purchase goods or services in the real world. The converse is also true: You can't transfer funds from a real PayPal account to the Sandbox.

✔ **You should access the Sandbox only through the** `https://developer.paypal.com` **link; you also need to make sure that the PayPal Developer Central logo is shown in the upper-left corner of the page when you sign into your developer account.** If not, you are not in the Sandbox environment!

✔ **When you send an eCheck or transfer funds to or from a real bank account to a PayPal account, there can be a lag of a few days before the funds clear.** This lag is duplicated in some of the Sandbox transactions. As a developer, you need to remember to manually clear (or fail) these transactions, after they take place.

✔ **The users aren't real . . . remember?** This means that their e-mail accounts aren't real either. E-mails that normally are sent to a real user go into a pseudo e-mail box, which you can access in the Sandbox environment.

✔ **This is your chance to be an actor.** All of the test accounts you create are linked to your developer account. If you ever wanted to be an actor, this is your chance, because you have to act the role of each test user you create. You have to log on as a test account user and perform the transactions you want to test against. (More information about how to do this is later in this chapter.)

✔ **The PayPal Sandbox generates credit card and bank account information for you.** Don't make any changes to this information when you create new credit card or bank accounts.

The address of a test user cannot be verified because a test user cannot have a real address.

✔ **Some of the options and features you find on PayPal are not available in the Sandbox environment.** These include:

- Phone number information linked to an account
- The ability to close an account
- The BillPay feature
- Anything points
- Monthly statements

- Shipping preferences
- Fraud checks
- Auction-related tasks
- PayPal shops
- PayPal Seller Protection policy

✔ **If you request an API Certificate for the PayPal production environment (also known as the real world), the request needs to go through a verification process.** If you request an API certificate in the Sandbox environment, it is issued automatically.

✔ **In the real world, PayPal offers technical support and member services if you run into trouble and need help.** These services are not available in the Sandbox environment, but you can ask for help on the PayPal Developer Forum.

Signing up for a personal test account

After logging on, you need to create at least two accounts that you use for testing transactions. You have the option of creating a Personal or Business test account. To get started, click the Sandbox tab, found at the top of the page. (Alternatively, you can also click the big Sandbox button, found to the right of the Developer Central welcome message.) Then, follow these instructions:

1. **Click the <u>Create Account</u> link, found at the top of the Test Accounts box.**

   See Figure 18-2, which shows what the Sandbox screen looks like.

   You see a screen that looks a lot like the PayPal Account sign-up screen, but there are a couple of very important differences: The PayPal Developer Central logo is shown at the upper-left corner of the screen and a "logged in as" message, along with your developer account ID, is shown at the upper-right corner of the page. Make sure you see these two, so you don't sign up for a real PayPal account! See Figure 18-3, which shows the screen you see when creating a test user.

2. **Choose either a Personal or Business test account and a country.**

3. **Click the Continue button.**

4. **Go through the "Account" Sign Up process.**

   Because this is a test account, you shouldn't use any personal information, including your real e-mail address and password! For your *fictional* user, you need to enter the requested information and click the Sign Up button:

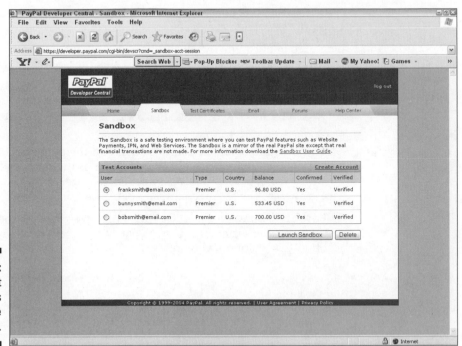

Figure 18-2:
Three test
accounts
in the
Sandbox.

Figure 18-3:
Before you
can start
testing, you
need to
create
at least
two test
accounts.
You need
two because
you transfer
funds from
one account
to the other
during
testing.

5. **The next screen lets you "confirm" the fictitious e-mail account you gave on the previous screen.**

   You need to confirm the e-mail address before the account can start getting payments from other test accounts. Click the Continue button.

   • **Go back to the Developer Central Web site and click the e-mail link.** You should see an e-mail to the e-mail address of the new test account. Click the <u>Activate Your PayPal Account!</u> link shown as the e-mail's subject header.

   • **The "e-mail" opens in a new instance of the browser.** Copy the URL shown in the body of the e-mail and paste it into the browser's address bar. In the Enter Password page, enter the password you assigned to the test account, and click the Confirm button.

   • **PayPal displays an Email Confirmed page.** Now that the account's e-mail address is confirmed, you can start receiving payments from other test accounts you create.

You can access your new account by going back to the main Developer Central screen and clicking the Sandbox tab. Select the new test user account and click the Launch Sandbox button. A Sandbox version of the PayPal welcome page appears and you can log on, using the password you just created.

Remember to write down the e-mail account and password that you created for your test user so you can "log on" to the Sandbox the next time you want to test with this account.

Signing up for a Business test account

The process of signing up for a Business test account is similar to signing up for a Personal test account. Log on to your Developer Central account and click the Sandbox tab, found at the top of the page.

1. **Click the <u>Create Account</u> link.** On the next page, select the Business Account option and the country for the test account. Click the Continue button.

2. **Enter business information for your test account, and click the Continue button.**

3. **Enter additional information for your Business account test user, and click the Sign-up button.**

   Don't enter any information (such as an e-mail address or a password) that pertains to a real PayPal account.

4. **On the next page, click the Continue button.**

You have the chance to enter more business information. Because this is not a real account, just enter anything you like and click the Go to My Account button.

5. **As you did when creating the Personal test account, you need to check your Sandbox e-mail to get the URL that lets you confirm the e-mail address associated with the account.**

A Sandbox version of the PayPal welcome page opens; you can log on using the password you just created for your test user.

Accessing your test account e-mail

When you conduct real transactions with your PayPal account, a lot of e-mail gets generated. You get e-mail when you first sign up for an account, when you get verified, and when you send or receive money.

E-mail is also generated when you are testing with the Sandbox. For you to see the e-mail, PayPal has created a Sandbox version of an e-mail "In Box." You access the test user's e-mail by logging on to your Developer Central account. Here's how:

1. **Click the Email tab.**

This displays the virtual e-mail box, which shows the e-mails that PayPal normally sends to real users. See Figure 18-4 for an example.

Figure 18-4:
It would be confusing if e-mails for your test users were sent to your real e-mail account, so the Sandbox has an Email screen, where you can see the e-mails that would have been sent to an actual user.

2. **You can click the subject header link of a specific e-mail to see the e-mail (which opens in a new instance of the browser).**

Up to 30 e-mails (the newest is at the top of the list) can display for your review.

Adding Funds to Your Testing Account

Right now, no funds are in your test user's PayPal account. Before you can do any testing, you need to link a "bank account" to your test user's e-mail account. After you add a bank account, you can also link a testing "credit card" to your test user's PayPal account.

Linking a bank account

Start by logging on to your Developer Central account, and click the Sandbox tab. Then follow these steps:

1. **Select the test user (if you have more than one) that you want to link a bank account to and click the Launch Sandbox button.**

   A Sandbox version of the PayPal welcome page loads.

2. **Type in the password that you created for your test account user and click the Log In button.**

3. **Click the <u>Add Bank Account</u> link, shown on the left side of the page.**

4. **On the Add U.S. Bank Account screen, enter the name of a fictional bank, whether you want a test checking account or savings account, and then click the Add Bank Account button.**

   The PayPal Sandbox generates the Routing Number and Account Number for you. It's important that you leave these numbers unchanged in order to be able to transfer "funds" from the testing bank account to your testing PayPal account. Figure 18-5 shows the Sandbox version of the Add U.S. Bank Account page.

   The Congratulations! You Have Successfully Added a Bank Account page loads in your browser and instructs you to check your bank balance so that you can enter the two small deposits made by PayPal.

5. **Because you are linking a test bank account in the Sandbox, you can ignore this information and just click the Continue button.**

   You are returned to the Account Overview page for your test account.

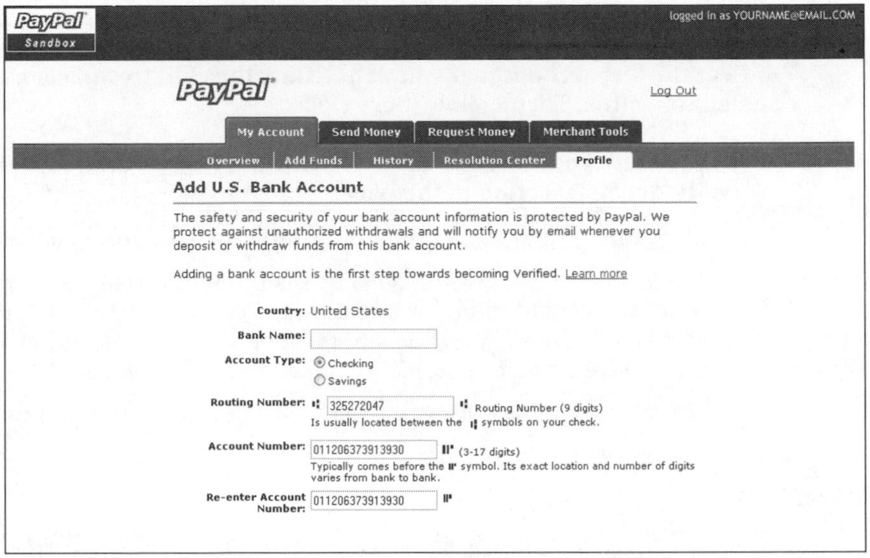

Figure 18-5:
When you
"add" a
bank
account
in the
Sandbox,
the account
and routing
numbers are
generated
for you. If
you want to
be able to
transfer
"funds" from
this account
to your test
PayPal
account,
don't make
any changes
to this
information.

6. **Click the <u>Confirm Bank Account</u> link shown on the left side of the page.**

   The Confirm Your Bank Account page appears. Because this is the Sandbox version, you won't have to enter the two small deposit amounts that you normally would with a real bank account.

7. **Click the Submit button.**

You see a page confirming your bank account and giving you the option to do an instant transfer from your newly-linked bank account to your PayPal account. (The instant transfer is only a Sandbox option, unfortunately . . . transferring from your real bank account to a real PayPal account still takes three to four business days.) In the "Clearing funds transferred into your account" section of this chapter, I show you how the test account can get access to funds right away.

After you link a bank account to your new test account, you need to add a credit card, which the next section covers.

Linking a credit card

You can add a credit card to your test account to fund transactions if there's not enough "money" in the test PayPal account. To link a credit card, start by logging on to your Developer Central account and clicking the Sandbox tab. Select the test account that you want to link the card to and click the Launch Sandbox button. Then, follow these steps:

1. **Log on to your test account and click the <u>Profile</u> link, found under the My Account section of the page.**

2. **Click the <u>Credit Cards</u> link, under the Financial Information column.**

   As shown in Figure 18-6, PayPal opens the Add Credit Card or Debit Card window. Account information for a credit card is already filled out for you. Don't make any changes to this credit card information, or you won't have a "valid" credit card linked to the test account.

3. **Leave the default billing address and click the Add Card button.**

Figure 18-6:
By leaving the credit card information that is filled in for you by the PayPal Sandbox, you can link a "credit card" to your test user account. You are now ready to use your test PayPal account!

(screenshot of the PayPal Sandbox Add Credit Card or Debit Card window)

Clearing funds transferred into your account

If you try to transfer funds from your "bank account" to your test PayPal account, the Add Funds screen indicates that it takes three to four days before the funds are transferred. Because I'm sure you don't want to wait that long before you start developing and testing, you need a way to speed up the process. Luckily, the Sandbox environment lets you speed up the process a little!

1. **Log on to your Developer Central account and click the Sandbox tab, found at the top of the page.**

2. **Select a test user account and click the Launch Sandbox button.**

3. **Log on to the test user account and click the <u>Add Funds</u> link (found under the My Account tab).**

   The Add Funds page loads.

4. **Click the <u>Transfer Funds From a Bank Account in the United States</u> link.**

5. **Select a bank account (if you have more than one listed) and enter the amount you want to be transferred into your testing account.**

   Make sure to transfer $1,000 or more into the test PayPal account. As long as you do your application testing with small payments, these funds should last you quite awhile. (Hey, you can live a little and transfer even more if you want to!)

   The Add Funds confirmation page shows the bank, the account name and number, and the amount. The page warns that it takes three to four days for the funds to clear (but as you soon see, this isn't the case for the Sandbox environment).

6. **Click the Submit button.**

7. **On the You've Added Funds page, click the <u>View the details of this transaction</u> link.**

   This page shows the standard PayPal details of the transfer, along with an expected clearing date. Down at the bottom of the page are two links, which are only available in the Sandbox: <u>Clear Transaction</u> and <u>Fail Transaction</u>.

   I started this chapter by listing some of the differences between the Sandbox and the PayPal production environment. The ability to clear or fail funds is one of the major differences. As a developer, it is your responsibility to either clear or fail the transaction; don't just leave the money waiting to clear (it never will, because the bank doesn't actually exist).

8. **Click either Clear Transaction or Fail Transaction.**

If you click Clear Transaction, the Transaction Details page shows that the money has been transferred into the test PayPal account. If you click Fail Transaction, the Transaction Details page looks as if the funds have been transferred; however, if you go to the Account Overview page, you see that no funds have transferred and the status of the transaction changes from Pending to Failed.

After you create two test accounts and add funds to at least one of them, you're ready to try out the process of sending a payment from one account to the other. As you would expect, the process is much like that of sending money with a real PayPal account.

Sending Money from a Test Account

After logging on to your Developer Central account and launching the Sandbox for one of your test accounts, you can send money. Try this:

1. **Click the Send Money tab, found at the top of the page.**

2. **On the Send Money page, enter the test e-mail account of the recipient.**

   This account needs to be one of the test accounts you created. PayPal lets you send payment to an e-mail address that is not linked to your developer account, but that defeats the purpose of the testing and the transaction has a status of Unclaimed.

3. **Enter the amount and the currency of the payment.**

4. **Enter the type of payment.**

   Unlike PayPal, the Sandbox does not let you send a payment that is connected to an auction, so you're limited to payments for other types of goods, services, or Quasi-cash.

   If you like, you can enter a subject header for the e-mail that is sent to the recipient, along with an e-mail message. Enter a header that is descriptive of the transaction (for example, Payment from Bob Smith). All of the e-mails for your test accounts are listed together and you won't be able to tell one payment from another because all payments are sent from payment@paypal.com.

5. **After entering the information about the payment, click the Continue button.**

   The Check Payment Details page appears. Here you can confirm the details of the transaction. If you want to change the way the test payment is funded, you can click the More Funding Options link. Even if a credit card has been linked to the test account that you're sending the money from, you can only choose to fund the payment from your PayPal balance or an eCheck, drawn against your test bank account.

6. **After selecting whether you want your shipping information included in the payment details, click the Send Money button.**

   PayPal displays the Money Sent confirmation page.

If this payment was being sent from an actual PayPal account, the steps to follow would end after viewing the confirmation page. But because we're working in the Sandbox environment, it's a good idea to check and see whether the transaction completed successfully. Here's how:

1. **Display the Account Overview page of the test account that sent the payment.**

   The transaction should show in the Recent Activity list, with a status of Completed. The amount in the test PayPal account should be reduced by the amount of the payment. From the standpoint of the test sender, the transaction has been completed successfully.

2. **Go back to the Developer Central page and click the Email tab.**

   You should see two new e-mails: one "Receipt for your Payment" e-mail that is sent to the sender and a second one sent to the recipient, which gives details about the payment.

3. **Go back to the Developer Central page and click the Sandbox tab.**

4. **Select the recipient of the money you just sent from the first test account and click the Launch Sandbox button.**

5. **Log on, using the e-mail account and password of the recipient.**

6. **On the Account Overview page, you should see the transaction, with a status of Completed, and the funds in the account should be increased by the amount of the payment, minus the PayPal fee.**

   You can see the fee amount by looking in the far right column of the transaction record.

Requesting Funds from a Test Account

The process of requesting funds from a test account can be manually initiated through the Sandbox interface. Start by logging on to your Developer Central account, selecting one of your test accounts from the Sandbox tab, and clicking the Launch Sandbox button. Then, follow these steps:

1. **Click the Request Money tab, found at the top of the page.**

2. **Enter the e-mail address of the test account you're requesting the payment from.**

   As with the Send Money transaction, the recipient of the e-mail needs to be one of the test accounts linked to your developer account.

    3. Enter the amount you are requesting and the currency.

    4. Select the type of payment (for goods, services, or Quasi-cash).

    5. Enter a descriptive e-mail subject header.

    This header helps you identify this e-mail from others you may already have for other test transactions.

    6. If you want, you can also enter text that displays with the body of the e-mail.

    7. After entering the information, click the Continue button.

    You see a page confirming your request for money. If the details are correct, click the Request Money button.

    8. Click the <u>View the details of this request</u> link.

    You see the details of the request (the status shows as Pending, until the payment is sent). From this page, you have the option of canceling the money request, editing the request (as long as the status remains Pending), sending an e-mail reminder, or returning to your account.

        • You should now confirm recipient of the payment request. Go back to the Developer Central Web page and click the Email tab. You should see two e-mails: one for the test account that requested the payment; and a second for the recipient of the money request.

        • Click the e-mail subject header of the e-mail that was sent to the test account, requesting money from the first test account.

        • The e-mail will open in a new instance of the browser. Because the e-mail has been formatted as plain text, instead of HTML, you won't see a Pay Now button. Instead, you need to copy and paste the URL shown in the body of the e-mail and paste it into your browser's address bar.

        • Log on by entering the password of the second test account and clicking the Continue button. On the Money Request Details page, you can see the details of the payment request. If they are correct, click the Pay button.

        • The funds are taken from money in the test PayPal account (if there are sufficient funds). If not, an eCheck is used to obtain the funds from the bank account of the test account. Click the Send Money button to send the payment.

As with the payment request, you should confirm the payment by checking to ensure that two e-mails have been sent (one from the account sending the money and the other from the account that sent the payment request). The correct amount of funds should be taken from the sender's PayPal account (or an eCheck should be used). The test account that receives the payment should have the correct amount deposited into the PayPal account, minus the PayPal transaction fee.

Testing Sandbox Payments Using Buy Now Buttons and IPN

Creating test accounts and transferring virtual money between them is fun, but the reason for using the Sandbox is to test whether your code works properly. To do that, you need to create a Web product page that includes a Buy Now button. Using one of your test accounts, you'll buy a product by clicking the Buy Now button and completing the transaction on the Sandbox version of the PayPal site.

After the transaction is complete, you can test whether your Instant Payment Notification code is working by checking whether you received the IPN data. (This section of the chapter gives a high-level overview of how the testing process works. For a more in-depth explanation of IPN, see Chapter 17.)

One of the complaints that often shows up in the PayPal Developer Forum is that the IPN script doesn't appear to be working. On closer examination, the problem is that the developer is trying to run IPN (which was set up to work in the Sandbox) with real PayPal user accounts. The converse is also true — you can't use an IPN script which you set up in the real PayPal environment and test it with Sandbox PayPal accounts.

Generating the test button code

Setting up IPN in the Sandbox is similar to setting it up on the PayPal production environment:

1. **Log on to Developer Central with your developer account and click the Sandbox tab.**

2. **Select one of your test accounts and click the Launch Sandbox button. (This test account will act as the merchant.)**

3. **Log on as the test user and click the Merchant Tools tab.**

4. **Click the <u>Buy Now Buttons</u> link (found under the Accepting Website Payments section of the page).**

5. **Use the Selling Single Items form to create the code for a Buy Now button.**

   Chapter 14 provides you with more information if you need help creating the button. If you decide to add additional button options, you can choose to set the URL of the Return and the Cancel pages, but it's not necessary for implementing IPN. If you want to test Payment Data Transfer (see Chapter 19 for details), you need to add these URLs before creating the button.

6. **After the button code generates (see the sample shown here), you can paste this into a product page on your Web site.**

```
<form action="https://www.sandbox.paypal.com/cgi-bin/
       webscr" method="post">
<input type="hidden" name="cmd" value="_xclick">
<input type="hidden" name="business"
       value="bunnysmith@email.com">
<input type="hidden" name="item_name" value="Sandbox
       Widget">
<input type="hidden" name="item_number" value="10030">
<input type="hidden" name="amount" value="20.00">
<input type="hidden" name="no_note" value="1">
<input type="hidden" name="currency_code" value="USD">
<table><tr><td><input type="hidden" name="on0"
       value="Size">Size</td><td><select
       name="os0"><option value="Small">Small<option
       value="Medium">Medium<option
       value="Large">Large<option value="X-Large">X-
       Large</select>
</td></tr></table><input type="image"
       src="https://www.sandbox.paypal.com/en_US/i/btn/
       x-click-but23.gif" border="0" name="submit"
       alt="Make payments with PayPal - it's fast, free
       and secure!">
</form>
```

When you look at the code for the Buy Now button, you notice a couple of differences when compared to the standard button code:

✔ The URL that the button code is posting to is for the Sandbox: `https://www.sandbox.paypal.com/cgi-bin/webscr`

✔ The second difference is that the value passed for the business name is your PayPal test account (not the e-mail address of a real PayPal user).

Creating an IPN script

Chapter 17 shows you in detail how to create an IPN script. Here, I give you just enough information to get you going. You can download one of the PayPal IPN scripts in a number of different languages including ASP.Net/C#, ASP.Net/VB, ASP/VBScript, Cold Fusion, Java/JSP, PERL, and PHP 4.1. Try this:

1. **To download one of PayPal's scripts, log on to your test account in the Sandbox and click the Merchant Tools tab.**

2. **At the bottom of the page, click the <u>Instant Payment Notification</u> link.**

The links shown on the left of the page can help you with your test IPN implementation by giving you a technical overview, letting you download the IPN manual, downloading code samples, giving you information on techniques and testing, and by providing links to additional technical support.

3. **For now, just click the <u>code samples</u> link; select the language you prefer to code in by clicking one of the links shown at the bottom of the page.**

I display the standard ASP/VBScript IPN script here, as an example:

```
<%@LANGUAGE="VBScript"%>
<%
Dim Item_name, Item_number, Payment_status,
        Payment_amount
Dim Txn_id, Receiver_email, Payer_email
Dim objHttp, str
' read post from PayPal system and add 'cmd'
str = Request.Form & "&cmd=_notify-validate"
' post back to PayPal system to validate
set objHttp = Server.CreateObject("Msxml2.ServerXMLHTTP")
' set objHttp =
        Server.CreateObject("Msxml2.ServerXMLHTTP.4.0")
' set objHttp = Server.CreateObject("Microsoft.XMLHTTP")
objHttp.open "POST", "https://www.paypal.com/cgi-
        bin/webscr", false
objHttp.setRequestHeader "Content-type", "application/x-
        www-form-urlencoded"
objHttp.Send str
' assign posted variables to local variables
Item_name = Request.Form("item_name")
Item_number = Request.Form("item_number")
Payment_status = Request.Form("payment_status")
Payment_amount = Request.Form("mc_gross")
Payment_currency = Request.Form("mc_currency")
Txn_id = Request.Form("txn_id")
Receiver_email = Request.Form("receiver_email")
Payer_email = Request.Form("payer_email")
' Check notification validation
if (objHttp.status <> 200 ) then
' HTTP error handling
elseif (objHttp.responseText = "VERIFIED") then
' check that Payment_status=Completed
' check that Txn_id has not been previously processed
' check that Receiver_email is your Primary PayPal email
' check that Payment_amount/Payment_currency are correct
' process payment
elseif (objHttp.responseText = "INVALID") then
' log for manual investigation
else
' error
end if
set objHttp = nothing
%>
```

You need to make one change to work with this code in the sandbox environment. When a buyer clicks the Buy Now button you just created, the Sandbox environment sends an IPN post to a script, located on a page that you specify. This post contains a number of transaction variables, plus a piece of encrypted code. When your page receives the notification, it needs to confirm the IPN by posting all of the data, along with a `"cmd=_notify-validate"` string, back to the PayPal server. PayPal then validates the transaction and returns a response of VERIFIED or INVALID.

When you receive an IPN post from the Sandbox environment, a new variable (`test_ipn`, which should have a value of 1) is sent, along with the standard IPN variables. By returning the test_ipn parameter when you confirm the rest of the post, you're indicating to PayPal that the IPN handler code should be run against the Sandbox environment — not against the real PayPal servers. When you're ready to test your code against the live servers, you just need to remove references to this variable (and make sure that you use the real Buy Now button code on your product pages!).

If you are using the `test_ipn` variable and are still running into problems, try updating the URL that you post back to, from your IPN script. Instead of:

```
objHttp.open "POST", "https://www.paypal.com/cgi-bin/webscr",
          false
```

You should change the string to:

```
objHttp.open "POST", "https://www.sandbox.paypal.com/cgi-
          bin/webscr", false
```

And try testing again!

Setting up IPN

After you add the test button code to a Web page and write your IPN test script, you need to set up IPN in the Sandbox. Start by logging back on to your test account (if you logged out previously), and click the <u>Profile</u> link, found under the My Account tab.

1. **Click the <u>Instant Payment Notification Preferences</u> link, found under the Selling Preferences column.**

2. **On the Instant Payment Notification Preferences page, click the Edit button.**

3. **Check the Instant Payment Notification check box and enter the URL for your test IPN handler code.**

4. **Click the Save button.**

You're ready to test your IPN code (see the following section for the steps you need to follow).

Testing IPN in the Sandbox

Start by going to the product page you created with the Sandbox version of the Buy Now button, then follow these steps:

1. **Click the Buy Now button.**

   You should be redirected to a PayPal Payment page *on the Sandbox.* (You need to confirm this by looking at the top of the screen — look for the PayPal Sandbox logo and a "Logged in as" message, followed by your PayPal Developer account. See Figure 18-7, which shows what the Sandbox version of the payment page looks like.)

Figure 18-7: Confirming that you're in the Sandbox environment when you first start testing IPN is very important!

PayPal Sandbox	logged in as YOURNAME@EMAIL.COM

Payments by **PayPal**

bunnysmith@email.com

Checkout   Secure Transaction 🔒

PayPal is the secure payment processor for your seller, **bunnysmith@email.com**. To continue, please enter the required information below. Learn more about PayPal.

Pay To: bunnysmith@email.com
Payment For: Sandbox Widget
Size: Small
Currency: U.S. Dollars
Amount: $20.00 USD
Shipping & Handling: $0.00 USD
Total Amount: $20.00 USD

If you do not currently have a PayPal account   [Click Here]

PayPal Login
Email Address: bobsmith@email.com
PayPal Password:

Forget your password?
Problems logging in?

2. **The PayPal address of your test seller appears at the top of the page.**
   You need to log on with one of your other test accounts, who serve as the buyer.

3. **Finishing paying for the test product.**

   It's now time to see whether everything worked as expected:

   • Make sure that the funds have been subtracted from the buyer's account.

- Log on as the seller and make sure the funds have been properly added to the seller's account.

- Testing whether IPN worked depends upon the functionality you added to your IPN script. You can add code that sends you an e-mail containing the IPN post results (or you can work with one of the Web sites that test IPN to see whether the basic code is working, before you add code to IPN to update a test product database). Chapter 17 contains a number of suggestions that you can implement to help with the testing process.

Requesting an API Certificate

After you get IPN and PDT to work, you're ready to begin working with PayPal APIs. But before you can make test calls, you need to obtain a test API Certificate from PayPal. Start by logging on to Developer Central with your developer account and clicking the Sandbox tab at the top of the page.

1. **Select one of your test accounts to be the seller.**

   Before you can apply for the test certificate, the account needs to be verified (that is, it needs to have a test bank account linked to the PayPal account).

2. **Log on to the test account and click the <u>Profile</u> link, found under the My Account section of the site.**

3. **Under the Account Information column, click the <u>API Access</u> link.**

4. **On the API Access page, click the <u>API Certificate Request</u> link, found in the middle of the page.**

5. **Fill in the fields on the application page (which can be seen in Figure 18-8).**

   These include:

   - The first and last name of your test account owner.

   - A fictitious company and department.

   - Anticipated online sales volume and expected use.

   - If you were applying for a real API certificate, you would need to provide an API account name (in the form of an e-mail address) and password. In the Sandbox environment, PayPal provides you the API account name, but you should add a password.

   - You need to agree to the terms of use and click the Continue button.

6. **On the API Certificate Request Review page, you have the opportunity to review the details of your request.**

   If everything is correct, click the Generate Certificate button.

Figure 18-8:
When
applying for
an API
Certificate
in the
Sandbox,
you are
provided
with an
e-mail
account
name, but
you need to
supply the
password.

7. **On the API Certificate page, click the Download button to download your certificate.**

   The File Download window prompts you to open or save the file. Click the Save button and save the `cert_key_pem.txt` file to your desktop. Certificates are made available immediately after the request is submitted in the Sandbox. When you apply for a real PayPal certificate, PayPal needs to verify your application before the certificate is issued.

   If you choose not to download your certificate immediately after generation (as you did in the previous step), you can download the certificate one of two ways:

   • Go back to Developer Central and click the Test Certificates tab, shown at the top of the page. Select the test account you used to generate the certificate, click the Download button, and save your certificate.

   • You can also go back to Developer Central and click the Email tab. Select the e-mail with the subject header "Your New API Certificate Request Confirmation." Copy the URL shown in the e-mail message and paste it into your browser's address bar. Log on as the test user and click the API Access link (found on the account Profile page). On the next page, click the API Certificate Information link. This takes you to a page where you can download the certificate.

The certificate needs to be renamed and then encrypted before you can use it. See Chapter 20 for more information about converting the certificate.

Chapter 19

Integrating PayPal Transactions into Your Site

*I*f you already have a catalog Web site that offers product information but cannot process orders, you may be ready to take the next step. Not only do you want to add shopping cart buttons to your Web site (see Chapter 16), you want to control the customer experience and track online sales using your database.

PayPal helps you do all this (and more) with a couple of technologies developed specifically for Web designers and developers: *Payment Data Transfer* (PDT) and *Instant Payment Notification* (IPN). In this chapter, I show you what these technologies can do for your site and how to implement them.

PDT's main function is to send data back to your Web site as soon as your customer has gone through the payment process. Among other uses, PDT data can be used to create a dynamic receipt page. IPN also sends data back to your Web site and gives the status of a payment (pending, completed, and so on) along with payment data that you can use to update your product database with transaction (customer and sale) information. Table 19-1 lists the differences between PDT and IPN.

Table 19-1	Differences between PDT and IPN	
Feature	PDT	IPN
Payment notification	Customer is immediately returned to your site and payment notification occurs immediately.	Happens whenever there is a change in payment status (payment status can be pending, completed, reversed, or refunded).
Trigger for process	Initiated by the actions of the merchant.	Initiated by PayPal because of change in payment status.
Primary function	Display payment transaction details to a buyer (but can also be used for updating a database or sending e-mail notifications).	Writing data to database (but can also be used for e-mail notifications). Because IPN lets you know when payment actually occurs (for example, after an eCheck clears), you can use IPN data as part of your fulfillment system.
Requirements	Auto Return must be enabled in your PayPal profile; special code needed to take advantage of data.	Special code needed to take advantage of data.
Possible problems	If the buyer closes the browser window before returning to your site, PDT data will not be sent to you.	Although usually a quick process, under special circumstances, IPN data can take hours to be returned to you.
Type of Data	A transaction token is passed to the URL of your return page; you can then use HTTP POST to request transaction details.	All payment data is sent to the URL you specify, you are required to authenticate the transaction data.

Don't worry if you're a little fuzzy about the differences between the two; the picture should get clearer as you read the information in the rest of this chapter.

Enabling Payment Data Transfer

Payment Data Transfer (which I call PDT for the remainder of the chapter) is transaction information that is sent to a URL you specify, as soon as the customer completes the payment process. You can use this data in any way: displaying transaction details to the customer or updating your product database with the transaction information.

It's important to remember that there can be a difference between when the customer makes a payment (triggering the PDT process) and when you actually get the money (which is what IPN tells you). While you may want to record a "sale" using the PDT data, fulfillment shouldn't be completed until after you get IPN notification. (Or, to put it another way, don't mail the product until the eCheck clears!)

Because you don't get PDT data until the sale is complete and the customer returns to your Web site, you need to set up Auto Return to enable PDT.

Enabling Auto Return

Even if you don't plan on using PDT, setting up Auto Return is a good idea when you're selling products through your Web site:

- **Auto Return lets you better control the customer experience.** By sending buyers back to your Web site after payment completion, you reinforce your company branding (instead of PayPal branding), which makes it more likely that customers will buy again from you.

- **Auto Return reduces the number of screens the user must go through to complete the PayPal payment process.** Because users don't like clicking through screen after screen just to make a purchase, Auto Return helps to improve overall customer satisfaction.

- **In addition to specifying which page customers go to after a successful sale, you can specify a page where customers can go if they cancel the purchase before payment is completed.** This gives you a page to convince them to complete the sale (or put up a feedback form to try to learn why the user didn't want to go through with the purchase).

To set up the PayPal Auto Return feature, start by logging on to your PayPal account. Here's how:

1. **Click the <u>Profile</u> link, found under the My Account section of the PayPal site.**

2. **Click the <u>Website Payment Preferences</u> link, which is located in the Selling Preferences column.**

3. **Under the Auto Return for Website Payments section of the page, make sure that the Auto Return "On" option is selected.**

   Figure 19-1 shows an example of the Website Payment Preferences page.

4. **Enter the URL that you want to use as your Return URL.**

   This URL is the Web page on your site that contains the code to process the PDT transaction token that is sent to you after the buyer completes a purchase. If you do not supply a valid Return URL (in the form of `http://www.YourSiteHere.com/YourPageWithCode.xxx`, where the `xxx` is replaced with an extension of `cgi`, `asp`, `aspx`, `php`, and so on), then PayPal sends the user to the standard Payment Done page.

   - The PayPal User Agreement requires you to supply content on your Return URL page that makes it clear to the user that they paid for the item and completed the transaction.

   - You also need to let the buyer know that transaction details are sent to them via e-mail. This is done automatically by PayPal so you're not required to send the e-mail receipt.

5. **Under the Payment Data Transfer section of the page, make sure to select the "On" option.**

   You also see a string of characters, which is your Identity Token. Copy and save this string somewhere accessible; you'll need it later, when you write the code for your Return URL page.

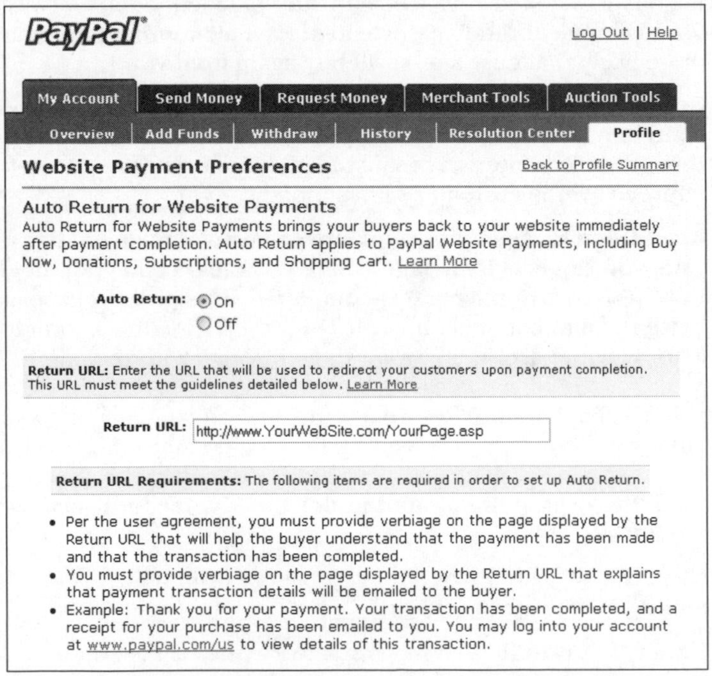

Figure 19-1: Setting the Return URL and Payment Data Transfer options on the Website Payment Preferences page are the first steps in implementing PDT successfully.

You can choose whether to leave the Account Optional feature on, which is the default setting. Account Optional lets a buyer purchase with a credit card, even if the buyer doesn't have a PayPal account. If the Account Optional feature is on, it has the potential to interfere with the PDT process. Buyers without PayPal accounts are given the option of returning to your site after paying (as opposed to returning automatically). If the buyer chooses not to return, then the PDT process will not be initiated.

6. **You can also set options for encrypting Web site payments and whether customers should include a contact number with their payment details.**

7. **After setting these options, click the Save button to save your Web site preferences.**

Although you haven't written the code for the Return URL page yet, jump ahead a moment to see what the customer experience is like after you enable PDT.

What happens when the customer pays?

At the most basic level, the PDT process starts with the customer clicking a button on your Web site, getting redirected to the PayPal Web site to make a payment, and being redirected a last time back to your Web site after the payment completes. The following steps provide a little more detail:

1. **Your site:** The customer clicks a Buy Now or Add to Cart button for a product displayed on your Web site.

2. **PayPal's site:** The customer is redirected from your site to the PayPal Payment Details page and fills out the payment details form.

3. **PayPal's site:** The customer is sent to a payment confirmation page and clicks the Pay button.

4. **PayPal's site:** A payment confirmation page lets the customer know the payment is complete. The customer is automatically redirected back to your site (or has the option of clicking a link to go back to your site without waiting).

5. **Your site:** The customer sees a page that confirms the purchase and reminds the customer that a receipt is coming in the mail. If you implement PDT, you can also choose to display detailed transaction information to your customer.

Now that you understand what the customer experiences, you're ready to "look behind the curtain" and see what happens when PDT is implemented.

The PDT process

After the payment process completes, the buyer is redirected back to your Web site to the Return URL you specified. During this redirection, a transaction token is passed, along with a number of parameters and a GET request header, which activates code you added to the Return Page.

Table 19-2 shows the parameters that get passed.

Table 19-2	Variables Specific to PDT	
Variable	*Description*	*Example*
tx	The transaction token, which you POST back to PayPal	tx=87P92385RE123456
st	The status of the transaction	st=Completed
amt	The amount paid for the item	amt=5.50
cc	The currency the amount was paid in (see previous variable)	cc=USD
cm	A custom message (usually left blank)	cm=

The code on your page needs to construct an HTTP POST response which is sent to https://www.paypal.com/cgi-bin/webscr. Your string needs to include the following:

- ✔ The transaction token sent by PayPal

- ✔ The identity token you were given after you enabled PDT

- ✔ A variable named cmd with a value of _notify-synch (for example, cmd=_notify-synch)

PayPal sends a response to your post with the word SUCCESS or FAIL displayed in the first line of the response. If the response is successful, the body of the response will provide the details of the transaction. Each of the details are displayed on a separate line, formatted as name=value pairs.

An example of a successful response looks like the following:

```
SUCCESS
first_name=Betty
last_name=Franklin
payment_status=Completed
payer_email=bettyfranklin@email.com
payment_gross=5.50
mc_currency=USD
```

Additional transaction details display in a similar fashion. The PayPal PDT response can be parsed and displayed on your Web page or written to a database.

Sample code

A great deal of help for implementing PDT is available on the PayPal Web site. Go to https://www.paypal.com/us/cgi-bin/webscr?cmd=p/xcl/rec/pdt-intro. The links on the left side of the page can take you to a technical overview of the PDT process, let you download the PayPal Integration Guide for developers (which includes a section on PDT), or let you download code samples. These are available for the following environments: ASP/VBScript, Cold Fusion, PERL, and PHP.

The following code is the ASP/VBScript sample, available from the PayPal Web site (I added comments, shown in bold to help you understand what the code is doing):

```
<%@LANGUAGE="VBScript"%>
<%


' declare your variables
Dim authToken, txToken
Dim query
Dim objHttp
Dim sQuerystring
Dim sParts, iParts, aParts
Dim sResults, sKey, sValue
Dim i, result
Dim firstName, lastName, itemName, mcGross, mcCurrency

' set the value of the authentication token assigned to you
          by PayPal
authToken = "Dc7P6fOZadXW-U1X8oxf8_vUKO9EHBMD7_53IiTT-
          CfTpfzkNOnipFKUPYy"

' retrieve the transaction token sent by PayPal
txToken = Request.Querystring("tx")

' POST your response which should contain the cmd variable
          along with the authentication and transaction
          tokens
query = "cmd=_notify-synch&tx=" & txToken &
"&at=" & authToken
set objHttp = Server.CreateObject("Microsoft.XMLHTTP")
objHttp.open "POST", "http://www.paypal.com/cgi-bin/webscr",
          false
objHttp.setRequestHeader "Content-type", "application/x-www-
          form-urlencoded"
objHttp.Send query
```

```
' retrieve the response to your POST
sQuerystring = objHttp.responseText

' if the response is SUCCESS then parse the remainder of the
            response for the transaction details
If Mid(sQuerystring,1,7) = "SUCCESS" Then
sQuerystring = Mid(sQuerystring,9)
sParts = Split(sQuerystring, vbLf)
iParts = UBound(sParts) - 1
ReDim sResults(iParts, 1)
For i = 0 To iParts
aParts = Split(sParts(i), "=")
sKey = aParts(0)
sValue = aParts(1)
sResults(i, 0) = sKey
sResults(i, 1) = sValue

Select Case sKey
Case "first_name"
firstName = sValue
Case "last_name"
lastName = sValue
Case "item_name"
itemName = sValue
Case "mc_gross"
mcGross = sValue
Case "mc_currency"
mcCurrency = sValue
End Select
Next

' format and present transaction confirmation to your buyer
' you can also write the transaction data to a database
            although that has not been included with this
            sample script
Response.Write("<p><h3>Your order has been
            received.</h3></p>")
Response.Write("<b>Details</b><br>")
Response.Write("<li>Name: " & firstName & " " & lastName &
            "</li>")
Response.Write("<li>Description: " & itemName & "</li>")
Response.Write("<li>Amount: " & mcCurrency & " " & mcGross &
            "</li>")
Response.Write("<hr>")
Else
' if the response to your POST request is ERROR then show an
            error message to the buyer
Response.Write("ERROR")
End If

%>
```

After getting a successful response, PayPal recommends you display the shipping address, buyer PayPal account e-mail, and the amount paid on the thank you page you show to the buyer.

When you receive a successful response, you should also check some of the PDT variables against data stored in your database. Specifically, you should check the following to make sure you're not being scammed:

- ✔ **Is the transaction ID a duplicate?** A duplicate means someone is trying to get you to send a product for a transaction that has already been paid for and fulfilled. (You don't want to send a product when you haven't received an actual payment!)

- ✔ **Has the payment sent to your PayPal account instead of the e-mail address associated with someone else's PayPal account?**

- ✔ **Are other transaction details (for example, the price of the item and number of items purchased) correct?**

When PDT fails

There may be several reasons why PDT doesn't return a successful response. The problem can result from a network error. (In this case, you can try reposting back to PayPal to determine if this was the case.) If the second try also fails, PayPal recommends that you look to see if there was a problem with your code. If you are having problems getting the code to work, several resources can help you.

PayPal Developer Central

`https://developer.paypal.com` is great place to ask for help. After signing up for a free developer account, you can post questions to the Developer's forum. Some of the forum participants are PayPal Evangelists (no really — that's their job title), and they can be very helpful when you experience a tough problem.

PayPalDev.org

Another good resource for help with PDT is `PayPalDev.org`. They have a forum focused specifically on PDT and IPN issues, organized by development environment. See Figure 19-2, which shows the home page of PayPalDev.org.

PayPalTech.com

`http://paypaltech.com` is like a cookbook for PayPal developers. You get sample code, instructions, demos, and links to other resources. The site offers a cool little PDT generator app (click the <u>PDT Generator</u> link, found on PayPalTech's home page). If you enter your authentication token and the language you want to use, the site generates the PDT code for you. You can also see working examples of PDT by going to `http://paypaltech.com/how-to/pdt`.

After you enable PDT, you may also want to implement IPN. If PDT lets you know when an item is purchased, IPN was created to integrate with your Web site's back-office operations and tracks the payment status of your sales.

Figure 19-2:
PayPalDev's
Developer
Support
Forums offer
help on a
variety of
develop-
ment topics.
If you're
struggling to
get PDT or
IPN to work,
you have a
good
chance
getting help
here.
Although
PayPalDev.
org is an
independent
forum (not
affiliated
with PayPal),
you'll find
that PayPal
support
personnel
are often
forum
participants.

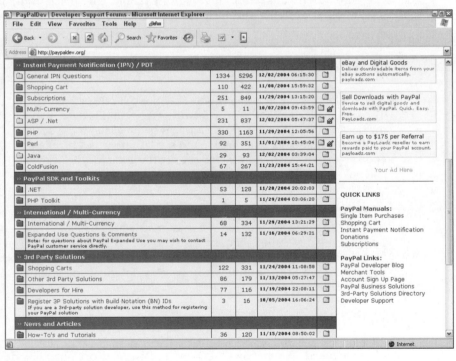

Setting Up Instant Payment Notification (IPN)

When you're trying to wrap your head around the differences between PDT and Instant Payment Notification (which I call IPN for the rest of this chapter), it helps to remember this: IPN is not triggered by a user event (that is, a purchase) but by a change in payment status. An IPN can occur at any time (for example, it could be days between the time a purchase is made and when an eCheck clears — which is when you actually are paid). As a general rule of thumb, if you use an automated process for fulfillment, you should set it up so the product won't be shipped until the IPN has updated your database to show the product is paid for.

This is just *theory*. In the real world, it may not always work out this way. If you sell digital goods or products, customers generally expect delivery as soon as the purchase completes. You either redirect the customer to a download page after the payment process completes, or you generate an e-mail that is sent to the customer containing a link to enable download of the product. Because you have no way of knowing when IPN will occur, you'll probably want delivery to be triggered by the PDT. In these cases, you should set up PayPal payment receiving preferences to block all eCheck payments. This keeps people from downloading the product before you are paid.

Because IPN gives you notification and authentication of PayPal payments, it can be used for a variety of purposes, including:

- ✔ Saving customer and transaction data to your own database
- ✔ Tracking affiliate sales
- ✔ Automating part (or in the case of digital products, all) of your fulfillment operations
- ✔ Sending e-mail confirmations (for example, sending an e-mail when the product is shipped) to your customers

The IPN process

When a customer purchases an item (or when there is a change in the payment status of a transaction), PayPal sends a post to a page you specified. This post contains a number of transaction variables, plus a piece of encrypted code. When your page receives the notification, it needs to confirm the IPN by posting all of the data, along with a `cmd=_notify-validate` string, back to PayPal's secure server. PayPal then validates the transaction and returns a response of either VERIFIED or INVALID.

If you receive a VERIFIED response, you still need to perform certain security checks (to make sure the order is valid) and then update your database with the transaction data.

If you receive an INVALID response, you need to do more research to determine if there's a problem with the transaction (or a problem with your IPN handler code).

Setting up IPN

Unlike PDT, IPN doesn't require that you set up Auto Return in your Website Preferences (because the IPN process is not always tied into a buyer's completion of a payment). Instead, you specify a URL that contains your IPN code. When PayPal needs to inform you of a change in payment status, it posts a notification to the URL you specified.

To set up IPN, you need to log on to your PayPal account and click the Profile link (found under the My Account section of the site). Try this:

1. **Click the Instant Payment Notification Preferences link, which you find under the Selling Preferences column.**

2. **Click the Edit button and enter the URL of a Web page that contains code you wrote to handle the IPN.**

   See Figure 19-3 for an example of the Instant Payment Notification Preferences setup page. This page is only designed to handle the IPN posts — your customers never see this page.

3. **Click the Save button.**

You can set up IPN through the PayPal interface (as described previously) but you can also set up IPN from within the Buy Now and Add to Cart button code that you write. Two variables (rm and notify_url) control the behavior of the Return URL and what that Return URL will be:

rm: Specifies how the buyer is sent back to the Return URL. If set to 1, the return uses a GET method. If set to 2, the return uses a POST method, which is what we need for IPN.

notify_url: Specifies the location of your script (the Return URL).

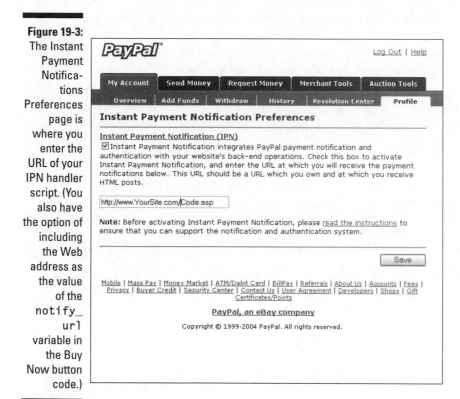

So to implement IPN, you need to add the following two lines to your button code:

```
<input type="hidden" name="rm" value="2">
<input type="hidden" name="notify_url"
        value="http://www.yourwebsite.com/yourcode.asp">
```

After setting up IPN (whether through PayPal or your button code), you're ready to write the code that manages the IPN notification.

IPN handler code

The code that resides on your server to respond to the IPN has several functions, in this order:

1. **Construct an HTTP** POST, **which is sent to** `https://www.paypal.com/cgi-bin/webscr`.

2. **The post-back (the message you send back to PayPal) needs to contain all of the form variables, exactly as they were received from the IPN.**

   IPN only returns variables for which it has information. It won't return subscription variables unless you're selling subscriptions.

3. **After the last variable, you need to append a** `cmd=_notify-validate` **string.**

Although you can write your own code from scratch, PayPal recommends starting with some of the sample code available from the PayPal Web site. Code samples are available for the following environments: ASP.Net/C#, ASP.Net/VB, ASP/VBScript, Cold Fusion, Java/JSP, PERL, and PHP. Go to `https://www.paypal.com/ipn` and click the <u>Code Samples</u> link, shown on the left side of the page.

The following code is the ASP/VBScript sample, available from the PayPal Web site. (In addition to the comments already added by PayPal, I add some of my own to help you understand what the code is doing.) Comments are shown in bold:

```
<%@LANGUAGE="VBScript"%>
<%
' declare a variable for each variable in the IPN
Dim Item_name, Item_number, Payment_status, Payment_amount
Dim Txn_id, Receiver_email, Payer_email
Dim objHttp, str

' read post from PayPal system and add 'cmd=_notify-validate'
str = Request.Form & "&cmd=_notify-validate"

' post back to PayPal system to validate
set objHttp = Server.CreateObject("Msxml2.ServerXMLHTTP")
objHttp.open "POST", "https://www.paypal.com/cgi-bin/webscr",
            false
objHttp.setRequestHeader "Content-type", "application/x-www-
            form-urlencoded"
objHttp.Send str

' assign posted variables to local variables
Item_name = Request.Form("item_name")
Item_number = Request.Form("item_number")
Payment_status = Request.Form("payment_status")
Payment_amount = Request.Form("mc_gross")
Payment_currency = Request.Form("mc_currency")
Txn_id = Request.Form("txn_id")
Receiver_email = Request.Form("receiver_email")
Payer_email = Request.Form("payer_email")
```

```
' Check notification validation
if (objHttp.status <> 200 ) then
' write an error message for HTTP handling
elseif (objHttp.responseText = "VERIFIED") then
' perform a series of additional checks as described below
elseif (objHttp.responseText = "INVALID") then
' write an error message and start trouble shooting
else
' error
end if
set objHttp = nothing
%>
```

The code itself is pretty straightforward, but can get lengthy because of the number of variables involved especially if the transaction was for a product with a number of options or for a subscription. (Later in this chapter, I list some of the more common variables in a table.)

You may wonder why you need to send a POSTback to PayPal for validation when all of the transaction information is passed in the IPN itself. Sending the data back to PayPal for validation is one way to know that the IPN actually came from PayPal and not from a hacker. Even after PayPal validates your post-back, you need to perform a few additional checks yourself to ensure the transaction is valid before you process the payment. Try this:

- ✔ **Write code to check whether the** Payment_status=Completed **before taking action on an order.** Unlike PDT, which lets you know when a purchase completes, an IPN is generated when there's a change in payment status.

- ✔ **Make sure that the transaction ID (**Txn_id**) has not already been processed.** In other words, make sure the order is actually a new order, not a spoof of an old order that has already been processed.

- ✔ **Make sure that the** Receiver_email **is actually your Primary PayPal e-mail account.** Do this to make sure that the payment is going to you.

- ✔ **You will also need to check whether the payment amount and currency match those in your product database.**

You received an invalid IPN response

There are a number of reasons why you may get an INVALID response to your post-back. The IPN may not have come from PayPal in the first place, or (more likely) PayPal may have changed one of the transaction's variables or there could be a problem with your code.

If IPN has been working like a charm and then breaks, the problem is likely on PayPal's end. You can try to get more information from a number of places about what the problem could be, including these:

✔ PayPal's Developer Network (https://developer.paypal.com)

✔ PayPalDev.org (www.paypaldev.org)

✔ The "What's New" section of the PayPal Web site (Log on to http://www.paypal.com and look at the column on the left side of the home page.)

✔ PayPalTech (www.paypaltech.com) (Scroll to the bottom of the home page where you can find a number of PayPal announcements.)

✔ The PayPalIPN (www.paypalipn.com) home page lists changes in the PayPal IPN service.

✔ The PayPal Developer Network Blog (http://paypal.typepad.com). This is a great place to go to read PayPal announcements, learn about scheduled network outages, and so on. You can also find out about the PayPal and eBay Developers Conference.

After doing a little research on the sites listed, it may be time to wonder if there's a problem in your code (especially if you've never gotten IPN to work properly).

The problem <sob!> is your code

Although the sample IPN code is pretty easy to follow, a quick glance through the PayPal Developer Forums shows you that a lot of people have a hard time getting IPN to work properly. You're not alone!

Sometimes the problem is with the way you're passing back variables. There may be times when the problem isn't really with your code, but with your ISP! (Some ISPs have firewalls that prevent external sites, such as PayPal, from running scripts on the server.) If you're tearing out your hair trying to get the sample code from the PayPal Web site to work for you, here are some tips that may save you hours of grief (and the rest of your hair!).

Try a different script

PayPal provides some good "starter" IPN scripts, but there are a lot of other freeware scripts you can try (and some that you can purchase for a small fee). Places to try include

✔ www.paypaltech.com: In addition to their PDT generator, they offer an IPN generator. You can choose from the following scripts:

- PERL – IPN and password management: Send variables in a simple e-mail or display variables in a simple HTML page.

- PHP: Write variables to a MySQL database, send a raw IPN post e-mail, send a customized e-mail to a buyer, or display variables in a simple HTML page.

- ASP: Send a raw IPN post e-mail, send a customized e-mail to a buyer, or display variables in a simple HTML page.

- Cold Fusion: Write variables to a text file or send a custom e-mail to a buyer.

✔ The PayPal Web site lists a number of third-party IPN support resources (`www.paypal.com/cgi-bin/webscr?cmd=p/pdn/3p-solutions-ipntools-outside`). A number of these resources provide instructions and IPN code samples.

✔ The PayPalIPN Forum is (as you may have guessed) a forum that covers IPN issues. A page on the site provides links to a number of scripts: `www.paypalipn.com/scripts.html`.

Get testing help

There are a number of sites that let you enter a series of variables, the URL of your IPN script, and let you know if your script is working correctly. Using one of these sites can be a lot cheaper, and quicker, than "purchasing" a product from your site multiple times using one PayPal account to test the IPN associated with your second PayPal account! Sites to check out include

✔ EliteWeaver (`www.eliteweaver.co.uk/testing/ipntest.php`) provides an IPN script testing environment. You enter the URL of your IPN handler code, enter a series of variables, select whether you want the IPN result to come back `VERIFIED` or `INVALID`, and click the Submit IPN button. You see a status report result, which lets you know the results of the test. A series of flag icons show at the top of the screen — click one of these to change the default currency used for your testing.

✔ BelaHost Web Hosting (`www.belahost.com/pp`) provides a very similar tool (along with a PHP version of an IPN script for you to download). You enter the variables and the URL of your script, and click the Submit IPN button. The site returns either a `VERIFIED` or `INVALID` result along with any variables prescribed by your script.

✔ OptionInsight (`www.optioninsight.com/IPNtestbed.html`) has a PayPal Instant Payment Notification Testbed. As with the other sites listed previously, you enter the URL of your script, your e-mail account, and the variable of the simulated sale, and click the Simulate Instant Payment Notification to your IPN Handler button. Unless the result comes back successfully `VERIFIED`, you don't get much information about where the problem may be as you do with the other two test sites.

If you want more information about why your script may not be working, you can use one of the testing services shown previously along with a small addition to your IPN script to generate an e-mail, which contains the variables in the body of the message. The example I show here is ASP/VBScript, but you can apply the same logic to whichever language you prefer to use.

This code snippet shows the section of my script that checks the notification validation sent by PayPal in response to my post. The new code (shown in bold) e-mails the variables to me.

```
dim rText
  rText = objHttp.responseText
If (objHttp.status <> 200 ) then
  response.write("status is not 200")
ElseIf (objHttp.responseText = "VERIFIED") then
  ' some code will go here
ElseIf (objHttp.responseText = "INVALID") then
  SET objMail = Server.CreateObject("CDONTS.NewMail")
  objMail.BodyFormat = 1
  objMail.MailFormat = 1
  objMail.From = "yourname@email.com"
  objMail.To = "yourname@email.com"
  objMail.Subject = "IPN Test"
  objMail.Body = Request.Form
  objMail.Send
  SET objMail = NOTHING
Else
  ' some code will go here
End If
```

After making the changes to your IPN script, use one of the test sites listed previously to send a simulated order to your script. Although the result of the test is invalid, an e-mail is sent to you containing the variables that you can use as a part of your testing process. The string e-mailed to you looks like the one shown here:

```
&ipnscript=http%3A%2F%2Fwww.yourwebsite.com%2Fyourcode.asp&ip
        nstatus=VERIFIED&receiver_email=yourname%40email.c
        om&business=yourname%40email.com&receiver_id=CHIJK
        FVRSTW28&paypal_address_id=ADFJPQ123X358&item_name
        =Chocolate&item_number=921&quantity=1&invoice=1234
        67&custom=Custom&payment_status=Completed&payment_
        date=16%3A35%3A01+Dec+02%2C+2004+PDT&payment_gross
        =19.95&payment_fee=0.58&mc_gross=19.95&mc_fee=0.58
        &mc_currency=USD&txn_id=HINRabhlop1234234&parent_t
        xn_id=EFABCQUefimoz4678&txn_type=web_accept&first_
        name=Jayson&last_name=Tester&address_street=13+Elm
        +Street&address_city=New+York&address_state=NY&add
        ress_zip=10185&address_country=United%2BStates&add
        ress_status=confirmed&payer_email=paypal%40theirdo
        main.com&payer_business_name=YourPayers+AMCE+Co.&p
        ayer_id=ACDGJLRWXZ578&payer_status=verified&paymen
        t_type=instant&notify_version=1.6&verify_sign=voKL
        s9D7mJd1c1234567COlEUtQShxM63VRraWubYPXBiNj8Z524zI
        kG
```

If you take a look at the string returned in the testing e-mail, you may notice that some of the text characters have been translated into URL encoding format (for example, **http://** becomes **http%3A%2F%2F**). For more information on HTML URL-encoding, see www.w3schools.com/html/html_ref_urlencode.asp.

IPN variables

As you may have guessed by now, there are a lot of IPN variables; too many to list them all here. If you want to get a copy of all of them, they can be found in Appendix A of the PayPal Integration Guide. (You can get a copy from www.paypal.com/en_US/pdf/integration_guide.pdf.)

In addition to Basic IPN and PDT variables (see Table 19-3), there are variables for advanced and custom information, shopping cart information, transaction information, currency and exchange information, auction information, security information, mass payment information, subscription information, and multicurrency information.

An IPN post contains only alphanumeric characters with a maximum field length of 127 characters with the exception of the custom and memo fields (which can contain up to 255 characters). The transaction ID posted by the IPN is always 17 characters in length. IPN (and PDT) variables are case-sensitive and most of the values are lowercase characters. (An exception to this rule is the payment_status variable, which returns one of the following values: Canceled_Reversal, Completed, Pending, Failed, Denied, Refunded, or Reversed.)

Table 19-3	PayPal IPN Basic Information Variables	
Variable	*Description*	*Character Limit*
business	The e-mail address of you (the merchant). This may be the e-mail address of the payment recipient but it does not have to be the primary e-mail address associated with the PayPal account.	127
receiver_email	The primary e-mail address associated with the PayPal account of the person receiving the payment. (Note: The value for the business and receiver_email variables is often the same but does not have to be.)	127

(continued)

Table 19-3 *(continued)*

Variable	Description	Character Limit
receiver_id	The unique PayPal account ID associated with the payment recipient. This is the same as the recipient's referral ID.	127
item_name	The name of the item you are selling. If the item is being sold through the shopping cart, a number will be appended to the item name (for example, item_name1, item_name2, item_name3, and so on).	127
item_number	An optional tracking number you can assign to a number (serves the same function as an SKU number).	127
quantity	The number sold of a specific item. If the item(s) are being sold through the shopping cart, a number will be appended to the quantity (such as, quantity1, quantity2, quantity3, and so on).	

Adding PayPal to Your Third-Party Shopping Cart

I use a number of tools to build e-commerce Web sites, but one of my favorites is a program called ClickCartPro (www.clickcartpro.com). (Among its other great features, it supports a large variety of payment methods and payment processors.) When I added support for PayPal to one of my Web sites, implementation took a grand total of five minutes (and that included some quick testing!).

When I looked at the code that ClickCartPro passes to PayPal, I realized that it's just one long POST with a lot of the same variables used in the PayPal button code. To put it another way . . . if you're a developer who's implemented a third-party shopping cart, adding support for PayPal payment processing can be quick and easy!

Passing aggregate product data to PayPal

There are two methods you can use when passing payment information to PayPal. The first (and simpler) method is to add up all the items in your application's shopping cart and pass the aggregate product data to PayPal through a Buy Now button. (So instead of passing the sales data for three separate widgets that cost $5.00 each, you pass a single item with a price of $15.00.)

Passing the aggregated sales data requires the form to submit four variables and the image for the "Submit" button:

✔ business — This is the e-mail address of the merchant's PayPal account.

✔ item_name — Because you won't be passing the name of the individual items, you can use a generic name for your shopping cart. Try to be as descriptive as possible because this is what the buyer sees in the PayPal account history. "The Widget Store" is a better item name than a nondescriptive name, such as "Product." You can also use the item_name field to pass a tracking ID (a unique order number or customer number pulled from your database).

✔ currency — One of the five PayPal-supported currencies — values are one of the following: USD, EUR, GBP, CAD, or JPY. (Please see Chapter 13 for more information about currency support.)

✔ amount — The aggregated (total) price of all items in the cart.

At its most basic level, the form to pass aggregated Widget sales data to a PayPal Buy Now button looks like the following:

```
<form action="https://www.paypal.com/cgi-bin/webscr"
         method="post">
<input type="hidden" name="cmd" value="_xclick">
<input type="hidden" name="business"
         value="yourname@email.com">
<input type="hidden" name="item_name" value="The Widget
         Company">
<input type="hidden" name="currency_code" value="USD">
<input type="hidden" name="amount" value="15.00">
<input type="image" src="http://www.paypal.com/en_US/i/btn/x-
         click-but01.gif" name="submit" alt="Make payments
         with PayPal - it's fast, free and secure!">
</form>
```

You don't need to restrict yourself to the variables shown here. Table 19-4 shows the additional variables you can use for passing aggregated data to the PayPal Buy Now button. (For more information about the Buy Now button code, see Chapter 14.)

Table 19-4	A List of the Variables to Use for Passing Aggregate Cart Data
Variable Name	*Variable Description*
quantity	The number of items being purchased. Show caution using the quantity variable when passing aggregate sales information because the value of the quantity is multiplied against the amount total.
item_number	An alpha-numeric, 127-character string that lets you track PayPal payments.
shipping	The cost of shipping the item.
shipping2	The cost of shipping each subsequent item.
handling	The handling cost for the order.
tax	The value of the tax variable (if you choose to use it) overrides any tax settings in your PayPal profile.
no_shipping	If the value is equal to 1, the customer is not required to provide a shipping address. If set to 0 or not included, the buyer is required to provide a shipping address.
cn	If you include a field to let the buyer send you a note, the cn variable provides the label that shows above the note field.
no_note	If the value is equal to 1, the customer can't add a note when paying for the item. If set to 0 or not included, there will be a field on the Payment Details page to let the buyer send a note.
on0	A 64-character, alphanumeric field that provides a field name for the first option, if there is one. (It doesn't make a lot of sense to have "options" for aggregated product data, but you have the capability if you need it.) The number at the end of each subsequent option name is incremented by one; so on1 is the second option, on2 is the third option name, and so on.
os0	The first set of values for the first option (200-character limit). os1 provides the set of values for the second option, and so on.
custom	This is an optional variable that is not shown to your customer but can be used by you for tracking purposes.
invoice	This is an optional variable that is not shown to your customer but you can use for the purpose of tracking invoices.

Variable Name	Variable Description
notify_url	If you plan on implementing IPN, the value for this variable is the URL where you find your IPN code.
return	If you want to send your customer to a specific page after completing payment, provide the URL as the value for the return variable.
cancel_return	The value will be the URL of a page users will be sent to if they cancel the transaction before completing the payment process.
image_url	The Web address of your 150-pixel-by-150-pixel logo displayed on customized payment pages.
cs	A variable to set the background color of your payment pages: A value of 1 is black; if omitted or set to 0, the page background is white.

In addition to the variables displayed previously, you can collect customer data (name, address, and so on) and pass these extended variables to PayPal (so the customer won't be required to fill out personal information twice). Before you can pass along the extended variables, you need to change the first line of your button code from:

```
<input type="hidden" name="cmd" value="_xclick">
```

to:

```
<input type="hidden" name="cmd" value="_ext-enter">
<input type="hidden" name="redirect_cmd" value="_xclick">
```

You can then pass along the following variables: email, first_name, last_name, address1, address2, city, state, zip, night_phone_a, night_phone_b, day_phone_a, and day_phone_b. For more information about extended variables, see the following page on the PayPal Web site: www.paypal.com/cgi-bin/webscr?cmd=_pdn_howto_checkout_outside#morevariables.

Passing separate items to PayPal

Although passing aggregate data to PayPal may seem easier, you'll provide a better shopping experience for your buyer if you pass the data for each separate item in the cart. When buyers go to their PayPal History to look at transactions, it is more informative for them to see the separate items that were purchased instead of a lump sum.

The process of passing detailed data from a third-party shopping cart is similar to that of upgrading from a Buy Now button to a PayPal Shopping Cart. (See the information shown in Chapter 16 if you need a reminder about how to do this.)

Start by upgrading the `cmd` variable that you pass from your application to PayPal and adding a new `upload` variable. The command variable for passing aggregate data is changed from:

```
<input type="hidden" name="cmd" value="_xclick">
```

to the following two lines:

```
<input type="hidden" name="cmd" value="_cart">
<input type="hidden" name="upload" value="1">
```

You still need to provide the following required variables, plus the button image: `business` and `currency_code`. The value for all monetary variables (shipping price, handling, and so on) default to the specified currency.

You then pass a series of variables for each item in the cart. Each of the variables has a number appended to the end, representing which item it is in the cart. For the first item in the cart, you pass `item_name_1`, `amount_1`, `item_number_1`, and so on. For the second item in the cart, you pass `item_name_2`, `amount_2`, `item_number_2`, and so on. Table 19-5 shows the variables that can pass for each item in your cart.

Table 19-5	Variables for Each Item Added to the PayPal Cart
Variable Name	**Variable Description**
`item_name_n`	The product name of the item added to the cart.
`item_number_x`	An alpha-numeric, 127-character string that lets you track PayPal payments.
`amount_x`	The price of the item added to the cart.
`shipping_x`	The cost of shipping one item.
`shipping2_x`	The cost of shipping each subsequent item (after the first).
`handling_x`	The item handling cost.

Variable Name	Variable Description
on0_x	A six-character, alphanumeric field that provides a field name for the first option, if there is one. The number at the end of each subsequent option name increments by one: on1_x is the second option; on2_x is the third option name, and so on.
os0_x	The first set of values for the first option (200-character limit) os1_x provides the set of values for the second option, and so on.

You find additional support for adding PayPal as a payment option with your current e-commerce solution by going to Developer Central (`https://developer.paypal.com`) and `PayPalDev.org`.

Generating Username/Password Combinations

If you sell subscriptions, you may want to provide access to members-only content for your customers. If desired, PayPal can generate a unique username and password combination, which is shown to a buyer who has completed the payment process. This username/password combo is stored on the buyer's subscription details page; you have the combo stored on your subscription details page as well.

To take advantage of this PayPal feature, you must manually track the subscriptions when buyers sign up, and activate the usernames and passwords on your server (and remember to deactivate them when the subscription period ends). This isn't very practical unless you have a very small subscriber base. A more logical solution is to write a script to manage the subscription process for you.

If this sounds too advanced for your coding capabilities, you'll be happy to know that PayPal provides a free PERL script that can do the work for you. (The script requires you to be using basic authentication for a site hosted by an Apache Web server on Linux.) You can download a copy of the script from `https://www.paypal.com/us/cgi-bin/webscr?cmd=p/xcl/rec/subscription-script-terms`. Click the button to accept the terms. You are taken to a page where you can download the instruction manual, along with a copy of the script.

To implement the PayPal password management, you need to set up IPN, which I cover earlier in this chapter. If you want to utilize subscription management, you cannot implement the PayPal Auto Return feature (because you want the buyer to receive the username/password combination, instead of being redirected to a thank you page).

Chapter 20

The PayPal APIs

You can customize your e-commerce Web site just by using PDT and IPN, but if you want to create a more robust application, then PayPal's newly launched Web Services can give you a whole new level of flexibility. Launched in 2004, the PayPal set of application programming interfaces (APIs) expands online payment capabilities for a new class of developers, along with third-party tool vendors and merchants. PayPal Web Services are based on SOAP (Simple Object Access Protocol) and WSDL (Web Services Description Language). For eBay application developers, PayPal's API architecture shares a common API structure with eBay's Web Services offerings.

For the rest of this chapter, I show you examples of working with PayPal Web Services. Because I'm most comfortable with Microsoft platforms (working there for six years will do that to you!), I'll be showing you .NET examples. If you prefer developing in Java, a wealth of information is on the Developer Central Web site. Please read this chapter to get a basic understanding for what you can do with PayPal APIs; you should be able to apply the same logic to your preferred environment. Additionally, a lot of help is also available from PayPalDev.org.

PayPal's Architecture Overview

Web services is a generic term used to describe how a Web-based application, using open standards, such as XML, SOAP, and WSDL, can communicate with code hosted on another server. XML tags are used to describe the data; and SOAP is the messaging protocol used to transmit the data through Web protocols (such as SMTP, HTTP, or MIME). WSDL describes the services that are available.

With Web Services, data is shared through a programmatic interface (as opposed to a browser making a request to a Web server). After the code has been developed to take advantage of a Web service, the developer can incorporate the code into an interface which is controlled by a user (such as a Web page or dedicated application). PayPal Web services let you write code in the language of your choice and share data with server-side APIs, without needing to know details about the other server's environment (and without having to write your own code to build or parse XML documents).

Not surprisingly, the architecture for PayPal Web Services shares a common API structure with eBay Web Services (which can make it easier for developers to create applications that work with both platforms). PayPal APIs use the foundation of eBay's Business Language (eBL) schema model and use many of the same versioning, naming standards, error handling, and error codes.

Because you're dealing with OPM (Other People's Money), there are certain restrictions on what you can do with PayPal Web services (that is, you won't be able to do everything through the APIs that you can do on the PayPal Web site). The API schema gives you access to only four functions:

- **TransactionSearch:** Lets you search for a specific transaction by a number of criteria.
- **GetTransactionDetails:** Lets you return the details associated with a transaction.
- **RefundTransaction:** Will reverse a specific transaction and issue a refund from one account to another.
- **MassPay:** Supports the transfer of funds to multiple recipients.

You find more detailed information about these APIs later in this chapter.

PayPal's Development Environments

As the first paragraph of this chapter may have suggested, PayPal's set of APIs are for developers who are familiar with Web Services and SOAP. To use the PayPal Web services, PayPal recommends that you use C# (on the .NET platform), Java, or C++, but you can actually program in any language that supports SOAP and WSDL.

Table 20-1 shows the client environments that PayPal has used in testing their APIs.

Table 20-1	PayPal-Recommended Development Environments	
Language	*SOAP Client*	*Required OS*
C# (Microsoft Visual Studio.NET 2003)	Microsoft .NET Framework, Version 1.1	Windows 2000 Windows XP Professional
C++	gSOAP	UNIX; Linux
Java (Version 1.4+)	Apache Axis, Version 1.1	Windows 2000 Windows XP Professional Linux

Although using one of the PayPal-sanctioned development environments is probably easier, any SOAP client should work as long as it meets the following requirements:

✔ The client needs to support document-style messaging (instead of RPC-style messaging).

✔ UTF-8 must be used as the encoding scheme in the SOAP messages.

PayPal used a public key security scheme to uniquely identify the application and confirm it is authorized to access PayPal Web Services. PayPal uses RSA's Public-Key Cryptography Standards, Component 7 (or PKCS#7), and Privacy Enhanced Mail (PEM).

Before you can begin development, you need to obtain a security certificate from PayPal. When you initiate a transaction, you must first pass a username/password combination to the API in a SOAP request header. If the authentication request succeeds, a security token returns to you. You can then make a call to the API.

The following example shows the SOAP request header that is used to make a PayPal API call:

```
<RequesterCredentials xmlns="urn:ebay:api:PayPalAPI"
            xsi:type="ebl:CustomSecurityHeaderType">
<Credentials xmlns="urn:ebay:apis:eBLBaseComponents"
            xsi:type"ebl:UserIdPasswordType">
<Username xsi:type="xs:string">username</Username>
<Password xsi:type="xs:string">password</Password>
</Credentials>
</RequesterCredentials>
```

More information about how to request and implement the security certificate is found later in this chapter.

PayPal's Software Development Quick Start

PayPal has a "Quick-Start" method for getting comfortable with their Web services. In the next few sections of this chapter, I show you how to perform the following:

1. **Get a Developer Central account and set up the Sandbox environment.**

   Information on how to set up your developer account is not included in this chapter, but is available in Chapter 18.

2. **Request an API Certificate.**

   You need to request one certificate in the Sandbox environment and a different certificate for the PayPal production environment. If you were setting up a standard e-commerce Web site, you would normally apply for an SSL certificate from a trusted authority (such as GeoTrust). PayPal does not allow you to use a certificate from a different authority, so you must request PayPal to generate your certificate.

3. **Download the necessary SOAP tools and files from the PayPal Web site and install them on your server.**

4. **Test the functionality of your environment by sending a payment from one of your test accounts to a second test account. See Chapter 18 for more information on sending payments in the PayPal Sandbox environment.**

5. **Make an API call to refund the payment you just sent.**

6. **Log on to the test account for your seller and confirm that the refund was successful.**

After signing up for a Developer Central account and setting up your Sandbox, you should get a copy of the API Reference Guide.

Downloading the API Reference Guide

To download a copy of the PayPal API Reference Guide, start by logging on to your Developer Central account (at `https://developer.paypal.com`).

1. **Click the Help Center tab (at the top of the page) or the big Help Center button (shown on the right side of the page).**

2. **Right-mouse click the <u>API Reference</u> link (shown under the Instruction section of the page).**

3. **Select the Save Target As option from the menu.**

   Select a folder where you want to save the file.

4. **Click the Save button.**

The API Reference Guide is saved to your computer. You should probably go through the same process to save a copy of the Sandbox User Guide as well.

Page 3 of the API Reference Guide contains instructions on how to quickly get started testing the PayPal Web service.

Getting a PayPal Certificate

After getting a copy of the API Reference Guide and setting up the Sandbox, you need to get a test version of a PayPal Certificate. In the following example, I request an API Certificate through the Sandbox, but you need to repeat the process to get a certificate for the production environment after you finish testing your code.

If you are a third-party developer, you will need to generate the API Certificate for your client. The API account name that is assigned to you needs to be sent to your client, who assigns API access to your ID. (More information about third-party API access is explained later in this section of the chapter.)

1. **Start by logging on to your Developer Central account and clicking the Sandbox tab.**

2. **Select the test user to act as a seller and click the Launch Sandbox button.**

3. **Log on as the test user and click the <u>Profile</u> link (found under the My Account section of the site).**

4. **Click the <u>API Access</u> link, found under the Account Information column.**

5. **Under the Request an API Certificate section of the page, click the <u>API Certificate Request</u> link.**

   In order to be issued a certificate, you need to provide seller information to PayPal (even if some of this information is redundant with the data already linked to the account). Fill out the form on the page and click the Continue button. The information you are asked to provide includes:

   - First name

   - Last name

   - Company

   - Department

   - The URL of your company's home page

   - Anticipated monthly volume

   - Expected use of the APIs (as an eBay seller, online merchant, third-party developer, and so on).

   - You are provided with a special API Account Name, in the form of an e-mail address. Write this e-mail account name down somewhere and the password associated with this account.

   - Your acceptance of the Terms of Use.

6. **After clicking the Continue button, you are redirected to a page where you can review the details of your request. If everything is okay, click the Generate Certificate button.**

7. **On the API Certificate page, click the Download button.**

   Save the `cert_key_pem.txt` to your desktop. See Figure 20-1, which shows the screen where you can download your new certificate file. If you choose not to download it now, you can download the file later by clicking the Test Certificates tab in Developer Central. This brings you to a page where you can download the certificate for any of your test accounts that applied for a certificate.

PayPal, an eBay company

Copyright © 1999-2004 PayPal. All rights reserved.
Information about FDIC pass-through insurance

Figure 20-1:
Click the
Download
button to get
your newly
acquired
certificate.

8. **If you are a merchant who has hired a third-party developer to create an application using your API Certificate, you'll need to give them access to the APIs associated with your account. To do this, start by clicking the** <u>Profile</u> **link, found under the My Account tab.**

- Click the <u>API Access</u> link, which is located under the Account Information column.

- On the API Access page, click the <u>API Access Authorization</u> link.

- Click the Add button to add an account (which can then be authorized to access your API).

- Enter the API Account Name that was assigned to your third-party developer during the process of requesting your certificate. Select which APIs to give your developer access. These include: RefundTransaction, GetTransactionDetails, TransactionSearch, Merchant-Initiated Payment, MassPay, BillAgreementUpdate, Encrypted Website Payments, or AddressVerify.

- Click the Save button, and the permissions are assigned to the API account you specified.

After you get your API Certificate, you need to convert it to a .P12 certificate. For information about how to do this is, read the next section of the chapter.

Converting Your API Certificate to a .P12 Certificate

After obtaining the certificate text file from PayPal, you need to convert it to *PKCS12* format. PKCS12, or PKCS#12, is a standard used for secure storage of private keys and certificates. One of the advantages of PKCS12 is that it can be imported and exported by Netscape 4.04 and Microsoft Internet Explorer 4.0 (and later versions of these browsers).

A PayPal API Certificate looks like the example shown here:

```
-----BEGIN RSA PRIVATE KEY-----
MIICXQIBAAKBgQCqzsXkzxkM3I1SVfmb2+gw40JMi/kPtDt6PT7egq6gS3Uz1
    yYf
AyfszLXBwyhRrragv7BYWKuHYdF/ydWqyYOnVGa9Q4917SCGeaVeoeWRzZ4Qd
    dn8
o30Mtzb1ZI9Kk4aa6ErHoOuNFipbE4/j2MCl8bf+BuPkws8Y6PBtDq6JWwIDA
    QAB
AoGBAIb2AIltVcbCzsI+6o5LMOjH+I/RHYdaCpDoqa9ZJK/FT6MZgaaJcNd7X
    LXw
BQCdgvH65FS6IzZChS1qhih/NOUKRPGr8Y1LYt3Wj5P1CwpjUTSnNiHVP3s2/
    jHt
ItDfwUv2NmF1pcOTKJm6Ngx4qvnQreDvXLvoxdFr77AsEljJAkEAOvT/ickc/
    hIL
iOVDkNOrjjm4hZuxNhxf3LqPo/rnEsM4Gox+0fNOjK8RSbyncU8Q9jk82asBw
    hAM
zfrGz3T8xQJBAM9HMiQCTvZxEQjCi5yl517cVRa8cWhhZD2LwMYv5JheW5VWv
    rwj
s4rcKmqimfC/fMojgCfjvCcbGSDVB8C+D58CQQCVQ3rn4CAeeWAl/aof/w4Jd
    Tfl
eXMbCVqeOHZAHZCQSwcQaeZ14V/PBzQhS1Xiq4Ih5f/zN7dnu3mD6PPw6CLNA
    kAN
MR/MOOTLpHiMES2ng5uNGwLDVqz1ErW5gQp80pF+7QpxH7s16CPGI6sDbGPVw
    aok
hOvhvgm8h2n6//P1XXNLAkAkgU9G+92PoOaZS5QMhK1JLtuPOR7BLrd8ojEMz
    vog
hD9zO84fDAvNp2ZfFPrKJ4M8BZPAMXt+ItyB6e3MZdeC
-----END RSA PRIVATE KEY-----

-----BEGIN CERTIFICATE-----
MIICnjCCAgegAwIBAgICCjMwDQYJKoZIhvcNAQEFBQAwgZ8xCzAJBgNVBAYTA
    lVT
MRMwEQYDVQQIEwpDYWxpZm9ybmlhMREwDwYDVQQHEwhTYW4gSm9zZTEVMBMGA
    1UE
ChMMUGF5UGFsLCBJbmMuMRYwFAYDVQQLFA1zYW5kYm94X2NlcnRzMRswGQYDV
    QQD
FBJzYW5kYm94X2NhbWVyY2hhcGkxHDAaBgkqhkiG9w0BCQEWDXJlQHBheXBhb
    C5j
```

```
b2OwHHcNMDQxMjAOMTczODAyWhcNMTQxMjAyMTczODAyWjB6MSIwIAYDVQQDF
                                         Bli
dW5ueXNtaXRoX2FwaTEuZW1haWwuY29tMRAwDgYDVQQKEwdTbWl0aENvMRUwE
                                         wYD
VQQLEwxPbmxpbmUgU2FsZXMxETAPBgNVBAcTCEJpZyBDaXR5MQswCQYDVQQIE
                                         wJD
VDELMAkGA1UEBhMCVVMwgZ8wDQYJKoZIhvcNAQEBBQADgYOAMIGJAoGBAKrOx
                                         eTP
GQzciVJV+Zvb6DDjQkyL+Q+OO3o9Pt6CrqBLdTPXJh8DJ+zMtcHDKFGutqC/s
                                         FhY
q4dhOX/JlarJg6dUZr1Dj3XtIIZ5pV6h5ZHNnhB12fyjc4y3NvVkjOqThproS
                                         sej
S4OWK1sTj+PYwKXxt/4G4+TCzxjo8GOOrolbAgMBAAGjDTALMAkGA1UdEwQCM
                                         AAw
DQYJKoZIhvcNAQEFBQADgYEAunaL36775zYIYh42/J3MsYmA1y6KV+oiPGYiu
                                         Jtr
ZzGCi2pQryPXQXSG4fKk2W90tDcEH9DI3Q3m8bt/X7UKp83V1PHu711YOzXPf
                                         GUV
WfRjHIXvO7qpdWFxpy19p1dlXObRYF91BtW+4UQ2uEhrOjRolltlol8jVcMYg
                                         9bB
djI=
-----END CERTIFICATE-----
```

To convert the certificate to PKCS12 format, follow these steps:

1. **Copy the text that begins with "**`-----BEGIN RSA PRIVATE KEY-----`**" and ends with "**`-----END RSA PRIVATE KEY-----`**" and save this text to a file named** `userkey.pem`.

2. **Copy the text that begins with "**`-----BEGIN CERTIFICATE----- `**" and ends with "**`-----END CERTIFICATE-----`**" and save this text to a file named** `usercert.pem`.

3. **You now need to use a cryptographic tool to convert these files to the correct format. PayPal recommends using OpenSSL for the conversion, but if you plan on developing with Microsoft Visual Studio.NET, you may find it easier to use the Win32 OpenSSL code from Shining Light Productions. You can get the code from** `www.slproweb.com/ products/Win32OpenSSL.html`. **(Use the recommend version of the code, instead of the latest version.)**

   Click the link to save the executable to your desktop and follow the instructions in the help file to install the code and convert your files.

If you're comfortable using OpenSSL to convert your test certificate to a PKCS12 certificate, I don't want to stop you from having fun. But if you're lazy, like me, there's an easier way to accomplish the task. PayPalTech.com (I really do love these guys . . .) has a beta conversion tool that generates the .P12 certificate for you. Start by going to `www.paypaltech.com/tools/ pem2p12.php`.

1. **Browse for the name of your key file.** (PayPalTech recommends a naming convention of `yourcomany_key.pem`.)

2. **Browse for the name of your certificate file.** (PayPalTech recommends using a naming convention of `yourcompany_cer.pem`.)

3. **Enter a password phrase you want to associate with your .P12 file.**

4. **Enter the name you want your .P12 file to have.** (PayPalTech recommends using a naming convention of `yourcompany.p12`.)

5. **Click the Generate button.**

6. **Click the** <u>Click here</u> **link to download your .P12 file.** After downloading the file, remember to click the Finish button to remove all your files from the PayPalTech servers.

If you plan on using the certificate with the Microsoft .NET environment, you will need to convert your .P12 certificate to a .CER certificate. Luckily, this is easy to do. Here's how:

1. **Double-click your .P12 file.**

   The Certificate Import Wizard begins. The wizard copies your certificate file to a certificate store. A *certificate store* is a location on your computer (in the registry, on the hard drive, and so on) where certificates are stored.

2. **After reading the first screen of the Wizard, click the Next button.**

   See Figure 20-2, which shows what the Certificate Import Wizard looks like. After using the wizard, you can confirm that the certificate was successfully installed by using Internet Explorer (select Internet Options from the Tools menu; click on the Content tab, then click on the Certificates button).

3. **Make sure that the filename displayed in the File to Import screen is the correct one and click the Next button.**

4. **Enter the password that you used to create the .P12 certificate and click Next.**

   Don't check any of the boxes on this Passport screen.

5. **On the Certificate Store screen, make sure that the "Automatically select the certificate store based on the type of certificate" option is selected and click the Next button.**

6. **At the final (Completing the Certificate Import Wizard) screen, click the Finish button.**

   You should see a message letting you know that the import was successful.

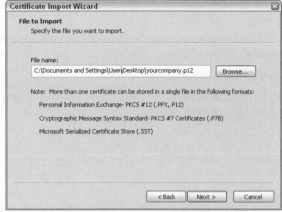

Figure 20-2:
The
Certificate
Import
Wizard
saves your
certificate
to a
certificate
store.

7. **Open Internet Explorer; from the Tools menu, select Internet Options.**

8. **Click the Content tab then click the Certificates button.**

   Under the Personal tab, you should see the certificate you created.

9. **Click the certificate name and then click the Export button.**

   The Certificate Export Wizard should open.

10. **Click the Next button.**

    The Export Private Key screen appears.

11. **Confirm that "No, do not export the private key" is selected and then click Next.**

12. **Keep the default setting (which should be the "DER encoded binary X.509 (.CER)" option and click Next.**

    You need to assign a name and a location to your .CER file. You can name the file something generic, such as "certificate." Click the Browse button to save the file to a location. The file needs to be saved to the same directory where you will be installing the PayPal API test package, so you may want to create the directory now (in preparation for steps you take later on in this chapter). PayPal recommends saving the files in a folder that is right off the root directory of your hard drive (that is, C:\APIClient).

13. **After selecting the filename and location, click the Next button.**

14. **Click the Finish button.**

    You should see a message letting you know the export was successful.

Close the Internet Explorer window, which is still open.

Now that you set up your certificate, you're ready to try downloading and running the PayPal test client package.

Running a Test Client

PayPal provides a test API Client that you can download and begin playing with to get an understanding of how the APIs work before you begin doing your own development. Clients are available for both Java and .NET.

I use the client for .NET in this chapter, but instructions for running the Java client are available in the PayPal API Reference Guide.

Downloading the test client package

Before you can run one of the test clients, you need to download the test client package from Developer Central. Try this:

1. **Log on to your Developer Central account at** `https://developer.paypal.com`.

2. **Click the Help Center tab at the top of the page.**

3. **Click the <u>For .NET</u> link, which you find under the API Client Tools section of the page.**

4. **Save the** `apiclient-CS.zip` **file to your hard drive and extract it to the same location where you saved your .CER certificate (for example, C:\APIClient).**

   This will install the files into the ApiClient folder.

5. **From the command prompt, go to the folder where you extracted the files.**

   Windows XP users can access the command prompt by clicking the Start button, selecting Run, typing **cmd** in the box, and then clicking OK.

6. **Type** APIClient **and press the Enter key.**

   A list of all available options displays in the command prompt window. Figure 20-3 shows the options that are displayed. Leave the command prompt window open for now.

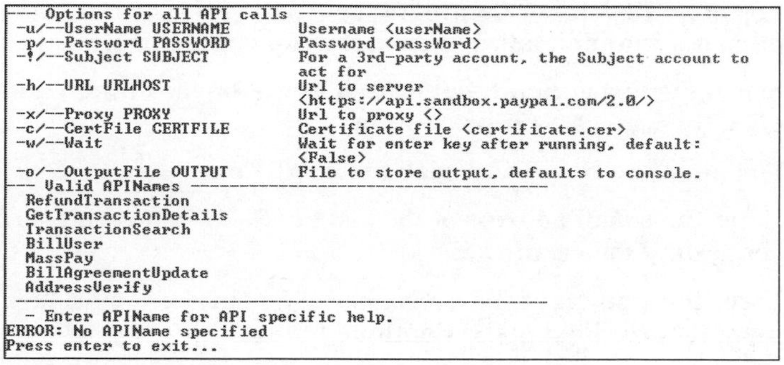

```
--- Options for all API calls ----------------------------
-u/--UserName USERNAME          Username <userName>
-p/--Password PASSWORD          Password <passWord>
-?/--Subject SUBJECT            For a 3rd-party account, the Subject account to
                                act for
-h/--URL URLHOST                Url to server
                                <https://api.sandbox.paypal.com/2.0/>
-x/--Proxy PROXY                Url to proxy <>
-c/--CertFile CERTFILE          Certificate file <certificate.cer>
-w/--Wait                       Wait for enter key after running, default:
                                <False>
-o/--OutputFile OUTPUT          File to store output, defaults to console.
--- Valid APINames ---------------------------------------
  RefundTransaction
  GetTransactionDetails
  TransactionSearch
  BillUser
  MassPay
  BillAgreementUpdate
  AddressVerify
----------------------------------------------------------
  - Enter APIName for API specific help.
ERROR: No APIName specified
Press enter to exit...
```

Figure 20-3:
After
installing
the API test
client, you
can see a
list of
options.

Compiling the client code

Now that you have a copy of the API test client, you need to compile the client code before you can begin testing. Here's how to do it:

1. **Open the folder where you unzipped the** APIClient **files and double-click the** APIClient.csproj **file.**

   The project opens in Visual Studio .NET.

2. **Using the Solution Explorer, double-click the Web References folder to expand it.**

3. **Right-click the PayPalSvc reference and select Properties.**

4. **Change the Web Reference URL to** http://api.sandbox.paypal.com/wsdl/PayPalSvc.wsdl.

5. **Right-click the APIClient project name, select Properties, Configuration Properties, and then Build.**

6. **Set the Output Path to** C:\APIClient **and click OK.**

7. **From the Visual Studio .NET Build menu, select Build APIClient to build your executable file and save it to the folder where you saved your** configuration.cer **file.**

Making a sample payment

After you compile the APIClient application, you need to make a sample payment (which you'll refund, using an API call, in a later step). You use the API Client Tool to refund this transaction in a few minutes. Follow these steps:

1. **Log on to Developer Central (**`https://developer.paypal.com`**) and click the Sandbox tab, shown at the top of the page.**

2. **Select the test account that is used as the buyer in this transaction and click the Launch Sandbox button.**

3. **Log on as the buyer and click the Send Money tab.**

4. **Enter the e-mail address of the test PayPal account you used when requesting the certificate.**

5. **Enter the amount of the transaction, the currency, and the type of payment before clicking the Continue button.**

6. **On the Check Payment Details page, confirm the details of the transaction and click the Send Money button.**

7. **Log out of the test account.**

Before you can try using the Refund API, you need to get the ID of the transaction you just implemented. Log on with the seller's account and click the <u>Transaction Details</u> link, which should appear on the Account Overview page. Figure 20-4 shows the Payment Details page, where you can find the Transaction ID.

Figure 20-4:
The
Transaction
Details page
shows the
transaction
ID to the
left of the
Payment
Received
header.
In this
example,
Transaction
ID is
4KC8289583
6601211.

Write down the Transaction ID and go back to the command prompt window, where you use the RefundTransaction API to refund the money you just transferred between your test accounts.

Refunding the transaction

In the command prompt window, type the following:

```
APIClient RefundTransaction -t (Transaction ID) -c
         (Certificate filename) -u (Test username) -p
         (Password)
```

To successfully execute the APIClient program as shown previously:

- ✔ *(Transaction ID)* is the transaction ID of the seller who received the funds from your test buyer.

- ✔ *(Certificate filename)* is the name you gave your certification file (for example, `certificate.cer`).

- ✔ *(Test username)* is the API account name assigned to your user. In my case, the test username is `bunnysmith_api1.email.com`.

- ✔ *(Password)* is the password associated with the test API account name.

To confirm the refund is successful, you should see `<Success>` listed as a transaction result and the Soap response should show as `completed` and `valid`. See Figure 20-5 for an example.

You should also log on to your test buyer account to confirm that the funds have transferred back from the seller's account. An e-mail should also appear in your Sandbox in-box, confirming the refund.

If you want to speed up your testing, you can enter your test username, password, and certificate filename into the `Class1.cs` file, which passes the information by default to the APIClient program (if you do not type them into the command line prompt when executing the program). Search for the "Set up the shared data" string in the `Class1.cs` file and replace the following variables with your test account information:

```
// Set up the shared data
    ApiArgs.sUserName = "api_username";
    ApiArgs.sPassword = "api_password";

    ApiArgs.sUrl = "https://api.sandbox.paypal.com/2.0/";
    ApiArgs.sProxy = "";

    ApiArgs.sCertFile = "certificate_filename";
```

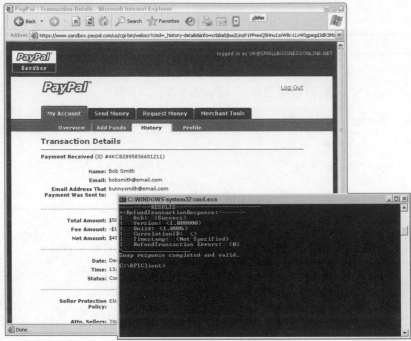

In the code sample shown previously, `https://api.sandbox.paypal.com/2.0/` should be used when you're testing against the sandbox and replaced with `https://api.paypal.com/2.0/` when you begin working with the PayPal production environment.

The eBay Business Language (eBL) Schema

PayPal APIs are built upon the foundation of the eBay Business Language (eBL) schema, specifically the following base type definitions `Abstract RequestType` and `AbstractResponseType`.

Tables 20-2 and 20-3 show the elements that comprise the `AbstractRequest Type` and `AbstractResponseType` definitions.

AbstractRequestType

The AbstractRequestType definition uses the following namespace:

```
Urn:ebay:apis:eBLBaseComponents
```

Table 20-2	AbstractRequestType API Call Elements	
Element	*Data Type*	*Description*
DetailLevel	xs:token	**Not Required:** An integer that defines the transaction detail level.
ErrorLanguage	xs:string	**Not Required:** A language identification tag. (See www.faqs.org/rfcs/rfc3066.html for more information about RFC 3066 language tags.)
Version	xs:string	**Required:** A string that describes the request payload schema version.

AbstractResponseType

The AbstractResponseType definition uses the following namespace:

```
Urn:ebay:apis:eBLBaseComponents
```

Table 20-3	AbstractResponseType API Call Elements	
Element	*Data Type*	*Description and Possible Values*
Timestamp	xs:dateTime	The date and the time in GMT format. Value depends upon the type of transaction.
Ack	xs:token	Application-level acknowledgement token. Values include the following: Success Failure SuccessWithWarning FailureWithWarning CustomCode

(continued)

Table 20-3 (continued)

Element	Data Type	Description and Possible Values
CorrelationId	xs:string	A string that can be used for application-level acknowledgment. Value depends upon the type of transaction.
Errors	xs:string xs:token (ErrorCode)	An error code that can be used to help in the debugging process and consists of a ShortMessage, LongMessage, and ErrorCode token. Value depends upon the type of transaction.
Version	xs:string	A string that gives the version of the response payload schema. Value is 1.0.
Build	xs:string	A string that gives the software build used to process the request and generate the response.

Data types

The eBL schema uses the following data types:

- ✔ Time values are returned in Greenwich mean time, using the ISO format.
- ✔ The core monetary type amount is derived from the string.
- ✔ In the case of numeric data types, int (32 bit) is used instead of integer; and float is used instead of decimal for percentages.

The PayPal schema

The components of the PayPal schema include

- ✔ The RefundTransactionRequest and RefundTransactionResponse
- ✔ The TransactionSearchRequest and TransactionSearchResponse
- ✔ The GetTransactionDetailsRequest and GetTransactionDetailsResponse
- ✔ The MassPayRequest and MassPayResponse

Downloading PayPal's SDK

After using the APIClient application to experiment with calling PayPal's APIs, you're ready to download the Software Development Kit (SDK) and begin writing your own applications. Try this:

1. **Log on to Developer Central (**`https://developer.paypal.com`**) and click the Help Center tab.**

   Or click the big Help Center button at the bottom of the page.

2. **Click the <u>PayPal SDKs</u> link, shown on the left side of the page.**

   The PayPal Software Developer Kits page (see Figure 20-6 for an example) provides links to a variety of resources, including Developer Toolkits for PHP, PERL, ColdFusion, and ASP. But if you're interested in writing applications that call PayPal Web Services, click the <u>SDK for ASP.Net developers</u> link, which is found in the middle of the page.

Figure 20-6:
You can download PayPal's SDK for ASP.NET directly from the PayPal site. The SDK includes documentation, controls, and code samples.

3. **After you click the link, you are redirected to a page that gives more information about the ASP.NET SDK; click the <u>Download</u> link found at the left side of the page.**

   This opens a new browser window, which contains links to three zipped files:

   - The PayPal ASP.NET Web Controls (`PayPal ASP.NET Web Controls.msi`), which lets you drag and drop PayPal button controls into your ASP.NET applications.

   - PayPal ASP.NET Commerce Starter Kit (`PayPal ASP.NET Commerce Starter Kit.msi`), which is a sample e-commerce application built with PayPal APIs. It includes a product catalog, shopping cart, customer signup page, and order processing.

   - The PayPal Order Management Application (`PayPal ASP.NET Commerce Starter Kit Order Mgmt.msi`), which is a sample desktop application that works with the Starter Commerce Kit application.

4. **After downloading the SDK files, you need to install the PayPal Web Controls into Visual Studio .NET 2003.**

   - Double-click the PayPal ASP.NET Web Controls `.msi` file to launch the installation wizard. Click the Run button to read the first screen and then click the Next button.

   - Select the "I Agree" option to accept the License Agreement and then click the Next button.

   - The next screen lists the system requirements for running the PayPal ASP.NET Controls. (You need to have Microsoft .Net Framework 1.1 and a PayPal Merchant account. You also need to have Visual Studio installed or Microsoft ASP.NET Web Matrix.) After reading the requirements, click the Next button.

   - You are prompted as to where you want the controls to be installed and who should be able to use them after installation. Accept the defaults and click the Next button. On the following screen, click next to start installing the files (which may take a few minutes to complete).

   - After the files finish installing, click the Close button to close the installation wizard. You need to restart your computer before you can begin using the Web Controls.

5. **After installing the Web Controls, open the** `Web.config` **file.**

6. **In the configuration section of the file, add an** `appSettings` **key named** `PayPal_BusinessEmail` **and set the value to be your PayPal account.**

The code should look like the example shown here:

```
<configuration>
    <appSettings>
        <add key="PayPal_BusinessEmail"
            value="yourname@email.com" />
    </appSettings>
</configuration>
```

After the files install, you can begin creating applications that take advantage of PayPal Web Services. Applications can be created in Visual Studio or in the Microsoft ASP.NET Web Matrix application (which I use for the following example).

1. **Start by giving a filename to a new ASP.NET page.**

2. **From the Tools menu, select the Add Local Toolbox Components option.**

3. **Click the PayPal.Web.Controls option in the list and then click the Add button.**

4. **In the Toolbox panel that displays on the left side of the Window, click the Custom Controls components.**

   See Figure 20-7, which shows the PayPal Controls that can be added to your new ASP.NET page.

5. **You can now select from one of the following PayPal controls:**

   - AddToCartButton
   - BuyNowButton
   - CheckoutCartButton
   - SubscriptionButton
   - UploadAggregateCartButton
   - UploadCompleteCartButton
   - ViewCartButton

6. **Drag one of the PayPal Web Controls and place it on your form.**

   In the example shown in Figure 20-7, I used the AddToCartButton control on the ASPX page.

7. **Click the control and set its properties; then click the Code tab to write the code that will control the functionality of your application.**

Figure 20-7:
After you install PayPal SDK, you can drag one of the button controls to your form and double-click the control to begin writing your code.

Using PayPal's Sample Applications

In addition to the Web Controls, PayPal's SDK comes with two sample applications that you can install and experiment with. You should have downloaded two .msi files from the PayPal SDK page: one for the Commerce Starter Kit and a second for an Order Management Application.

Installing the applications

Before you can install the Commerce Starter Kit, you need to make sure your environment meets these requirements:

✔ Windows 2000, Windows XP, or Windows Server 2003.

✔ Microsoft .NET Framework 1.1.

✔ SQL Server 2000 or MSDE.

✔ IIS (or Cassini) must be installed.

✔ Finally, you need to have administrative privileges for your machine.

Products such as Microsoft SQL Server can be expensive, but you can download many of the Commerce Starter Kit component requirements for free from Microsoft.

> ✔ For the Cassini Web server, go to `www.asp.net/Projects/Cassini/Download`.
>
> ✔ For the .NET Framework, go to `www.asp.net/download-1.1.aspx`.
>
> ✔ For the MSDE (Microsoft Database Engine), go to `www.asp.net/msde`.

Double-click the `.msi` file for the Commerce Starter Kit to launch the installation wizard.

After installing the Commerce Starter Kit, double-click the `.msi` file for the Order Management Application. Follow the instructions to install the application.

Using the applications

Take a little time to try using the applications before looking at the sample code. Launch the code by going to `http://1yourwebserver/PayPal Commerce`. (I installed the applications to run from my computer's IIS server, so I go to `http://localhost/PayPalCommerce`.)

You should see a page that has a "Welcome to the ASP.NET Commerce Starter Kit" heading (see Figure 20-8). You can click one of the category links (shown in the navigation bar on the left side of the page) to see products that can be added to the cart. Practice adding items to the cart and checking out, as if you were a real buyer.

At the upper-right side of the Commerce Starter Kit pages is a <u>Services</u> link. Click this link to get more information about the `OrderItem` and `Check Status` methods used by the program. If you click the <u>OrderItem</u> link on the InstantOrder page (`http://localhost/PayPalCommerce/Instant Order.asmx`), you can test the operation by filling out a form and clicking the Invoke button.

You can also test the `CheckStatus` operation in a similar fashion by clicking the <u>CheckStatus</u> link that is displayed on the first InstantOrder page (under the <u>OrderItem</u> link).

After making some test purchases, you can begin testing the Order Management application, which is located in a folder called `Default Company Name\ PayPalTestAppSetup`, located under your Program Files folder. (Default Company Name is the name you gave the folder when you installed the application.) After locating the folder, double-click the `PayPalTestApp` executable, which launches the ASP.NET Starter Kit application. See Figure 20-9, which shows what the application looks like when you first launch it.

Figure 20-8:
The
Commerce
Starter Kit
offers the
functionality
of a real
online store;
after playing
with the
application,
you can edit
the code to
adapt it to
your
require-
ments.

Figure 20-9:
The PayPal
Order
Manage-
ment
application
lets you
search for
orders that
were placed
through the
Commerce
Starter Kit
interface.

All of the data for the Commerce Starter Kit application is stored in a PayPalCommerce database. You can use SQL Enterprise Manager to look at the order tables and confirm that the Order Management application is retrieving the orders correctly.

When you're ready to start making changes to the source code, you can click the Windows Start button, click Programs, and then click ASP.NET Starter Kits.

Additional Resources

Showing you examples of how to write C# code to create sample PayPal applications is beyond the scope of this book. But if you need help with your coding, I would recommend any of the books shown here:

- ✔ *.NET Web Services For Dummies* by Anthony T. Mann
- ✔ *C# For Dummies* by Stephen Randy Davis
- ✔ *Visual Studio.Net All in One Desk Reference For Dummies* by Nitin Pandey and Senthil Nathan

If you need help getting your code to work with PayPal Web Services, the following are invaluable resources:

- ✔ **PayPal Developer Central** (`https://developer.paypal.com/cgi-bin/devscr?cmd=help/main#`): I find that the people who participate in the forums are very helpful and generous with their time.

- ✔ **PayPalTech.com** (`www.paypaltech.com/demo_site/purchase.html`): This demonstration logs you on to Developer Central to buy a product, refund a transaction, and get details about a transaction. Best of all, you can download code samples to see how the demos were created. *Hint: PayPalTech resources are added to, on a regular basis, so it's worthwhile to check our their site map periodically to see if there's anything new.*

- ✔ **PayPalDev.org:** A section of the PayPalDev.org forum is dedicated to SDK-related issues. If you are having trouble and need some help in getting the problem fixed, go to `http://paypaldev.org/default.asp?CAT_ID=13` and select your development environment.

- ✔ **eBay Developer's site:** This site offers online presentations about a variety of eBay-related topics. PayPal SDK information is available in Course 0201: Advanced .Net SDK (see `http://developer.ebay.com/education/educationcatalog.aspx` for more details).

✔ **PayPal Connect! Conference:** A lot of information is available from the online resources created for the PayPal Connect! Conference. You find resources from the Developer's Track at `http://paypal.sitestream.com/developer.html`.

If you decide that you would prefer to buy an off-the-shelf solution, based on PayPal APIs (instead of coding your own), you can find a list of solutions by going to `https://www.paypal.com/cgi-bin/webscr?cmd=p/pdn/3p-solutions-outside`. Solutions are available in the following categories:

✔ Accounting and Financial IPN Tools

✔ Affiliate Software Logo/Image Hosting

✔ Auctions

✔ Membership Systems

✔ Code Samples Shipping & Fulfillment

✔ Customer Tracking Shopping Carts & Storefronts

✔ Digital Goods Software Components

✔ E-mail Marketing Website Editing Tools

✔ HTML Templates Other Solutions

✔ International

If you are looking for software components, based on PayPal Web Services, the following products may be of interest to you. Here is a list of Software Component solutions, controls, and extensions that work with PayPal:

✔ ColdFusion Tags for PayPal, by HappyToad Design: These tags let you add Buy Now and Shopping Cart functionality to your e-commerce Web site.

✔ ComponentOne: This is a free e-commerce control that provides credit card processing for ASP.NET Web sites and applications.

✔ ANYR&D: Provides PayPal drag-and-drop components to let you add e-commerce capability to a Web site designed using Flash.

✔ nAlliance nIPN: A free IPN handler written in .NET.

✔ MercSoft: A database and IPN handler for Macromedia ColdFusion.

✔ OS Commerce: A PayPal plug-in for the OS Commerce open source e-commerce storefront.

- PayMate by Effengud Software: A self-contained VB/ASP e-commerce application developed using PayPal IPN to update sales reporting in real-time.

- PayPal Extension Suite: ShoreComp, a set of extensions to let you add PayPal functionality (such as Buy Now buttons, Subscription buttons, Donations buttons, Shopping Carts, Recurring Payments, and so on) to your e-commerce Web site built using Macromedia Dreamweaver.

- ShoreComp PayPal IPN for ASP.NET: A .NET class that provides IPN processing for notification and response, transaction verification, and error handling.

- WebAssist eCart: A shopping cart extension for Macromedia Dreamweaver designers. The eCart includes sample databases and templates, along with a Merchandising Wizard that lets you create discounts and special offers.

- Xheo PayPal Components: A set of common utility classes and controls to help you integrate PayPal functionality into the ASP.NET applications you develop.

A few other resources you may want to check out include

- GoDaddy.com SSL Web server certificates: If you signed up for an account with the PayPal Developer Network, you can receive a discount when purchasing 128-bit encryption SSL certificates from GoDaddy.com.

- 3D3 ShopFactory: If you are building an e-commerce application that will be available in multiple countries (or in multiple languages), this shopping cart and store-building solution from ShopFactory can help you in your efforts.

- StoreFront: LaGarde offers a shopping cart/online store solution used by Web designers who work with Microsoft FrontPage, or developers who code ASP.NET applications. StoreFront now offers integrated support for PayPal.

Part VII
The Part of Tens

The 5th Wave · By Rich Tennant

SINCE THEN WE DISCONNECT THE ONLINE SHOPPING FUNCTION DURING THE HOURS "LIFESTYLES OF THE RICH AND FAMOUS" IS ON.

In this part . . .

It wouldn't be a . . . *For Dummies* book without the Part of Tens, and this book is no exception. In this section, I give you ten reasons to add PayPal to an existing Web site and provide ten helpful PayPal resources for you to check out when you want more information.

Chapter 21

Ten Reasons to Add PayPal to Your Web Site

In This Chapter

▶ PayPal is the easiest way to add e-commerce to your Web site

▶ You don't need to apply for a merchant license

▶ You can specify payment preferences

▶ The buttons are free

▶ Easy encryption

▶ Many e-commerce solutions already support PayPal

▶ Setting up subscription payments is easy

▶ No setup fees

▶ Detailed transaction data

▶ Promotion through PayPal shops

*I*f you think PayPal is just for eBay sales, then you're missing out on a great opportunity to get revenue (or more revenue) from your Web site. If you're not already selling products from your Web site, adding Buy Now buttons or the PayPal Shopping Cart is the easiest way to turn a marketing site into an e-commerce site. If you're already accepting credit card payments, then offering PayPal as an additional payment option widens your customer base because people who don't want to use a credit card can still make purchases. The following paragraphs give ten good reasons why you should add PayPal to your Web site.

PayPal Is the Easiest Way to Add E-commerce to Your Web Site

If you don't know how to code, but you're comfortable using FrontPage to create a Web site, you can integrate e-commerce quickly and easily with

PayPal's free tools for Microsoft FrontPage. These tools let you add Buy Now buttons, a Shopping Cart, or set up subscriptions and recurring payments while you're designing with FrontPage. For information on how to install and use the tools, see Chapter 17.

You Don't Need to Apply for a Merchant License

In order to sell and accept credit cards online, you normally need to work with a credit card processing company or bank. The role of the processor is to validate buyer's credit cards at the time of purchase. Credit card processors help prevent you from fraud by checking whether the buyer's credit card is valid, and blocking IP addresses, e-mail addresses, or names of known problem buyers. Additionally, the processor can block a payment that sends the user over their credit limit.

You get a lot of peace of mind when working with a processor, but the application process can be a pain. (You need to provide a lot of information about your company, have a business bank account, and so on.) After you're approved by the processing company, you need to set up your Web site to accept secure payments and to configure your e-commerce software to send payment data to your processor's payment gateway. To work with a credit card processor, you spend a lot of time and resources before selling your first item.

PayPal also lets you accept secure payments, even credit card purchases, but the application process is as easy as providing your country, name, address, home telephone number, and e-mail address, and accepting the PayPal User Agreement. You can decide to open an e-commerce shop in the morning and start accepting payments in the afternoon.

You Can Specify Payment Preferences

If you accept PayPal payments, you can set up your Payment Receiving Preferences to block certain types of buyers. You can decide not to sell internationally or to block purchases from buyers who have not confirmed their address. This adds another layer of protection for you as the seller. Additionally, you can decide to accept payments only if they are made in a specific currency, and you can block buyers who try to purchase with a credit card when they have a bank account linked to their credit account.

In addition to deciding whether to block certain types of buyers, you can easily change your credit card company name (the one that is shown on the buyer's credit card statement).

The Buttons Are Free

Most credit card companies charge you a monthly fee, even if you don't receive any payments. The credit card processor I work with for my Web design business charges approximately $35 a month, plus a 2.5 percent fee on every transaction made. If I don't have many credit card sales in a month, I really get stung by the ongoing fee.

In contrast, adding PayPal e-commerce buttons to a Web site costs you nothing — if you don't sell anything, you don't pay. When you do sell an item, you pay $0.30 for each transaction, plus 2.9 percent of the selling price. The percentage can drop as low as 1.9 percent, depending upon your monthly volume of sales.

Easy Encryption

When you want to set up a secure e-commerce Web site, there are a number of steps you must take. First, you need to apply for an SSL (Secure Sockets Layer) license. SSL is a protocol used to send secure data over the Internet. SSL encrypts data that is sent from the browser; the data is decrypted when it gets to the server. After you implement SSL, you need to build an e-commerce Web site that works with SSL to transmit data securely (usually to a credit card processor).

Compare this to the ease of encrypting buttons with PayPal! When creating a button with the Button Factory, all you have to do is click the Yes option to have your button's code encrypted. When you copy the encrypted code to your Web site page, snooping eyes won't be able to see any personalized information by viewing the source code for the Web page.

Many E-commerce Solutions Already Support PayPal

I like using an e-commerce application called ClickCartPro (www.clickcart pro.com) when I'm designing an e-commerce Web site. It gives me a lot of control over the design and makes it easy to integrate some pretty sophisticated e-commerce features. So I wasn't surprised to find that ClickCartPro provides support for the PayPal IPN (Instant Payment Notification). See Chapter 18 for more information.

What did surprise me was how easy it was to set up — it took two minutes, and I was able to accept PayPal payments online. (See Figure 21-1 for the ClickCartPro PayPal integration page.) Another reason to add PayPal to your Web site is that so many shopping cart and storefront applications already have integrated PayPal support. The PayPal Business Resource Center `https://www.paypal.com/us/cgi-bin/webscr?cmd=p/sell/ small-biz-3p-stores` lists dozens of tools that you can use to develop a PayPal storefront.

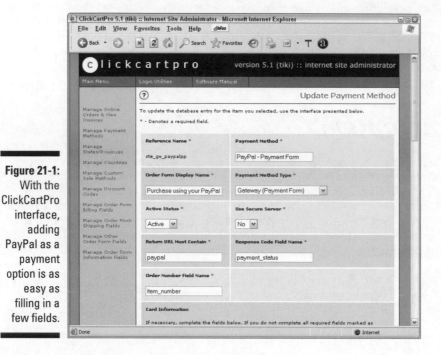

Figure 21-1: With the ClickCartPro interface, adding PayPal as a payment option is as easy as filling in a few fields.

Setting Up Subscription Payments Is Easy

PayPal makes it easy to set up subscriptions and recurring payments and frees you from the hassle of sending out periodic invoices. When you set up your subscription, you can specify up to two trial periods (for example, the subscriber can be billed $0.00 for the first month, and $20 for every month after the trial period has ended). You can set your billing cycle to be days, weeks, months, or even years.

You have the option of setting up *recurring payments,* in which the buyer pays the specified amount every month, without end. You can also set up payment installments; for example, you can charge the buyer $20 for five installments to purchase a $100 product.

Finally, PayPal can generate unique username and password combinations if you want to give buyers access to "members-only" content, stored in a special folder of your Web site. See Chapter 15 for more information about setting up subscriptions or recurring payments.

No Setup Fees

Usually setting up an online store involves some type of setup fee — either you have to pay for the price of the e-commerce software, a setup fee if you're using an online service, or you have to pay a developer to write custom code. Not with PayPal. . . . You have no upfront fees to open an online store if you use the PayPal Buy Now buttons or the Paypal Shopping Cart. With PayPal, you don't pay a thing until you actually sell something!

Detailed Transaction Data

When you use PayPal for e-commerce transactions, you can use the PayPal History Reporting Tools to download and analyze detailed information about every sale made. You have the option of including Shopping Cart details in the report. You can also do an advanced search to find transactions linked to an e-mail address, transaction ID, buyer's name, receipt ID, or item number. You can import the downloaded file into Excel, Quicken, or QuickBooks for additional tracking and analysis. You can also look at summary information available from the Merchant Sales Report.

Promotion through PayPal Shops

If you accept PayPal payments on your Web site, you can enroll your online store in PayPal Shops, a directory of Web sites that accept PayPal. After you enroll, PayPal members can search for the products and services you sell.

There is no cost to list your site with PayPal Shops, but you do need to have a Premier or Business PayPal account. Additionally, you need a bank account and credit card linked to your PayPal account and you need to invest in the PayPal Money Market Fund. To enroll in the fund, you need to provide a social security number or an employer identification number.

Chapter 22

Ten Helpful PayPal Resources

I've tried to provide you with a lot of information in this book, but there's always more to discover because PayPal offers so many great features to take advantage of. In this chapter, I give you ten resources to help you whether you want to find out more about developing with PayPal APIs, or you need design help to build a professional-looking e-commerce Web site.

PayPal Connect

PayPal Connect is available at `http://paypal.sitestream.com`. PayPal Connect is like going to the PayPal Developer Conference without leaving home. You can watch video clips of presentations that were given at the conference, download PowerPoint slides displayed during the conference, and download manuals on specific topics. You also find links back to the Help section on the PayPal Web site so you can look up specific how-to topics.

If you're a developer, the PayPal Connect site can be an invaluable resource. (In fact, the site is hosted by the PayPal Developer Network.) But the site can also be very helpful if you're a merchant who never intends to write code. A merchant track gives information about how to sell on eBay, how to manage your sales reporting, and how to protect yourself from fraud.

Because PayPal Connect offers content in a variety of formats (streaming video and PowerPoint slides), you need specialized applications installed on your computer to take advantage of everything. Luckily, these applications can be downloaded and installed for free:

Microsoft Windows Media Player

`www.microsoft.com/windows/windowsmedia/mp10/default.aspx`

Adobe Acrobat Reader

`www.adobe.com/products/acrobat/readstep2.html`

Microsoft PowerPoint Viewer (if you don't have Microsoft PowerPoint)

`www.microsoft.com/downloads/details.aspx?FamilyID=428d5727-43ab-4f24-90b7-a94784af71a4&displaylang=en`

The PayPal Business Resource Center

For the Business Resource Center, log on to your PayPal account and go to `https://www.paypal.com/us/cgi-bin/webscr?cmd=p/sell/small-biz-3p`. If you need help implementing a PayPal feature but are unsure to whom to turn, PayPal has a list of companies to contact for help. Third-party companies can provide support for

- Affiliate programs
- Auction tools
- Customer tracking
- Digital goods
- E-mail marketing
- HTML templates
- International logo/image hosting
- Membership systems
- Online stores

> ✔ Shipping
>
> ✔ Shopping carts
>
> ✔ Other solutions

PayLoadz

PayLoadz is available at www.payloadz.com. If you sell items from your Web site, the delivery process is straightforward. As soon as you receive notification that a payment has been sent to your PayPal account, you can ship the item to the buyer. But what if you want to sell digital items online? You can just wait until you receive payment and then e-mail a link to let the buyer download an item, but this is cumbersome (and buyers usually want their eBook, screen saver, MP3 file, or software right away).

That's where PayLoadz comes in . . . it's a service that integrates with your PayPal account and sends the digital file as soon as the money transfers into your PayPal account. Setup is pretty straightforward — basically, you enter a PayLoadz URL into the Instant Payment Notification Preferences form on the PayPal Web site. Use PayLoadz to generate the Pay Now button code you add to your Web site. As soon as a sale is made, you get your money and the buyer gets the file.

You pay a monthly fee based upon the value of your monthly transactions and the file space you use on the PayLoadz servers. Fees for Basic and Premium accounts can run between $15 and $70 a month for sales volume above $250.

Allwebco Design

Allwebco Design is available at http://allwebcodesign.com. You want to build a PayPal e-commerce Web site and you're comfortable tweaking HTML code. Unfortunately, your design skills are limited to drawing stick figures and you don't have the cash to pay a high-priced designer. You can still have a professional design by going to the Allwebco Design site.

Allwebco offers great Web design templates (some even include flash animations). After paying for the template (usually under $50), you download the source files and add your own content. Best of all, they have templates that are specifically designed for PayPal e-commerce Web sites. See Figure 22-1 for a sample Allwebco PayPal template.

Beauty is in the eye of the beholder . . . I happen to like many of the Allwebco designs, but you may not. PayPal has a list of other HTML companies from which to choose. Log on to your PayPal account and go to `https://www. paypal.com/us/cgi-bin/webscr?cmd=p/sell/small-biz-3p`. By adding your own content to a well-designed template, you can have a professional-looking site, even if you can't draw a straight line.

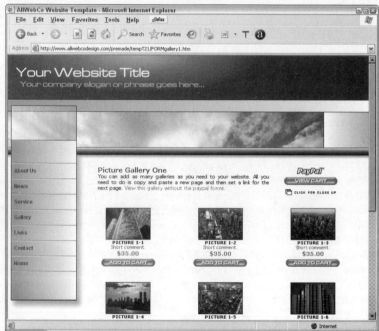

Figure 22-1: Allwebco Design templates include pages designed to work with your PayPal account, making it easy to create an e-commerce Web site.

PayPal Developer Central

PayPal Developer Central is available at `https://developer.paypal.com`. PayPal Developer Central is an essential resource if you want to develop PayPal applications or create custom e-commerce solutions for your Web site. Developer Central provides sample code, instruction manuals, support forums, and a testing environment (so you can test your code without having to transfer money between accounts).

You need to sign up for an account before you can access any of the Developer Central resources. After you sign up, Developer Central displays customized content, depending on whether you signed up as a merchant or a developer.

PayPalDev.org

PayPalDev.org is available at www.paypaldev.org.

PayPalDev.org is an independent forum that supports developers who work on PayPal applications. PayPalDev.org is a good resource when you need to have a specific question answered, or you want to search for information about how another developer solved a similar problem. Think of PayPalDev.org as a backup resource, if you can't find the answer you're looking for on PayPal Developer Central.

PayPalDev.org should not be confused with PayPal Developer Central.

AuctionPix Image Hosting

AuctionPix is available at www.auctionpix.com.

If you don't have your own Web site but you want to add a logo image to your PayPal invoices, you can have your image hosted on AuctionPix. (You can also host the images you want displayed in your eBay listings.) You have a variety of packages from which to choose: You can host images for a certain number of days, pay by the month if you want to have the images hosted indefinitely, host on a dedicated server, e-mail photos that are then edited by AuctionPix, or have your photos scanned. Prices vary, according to the level of service you require.

Constant Contact

Constant Contact is available at http://paypal.roving.com. I use Constant Contact to market my Web design company and I love the service! You enter e-mail addresses to build a list of subscribers. (Constant Contact also provides code to add a sign-up link on your Web site.) You can send personalized e-mail campaigns to your list and track how many people respond to the e-mail (by opening the e-mail or clicking the links).

You can link your PayPal account to Constant Contact. When using e-mail templates with specific products, you can choose to add a PayPal "click to buy" button. The subscriber can buy the item (or make a donation) right from within the e-mail. The monthly rate is very reasonable, depending on the number of e-mails you send per month; PayPal subscribers get the service free for 60 days by signing up online at http://paypal.roving.com.

SendPal

SendPal is available at www.sendpal.com. PayPal's integration with USPS and UPS is very cool when you want to pay for a shipping label and print it from your computer. Unfortunately, PayPal doesn't let you accurately determine the shipping costs at the time you're pricing the item. Any amount you add to the price to cover shipping costs is just a rough estimate. SendPal overcomes this obstacle by letting you get an accurate shipping cost before you ask the buyer to send payment. After signing up for a SendPal account, you use the SendPal service to generate your "Add to Cart" buttons. The actual shipping cost is calculated and added to the price of the item at the time the purchase is made. SendPal only charges a fee of $0.05 per rate quote, and it can save you a lot of money in misjudged shipping costs!

LeverUp

LeverUp is available at www.leverup.com. LeverUp is an order management service that can be very useful for sellers with a lot of transactions. You can view and analyze sales data more intuitively than with the PayPal Post-Sale Manager. LeverUp Basic service is free; setup is simple. You add the LeverUp URL to the PayPal Instant Payment Notification preferences; then enter your e-mail address into a form on the LeverUp home page. You get detailed purchase information for each transaction and summary data, ordered by total sales, item popularity, customers by zip code, and so on. For the free service, the data is retained for three days. For $10 a month, 60 days of data is saved; for $15 a month, up to 15 months of data is saved.

Index

BUSINESS, CAREERS & PERSONAL FINANCE

0-7645-5307-0

0-7645-5331-3 *†

Also available:

- Accounting For Dummies †
  0-7645-5314-3
- Business Plans Kit For Dummies †
  0-7645-5365-8
- Cover Letters For Dummies
  0-7645-5224-4
- Frugal Living For Dummies
  0-7645-5403-4
- Leadership For Dummies
  0-7645-5176-0
- Managing For Dummies
  0-7645-1771-6

- Marketing For Dummies
  0-7645-5600-2
- Personal Finance For Dummies *
  0-7645-2590-5
- Project Management For Dummies
  0-7645-5283-X
- Resumes For Dummies †
  0-7645-5471-9
- Selling For Dummies
  0-7645-5363-1
- Small Business Kit For Dummies *†
  0-7645-5093-4

HOME & BUSINESS COMPUTER BASICS

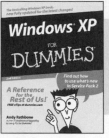

0-7645-4074-2

0-7645-3758-X

Also available:

- ACT! 6 For Dummies
  0-7645-2645-6
- iLife '04 All-in-One Desk Reference
  For Dummies
  0-7645-7347-0
- iPAQ For Dummies
  0-7645-6769-1
- Mac OS X Panther Timesaving
  Techniques For Dummies
  0-7645-5812-9
- Macs For Dummies
  0-7645-5656-8

- Microsoft Money 2004 For Dummies
  0-7645-4195-1
- Office 2003 All-in-One Desk Reference
  For Dummies
  0-7645-3883-7
- Outlook 2003 For Dummies
  0-7645-3759-8
- PCs For Dummies
  0-7645-4074-2
- TiVo For Dummies
  0-7645-6923-6
- Upgrading and Fixing PCs For Dummies
  0-7645-1665-5
- Windows XP Timesaving Techniques
  For Dummies
  0-7645-3748-2

FOOD, HOME, GARDEN, HOBBIES, MUSIC & PETS

0-7645-5295-3

0-7645-5232-5

Also available:

- Bass Guitar For Dummies
  0-7645-2487-9
- Diabetes Cookbook For Dummies
  0-7645-5230-9
- Gardening For Dummies *
  0-7645-5130-2
- Guitar For Dummies
  0-7645-5106-X
- Holiday Decorating For Dummies
  0-7645-2570-0
- Home Improvement All-in-One
  For Dummies
  0-7645-5680-0

- Knitting For Dummies
  0-7645-5395-X
- Piano For Dummies
  0-7645-5105-1
- Puppies For Dummies
  0-7645-5255-4
- Scrapbooking For Dummies
  0-7645-7208-3
- Senior Dogs For Dummies
  0-7645-5818-8
- Singing For Dummies
  0-7645-2475-5
- 30-Minute Meals For Dummies
  0-7645-2589-1

INTERNET & DIGITAL MEDIA

0-7645-1664-7

0-7645-6924-4

Also available:

- 2005 Online Shopping Directory
  For Dummies
  0-7645-7495-7
- CD & DVD Recording For Dummies
  0-7645-5956-7
- eBay For Dummies
  0-7645-5654-1
- Fighting Spam For Dummies
  0-7645-5965-6
- Genealogy Online For Dummies
  0-7645-5964-8
- Google For Dummies
  0-7645-4420-9

- Home Recording For Musicians
  For Dummies
  0-7645-1634-5
- The Internet For Dummies
  0-7645-4173-0
- iPod & iTunes For Dummies
  0-7645-7772-7
- Preventing Identity Theft For Dummies
  0-7645-7336-5
- Pro Tools All-in-One Desk Reference
  For Dummies
  0-7645-5714-9
- Roxio Easy Media Creator For Dummies
  0-7645-7131-1

* Separate Canadian edition also available

† Separate U.K. edition also available

Available wherever books are sold. For more information or to order direct: U.S. customers visit www.dummies.com or call 1-877-762-2974.
U.K. customers visit www.wileyeurope.com or call 0800 243407. Canadian customers visit www.wiley.ca or call 1-800-567-4797.

 WILEY

SPORTS, FITNESS, PARENTING, RELIGION & SPIRITUALITY

0-7645-5146-9

0-7645-5418-2

Also available:
- Adoption For Dummies
  0-7645-5488-3
- Basketball For Dummies
  0-7645-5248-1
- The Bible For Dummies
  0-7645-5296-1
- Buddhism For Dummies
  0-7645-5359-3
- Catholicism For Dummies
  0-7645-5391-7
- Hockey For Dummies
  0-7645-5228-7

- Judaism For Dummies
  0-7645-5299-6
- Martial Arts For Dummies
  0-7645-5358-5
- Pilates For Dummies
  0-7645-5397-6
- Religion For Dummies
  0-7645-5264-3
- Teaching Kids to Read For Dummies
  0-7645-4043-2
- Weight Training For Dummies
  0-7645-5168-X
- Yoga For Dummies
  0-7645-5117-5

TRAVEL

0-7645-5438-7

0-7645-5453-0

Also available:
- Alaska For Dummies
  0-7645-1761-9
- Arizona For Dummies
  0-7645-6938-4
- Cancún and the Yucatán For Dummies
  0-7645-2437-2
- Cruise Vacations For Dummies
  0-7645-6941-4
- Europe For Dummies
  0-7645-5456-5
- Ireland For Dummies
  0-7645-5455-7

- Las Vegas For Dummies
  0-7645-5448-4
- London For Dummies
  0-7645-4277-X
- New York City For Dummies
  0-7645-6945-7
- Paris For Dummies
  0-7645-5494-8
- RV Vacations For Dummies
  0-7645-5443-3
- Walt Disney World & Orlando For Dummies
  0-7645-6943-0

GRAPHICS, DESIGN & WEB DEVELOPMENT

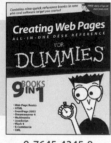

0-7645-4345-8

0-7645-5589-8

Also available:
- Adobe Acrobat 6 PDF For Dummies
  0-7645-3760-1
- Building a Web Site For Dummies
  0-7645-7144-3
- Dreamweaver MX 2004 For Dummies
  0-7645-4342-3
- FrontPage 2003 For Dummies
  0-7645-3882-9
- HTML 4 For Dummies
  0-7645-1995-6
- Illustrator CS For Dummies
  0-7645-4084-X

- Macromedia Flash MX 2004 For Dummies
  0-7645-4358-X
- Photoshop 7 All-in-One Desk
  Reference For Dummies
  0-7645-1667-1
- Photoshop CS Timesaving Techniques
  For Dummies
  0-7645-6782-9
- PHP 5 For Dummies
  0-7645-4166-8
- PowerPoint 2003 For Dummies
  0-7645-3908-6
- QuarkXPress 6 For Dummies
  0-7645-2593-X

NETWORKING, SECURITY, PROGRAMMING & DATABASES

0-7645-6852-3

0-7645-5784-X

Also available:
- A+ Certification For Dummies
  0-7645-4187-0
- Access 2003 All-in-One Desk
  Reference For Dummies
  0-7645-3988-4
- Beginning Programming For Dummies
  0-7645-4997-9
- C For Dummies
  0-7645-7068-4
- Firewalls For Dummies
  0-7645-4048-3
- Home Networking For Dummies
  0-7645-42796

- Network Security For Dummies
  0-7645-1679-5
- Networking For Dummies
  0-7645-1677-9
- TCP/IP For Dummies
  0-7645-1760-0
- VBA For Dummies
  0-7645-3989-2
- Wireless All In-One Desk Reference
  For Dummies
  0-7645-7496-5
- Wireless Home Networking For Dummies
  0-7645-3910-8